SKILLS & VALUES: ALTERNATIVE DISPUTE RESOLUTION

Negotiation, Mediation, Collaborative Law, and Arbitration

SKILLS & VALUES: ALTERNATIVE DISPUTE RESOLUTION

Negotiation, Mediation, Collaborative Law, and Arbitration

John Burwell Garvey
Professor of Law and Director,
Daniel Webster Scholar Honors Program
University of New Hampshire School of Law

Charles B. Craver
Freda H. Alverson Professor
George Washington University Law School

ISBN 978-0-7698-5119-8
Ebook ISBN: 978-0-327-17972-6

Library of Congress Cataloging-in-Publication Data

Garvey, John Burwell.
Skills & values. alternative dispute resolution : negotiation, mediation, collaborative law, and arbitration / John Burwell Garvey, Professor of Law and Director, Daniel Webster Scholar Honors Program University of New Hampshire School of Law; Charles B. Craver, Freda H. Alverson Professor, George Washington University Law School.
pages cm. -- (Skills & values series)
ISBN 978-0-7698-5119-8
1. Dispute resolution (Law)--United States--Problems, exercises, etc. 2. Negotiation in business--United States--Problems, exercises, etc. 3. Communication in law--United States--Problems, exercises, etc. I. Craver, Charles B. II. Title. III. Title: Skills and values. IV. Title: Alternative dispute resolution.
KF9084.G37 2013
347.73'9--dc23   2013004868

NOTE TO USERS
To ensure that you are using the latest materials available in this area, please be sure to periodically check the LexisNexis Law School web site for downloadable updates and supplements at www.lexisnexis.com/lawschool.

Editorial Offices
121 Chanlon Rd., New Providence, NJ 07974 (908) 464-6800
201 Mission St., San Francisco, CA 94105-1831 (415) 908-3200
www.lexisnexis.com

MATTHEW◆BENDER

ACKNOWLEDGEMENTS

There are many people who helped prepare this book and we appreciate it. In particular, we thank the Daniel Webster Scholars of the University of New Hampshire School of Law Class of 2013 and the UNH Law Students taught by Professor Melinda Gehris, who field tested this material.

PREFACE

1. THIS BOOK IS YOUR BOOK

This book was written primarily for law students. If you are like most students, you bought it because it was assigned by your professor. You just paid good money and would like to know what you can hope to get for it. That is a fair request, and we will try to give you a clear answer.

But first, if you are using this book for a course involving any aspect of alternative dispute resolution, including negotiation, mediation, collaborative law, and arbitration, we commend you on your course selection! You probably signed up for the course because you were interested in learning the subject. We think this is a smart decision on your part. Although nearly all lawyers are repeatedly involved in some way with aspects of alternative dispute resolution, most law schools do not require any training. If you apply yourself, we predict that this will be one of the most useful courses you take in law school. Please let us know if you agree after you have been in practice for a few years. We would like to hear from you.

2. WHAT YOU CAN GET FROM THIS BOOK

This book is designed to give you both theory and practical application for the skills and values which come into play during the various forms of alternative dispute resolution, including negotiation, mediation, collaborative law and arbitration. This book is not intended to be the last word on alternative dispute resolution theory, although it will direct you to lots of further discussion. It is not intended to be a comprehensive treatise on the law and specific rules. Your professor may choose to use it as a practical supplement to a standard text or as a stand-alone course book. This book is designed to provide a practical, hand's on experience so that you can practice and reflect upon what you will be doing as a lawyer. Think of it as "practice practice"! Each chapter focuses on a different aspect of the dispute resolution process. The idea is to read the material and then test and develop your knowledge through exercises and simulations. Some of the hands-on materials are in the book, some of them are online, and some of them will be distributed by your professor. When the material is online, you will be asked to visit the **LexisNexis Webcourse** for the chapter you are reading. After each experience, you will be given an opportunity to evaluate and reflect upon your performance. If you work through the exercises before you "peek" at the self-study sections, you will get more out of the experience.

The **LexisNexis Webcourse** for this book provides supplemental reading and reference materials. In addition, there are online videos. You can watch examples of lawyers doing the various things that are discussed in the book. There are some commentaries by us further discussing the materials and links to other video commentaries. **We encourage you to read each chapter in conjunction with the LexisNexis Webcourse for that particular chapter, since the Webcourse materials are intended to complement the reading.**

3. THE POWER OF REFLECTION

Many attorneys go from case to case without ever reflecting on what they learned from the interactions. Most people who do not reflect do not improve and are doomed to make the same mistakes over and over. During this course, you have an opportunity to practice good

PREFACE

habits by reflecting after each exercise. By doing this consciously in the beginning, you can train yourself to internalize the process and do it even without realizing that you are doing it. This will make you a more *intentional* lawyer and you will actually be able to observe and mark your progress. Your results will be consistently better, your career will be more rewarding and your clients will be better served.

TABLE OF CONTENTS

TABLE OF CONTENTS

TABLE OF CONTENTS

TABLE OF CONTENTS

TABLE OF CONTENTS

TABLE OF CONTENTS

TABLE OF CONTENTS

Chapter 1

INTRODUCTION TO ALTERNATIVE DISPUTE RESOLUTION

A. WHAT IS ALTERNATIVE DISPUTE RESOLUTION?

Alternative Dispute Resolution ("ADR") is a collective term used to categorize any of the numerous conflict resolution alternatives to traditional adjudication by a judge or jury. In this book, we will separately consider *negotiation, mediation* (a particularized form of negotiation), *collaborative law* (another form of negotiation), and *arbitration* (adjudication by an arbitrator or arbitrators instead of a judge or jury).

B. DEVELOPMENT OF THE ADR MOVEMENT

The ADR movement was slow in coming, and developed from a sense that the traditional methods of litigation were often not addressing the needs of the litigants.[1] Although the various forms of ADR have been around in one form or another for many years, the American ADR movement as we know it today had its genesis at the ABA Sponsored Pound Conference of 1976.[2] Led by Chief Justice Warren Burger, this conference reviewed the paper presented at the 1906 ABA Annual Meeting by Professor Roscoe Pound entitled, "The Causes of Popular Dissatisfaction with the Administration of Justice."[3] As a result of the Pound Conference, the ABA created the Special Committee on Resolution of Minor Disputes in 1976.[4] In 1993, this committee metamorphosed to become the ABA Section of Dispute Resolution. According to the ABA, it "is one of the ABA's newest and fastest growing Sections . . . ."[5]

---

[1] "It is time, therefore, to ask ourselves whether the tools of procedure, the methods of judicial process that developed slowly through the evolution of the common law, and were fitted to a rural, agrarian society, are entirely suited, without change, to the complex modern society of the late 20th and the 21st centuries." Chief Justice Warren E. Berger, *Keynote address*, pp. 23-35 of THE POUND CONFERENCE, on page 32, 70 F.R.D. 79 (1976).

[2] ABA Criminal Justice Section Report to the House of Delegates p. 2, October 2008.

[3] Rex E. Lee, *The Profession Looks at Itself — The Pound Conference of 1976*, 1981 B.Y.U. L. REV. 737 (1981).

[4] ABA JOURNAL Jan. 1979, Vol. 65, p. 5 (written by ABA Pres. S. Shepard Tate).

[5] http://www.americanbar.org/groups/dispute_resolution/about_us.html. Last visited July 27, 2011.

C. HOW PREVALENT IS ADR?

You are preparing to practice law at a time when the term "ADR" has become a misnomer. This concept has gained acceptance in American law today to the point that it is no longer really considered "alternative" but mainstream. (Note that the name of the ABA Section of Dispute Resolution does not include the word "alternative".) There are now ADR programs in all federal trial courts, most state trial courts, and many appellate courts. Even when parties decide to litigate in the first instance, courts now routinely require some form of ADR (usually mediation) prior to trial. Many cases are now routinely mediated even when it is not required. In most courts, *fewer than five percent* of civil and criminal matters are adjudicated. More and more family law matters are being resolved through either mediation or a collaborative law process with trained collaborative lawyers. There are mediation and arbitration programs for resolving many disputes with federal, state and private employees. Insurance contracts usually contain arbitration language for the settlement of disputes between the insurance company and the insured. Business contracts routinely include dispute resolution procedures. Many consumer contracts contain mandatory arbitration agreements which the Supreme Court has found to be enforceable — even when the seller eliminates the right to class actions.[6]

ADR is everywhere. Whether you draft business agreements, real estate contracts, employment agreements, consumer contracts or many other kinds of documents, dispute resolution procedures will be part of the equation. If you are an employment lawyer, ADR will often be involved. If you litigate, you will see ADR much more often than you see a jury! In short, ADR is now ubiquitous.

---

[6] *AT&T Mobility LLC v. Concepcion*, 131 S. Ct. 1740 (2011).

Part One

NEGOTIATION

3

Chapter 2

INTRODUCTION TO NEGOTIATION

A. THE IMPORTANCE OF NEGOTIATION SKILLS

Negotiation is not limited to the ADR process but is a crucial component of it. Therefore, a substantial portion of this book is devoted to helping you understand the science and skills that should be considered when negotiating. The information that you will learn about negotiating will be applied throughout the exercises in every part of this book.

Everyone negotiates, even though they are often not aware of it. Babies negotiate by crying. They agree to quit crying if you give them what they want.[1] Teenagers negotiate curfews — "I'll be home by midnight and I'll fill the tank and clean the car if I can drive to the concert". College students negotiate roommate disputes — "I'll agree to tutor you in Spanish if you'll agree to have the party in our room on a night *after* my Chemistry midterm exam."

Law students negotiate constantly. They negotiate to get into selective courses, work with study groups, and deal with roommates. They negotiate to obtain interviews with firms, companies, government agencies, etc. At interviews, they endeavor to convince the interviewer that they should make the hire. Once employment offers are obtained, prepared candidates politely ask whether the parties may negotiate over the terms being offered. Even where the prospective employer has set salary policies, prepared students are sometimes able to negotiate for the cost of bar review courses and bar examinations, moving expenses, and the cost of attending continuing legal education programs that will enhance their lawyering skills.

Lawyers negotiate with their partners, associates, legal assistants, and others within their own firms and agencies. They negotiate when they interact with prospective clients and with current clients. They negotiate when they interact with others on behalf of their own clients. Business transactions are almost always structured through bargaining discussions. Buy/sell agreements, commercial property transactions, patent/copyright licensing terms, joint ventures, international business deals, and similar arrangements are all structured through negotiations.

The vast majority of litigated legal disputes are disposed of through negotiated settlement agreements. In most states, fewer than five percent of civil and criminal matters are adjudicated. The remaining ninety-five percent are dismissed, withdrawn, or resolved through negotiated arrangements. Even with respect to the few cases that

---

[1] *See* Charles B. Craver, *Everything You Need to Know to Be a Great Negotiator You Learned Before Kindergarten*, THE NEGOTIATOR MAGAZINE (Feb. 2005), http://www.negotiatormagazine.com/article248_1.html.

are actually litigated to conclusion, effective lawyers often employ their negotiation skills to narrow the legal and factual issues and to streamline the discovery process.

The ability to effectively negotiate is a major factor in the early and ongoing success of any lawyer. Because of this, we hope that you are motivated to learn all that you can about negotiating — it needs to be a lifelong skill!

B. LIMITED LAW SCHOOL TREATMENT OF NEGOTIATION

Law schools have traditionally had few formal courses designed to teach students how to prepare for and conduct legal negotiations. As recently as ten or fifteen years ago, many schools did not even offer courses on Legal Negotiating. Faculty members thought that such skills courses did not fit within their theoretical and sophisticated curricula. Law professors seemed to believe that students either knew how to negotiate from their prior endeavors, or would learn such practical skills once they entered practice. Fortunately for you, this is no longer the case!

Almost all law schools have begun to appreciate how important negotiation skills are and the need to teach such skills to law students. Some now have first year lawyering skills courses that include client counseling, legal research and writing, and negotiation. Others incorporate negotiation skills training in Alternative Dispute Resolution courses, while others have separate courses devoted to negotiation practice.

Effective Negotiation courses must be both practical and theoretical — and highly interdisciplinary. Individuals can read everything ever written on the negotiation process and not improve their bargaining skills. They can alternatively engage in numerous negotiation exercises without gaining a real appreciation of the factors that influence bargaining encounters. Negotiation involves an *experiential lawyering skill*; it must be learned both through an understanding of the theoretical underpinnings and through exercises designed to teach students the practical application of the underlying concepts being explored. That is what you will be doing as you work through Part One of this book; you will be able to apply this knowledge and experience as you move forward in the other parts of the book and during your career.

C. CHARACTERISTICS OF EFFECTIVE NEGOTIATORS

Effective negotiators have to appreciate the impact of psychological and sociological concepts, the importance of verbal and nonverbal communication, and the application of economic game theory. They have to appreciate the structured nature of bargaining interactions, to enable them to know what they should be trying to accomplish during each separate stage of the process. They need to understand the different negotiating techniques, both to enable them to decide which tactics they should employ in particular circumstances and to recognize and effectively counteract the techniques being employed against them.

What personal characteristics make individuals proficient negotiators? For example, are students with higher GPAs more effective negotiators? Although one might think that better students should achieve better negotiation results than less proficient students based upon their supposed intellectual superiority, we have found no correlation between student GPAs and the results students achieve on negotiation exercises. GPAs tend to reflect student abstract reasoning skills, while negotiation results usually reflect student interpersonal skills. This is why there are so many stories about highly successful lawyers who did not do particularly well in the formal academic setting. In an unpublished study conducted several years ago, Charles Craver and Psychologist Allison Abbe sought to determine whether there was any statistically significant correlation between student emotional intelligence scores and their performance on negotiation exercises, and they found none.

The good news is that negotiating is a skill that can be learned. Like any skill, it takes a lot of practice to get good.[2] Skilled negotiators usually outperform less skilled bargainers. They know how to prepare for such interactions, and they know what to do during each stage of the process. They know what tactics to employ and how to counter the techniques being used against them. They are **intentional** — they have prepared for the negotiation, carefully considering the facts and the law. They have fully explored the strengths and weaknesses of the parties *and* the lawyers. They know their own client's **needs and interests**[3] *and* they have done what they can to identify the other side's **needs and interests**. They are fully prepared. They know the difference between items they would *like* to obtain and items they *must* obtain to reach agreement. This enables them to exude an ***inner confidence*** that disconcerts less certain opponents and usually causes less confident negotiators to move in their direction.[4] We will specifically discuss the skills you need to develop in order to maximize your results as a negotiator.

D.   THE IMPACT OF CULTURE ON NEGOTIATION

Most Americans are not skilled negotiators. For the most part, corporate retail America does not encourage a negotiating culture with its customers.[5] We go to supermarkets and other retail stores and pay the stated prices or refrain from buying the items in question. Many of us think that negotiating over price or conditions is impolite and unsavory. We may "negotiate" by price shopping — forcing the sellers to stay competitive — but we do not often "confront" the seller and directly negotiate for a lower price.[6] One of the few expected negotiations that take place in retail America is the purchase of a car. Many Americans find this type of haggling extremely distasteful.

---

[2] Some researchers have found that the "magic number" of practice hours for becoming an expert at anything is 10,000! MALCOM GLADWELL, OUTLIERS, THE STORY OF SUCCESS 40 (Little Brown and Co. 2008).

[3] Needs and interests are discussed further in Chapter 4.

[4] In collaborative law, which you will read about in Part Three, there is no attempt made to disconcert the opponent but ***inner confidence*** is still valuable.

[5] Many immigrant communities bring a negotiating culture to small retail local markets. It will be interesting to see whether those cultures eventually put enough economic pressure on American corporate retail to change the negotiating culture or whether they assimilate. While you are taking this course, we hope you will seek out these communities in your area to practice your negotiating skills.

[6] Some stores now advertise "lowest price guarantees" which encourages the consumer to bring lower prices to the seller's attention. But this is still a lot different than the kind of direct negotiation that is common in many countries.

In many other countries, however, nearly everything is negotiable. Citizens negotiate constantly with respect to almost everything they need or want. As a result, they are comfortable with the bargaining process, and they actually look forward to negotiation situations. Although certain negotiators may be considered "impolite" — as with any situation — the *act* of negotiating is perfectly normal and proper.

Americans should not fear bargaining encounters, nor should they view them as unpleasant or impolite situations. They should instead view such encounters as **opportunities** providing them with the chance to improve their current positions. If the other side did not have the ability to enhance their circumstances, the parties would not be negotiating! Even in the dominant American culture, it is amazing how often things are negotiable if people ask politely.

E. GETTING MENTALLY PREPARED TO LEARN HOW TO NEGOTIATE

Many American law students have been raised in the American corporate retail culture and initially find formal negotiating emotionally stressful. However, putting aside America's aversion to retail negotiation, remember that you **need** to negotiate effectively if you are to succeed as a lawyer. It is not impolite. It does not make you a bad person! It is **essential**. As you begin to learn the skill of intentional negotiation in this course, confront any discomfort you may have. In the negotiation exercises that follow, **be mindful of making concessions based on personal discomfort or a desire to please.** Firm, fair and friendly negotiation is totally appropriate **and you must not be apologetic**. When you feel yourself getting uncomfortable, say to yourself: "**Good lawyers are good negotiators.**" With practice, you will be comfortable and actually enjoy negotiating.

Finally, do not forget that you have been "negotiating" for years — with your parents, siblings, friends, and even strangers — but probably have not thought about these regular occurrences. You may have forgotten the many tools you learned intuitively as a child. Negotiation is not actually new to you, but now you are going to study it and consider it in an intentional way. This course will provide you with the opportunity to rethink ideas you learned as a child and to learn new concepts that will enhance the skills you already possess.

F. ETHICAL CONSIDERATIONS

We just assured you that negotiation is good. But there are rules of behavior. As you work on the exercises in this book, consider the ethical implications of your actions. It is common at the beginning of interactions for negotiators to demand more or offer less than they really hope to obtain or are willing to pay. Individuals requesting money embellish their circumstances, while those being asked to provide money understate the value of the transactions being discussed. Does such behavior contravene the ethical standards applicable to attorneys?

Although we will explore this topic in depth in Chapter 5, it is important to recognize here that Model Rule 4.1 provides that "a lawyer shall not knowingly: (a) make a false statement of material fact or law to a third person." Rule 4.1(a) would appear to proscribe exaggeration, puffing, and embellishment. Nonetheless, Comment 2 acknowledges the different expectations indigenous to bargaining encounters. "Under generally accepted conventions in negotiation, certain types of statements ordinarily are not taken as statements of material fact. Estimates of price or value placed on the subject of a transaction and a party's intentions as to an acceptable settlement of a claim are ordinarily in this category . . ." It is thus ethical for negotiators to demand more or offer less than they are willing to accept or pay. It is similarly ethical for negotiators to understate or overstate the value of items being discussed for strategic purposes. When Side A asks for Item 1, Side B may indicate a reluctance to give up that item even when that item has no value to Side B. Side B can do this hoping to obtain a concession from Side A in exchange for Item 1 which Side A does value.

It is ironic that Comment 2 permits negotiators to misrepresent their side's *settlement intentions* and how they *value the items being exchanged*, since these are the most material matters during bargaining interactions! The facts, law, economic, political, and cultural issues are all secondary. What each negotiator must truly ascertain concerns two fundamental issues: (1) what does the other side really want; and (2) how much of each item must this side give up to induce the opposing side to enter into a mutual accord.

As you work on the various exercises in this book, contemplate the difference between acceptable puffing and embellishment and unacceptable misrepresentation of material fact. Just like in real practice, individuals who make false statements that are not exempt from Rule 4.1 will develop negative reputations among class members; this will usually affect them negatively when they subsequently interact with the same opponents *or* with other persons who have been informed of their questionable behavior. As a lawyer, you are bound to follow the ethical rules in your jurisdiction, and doing so is the best way to develop a strong reputation which will benefit you and your clients.

Chapter 3

THINKING ABOUT NEGOTIATING

Before you begin to dissect and examine the elements of negotiation in an intentional manner, we want you to try a couple of exercises using your gut. Although the skills you are going to learn later will make you much more effective, these exercises will help you think about what is happening when you negotiate.

EXERCISES

EXERCISE 3.1
SILENT NEGOTIATION EXERCISE

"ALL OR NOTHING"

GENERAL DESCRIPTION OF EXERCISE: You will receive instructions in class.

PARTICIPANTS NEEDED: You will be divided into pairs in class.

ESTIMATED TIME REQUIRED:

35 minutes

LEVEL OF DIFFICULTY (1-5):

EXERCISE 3.2
SILENT NEGOTIATION EXERCISE

"NEGOTIATING FOR A CLIENT"

GENERAL DESCRIPTION OF EXERCISE: In-class negotiation of personal injury suit under certain constraints.

SKILLS INVOLVED: Adaptability and self-observation.

PARTICIPANTS NEEDED: You will be divided into pairs in class.

ESTIMATED TIME REQUIRED:

35 minutes

LEVEL OF DIFFICULTY (1-5): 1

ROLES IN EXERCISE: You are acting as a lawyer for a party as identified in the exercise.

THE EXERCISE

You will be divided into pairs. One person will represent the plaintiff and the other person will represent the defendant. Start by reading the General Information below. Then read the "Confidential" Information for both the Plaintiff **and** Defendant. Your professor will give you final instructions before you begin the exercise.

GENERAL INFORMATION

An unmarried twenty-year old female Plaintiff was injured in an automobile accident with the Defendant. Due to flying glass, the Plaintiff lost the sight in one eye and suffered permanent facial scars. She still suffers from occasional bad headaches. Her unpaid medical bills to date amount to $20,000. The Defendant has admitted negligence, but has alleged contributory negligence by the Plaintiff in a jurisdiction where contributory negligence is still a bar to recovery. A lawsuit for $300,000 has been filed.

EXERCISE 3.2: CONFIDENTIAL INFORMATION FOR PLAINTIFF

Your client is financially destitute and emotionally distraught. The accident, the injuries, the medical bills, and the pending litigation have drained her financially and psychologically. She has recently been seeing a psychiatrist and is prepared to put this entire incident behind her. The headaches have abated, but her mental state has deteriorated due to the pending litigation. She wants to obtain $20,000 to pay off her medical bills and be through with everything. Her psychiatrist has informed you, with her permission, that if this case is not resolved quickly, she is likely to suffer an emotional relapse and commit suicide. The Plaintiff has instructed you to settle this matter immediately for any amount over $20,000. You should assume that you are representing the Plaintiff on a pro bono, no-fee basis, thus she will obtain any sum agreed upon to settle this case.

EXERCISE 3.2: CONFIDENTIAL INFORMATION FOR DEFENDANT

Your insurance firm is overburdened with other claims and believes the Plaintiff will be an appealing witness. It fears a verdict in excess of the modest $300,000 being sought, and will be obliged to pay the entire judgment if that fear is realized. You have thus been instructed to settle this case immediately for any amount up to $300,000. If you fail to achieve an immediate resolution of this matter, you will be terminated.

EXERCISE 3.3

WHO AM I?

As you prepare for negotiation and all forms of ADR, it is important to understand that personalities have a big impact on the process. To begin with, you want to know as much as you can about yourself. How do you react when faced with a dispute or conflict? Is your primary focus on solving the problem? Reaching a compromise? Winning? Avoiding the dispute? Developing a good relationship? It is important to identify your tendencies so that you can be aware of them as you negotiate. If you are a person who does not like disputes, how will you handle negotiations with someone who wants to win at all costs? Will you accede to her demands in order to avoid the conflict? That probably will not make your client very happy! There are many free personality inventories available online that can help you better understand yourself. Knowledge of yourself really is power.

Go to the **LexisNexis Webcourse** and follow the instructions.

EXERCISE 3.3
WHO AM I?

REFLECTION

Reflect on what you have learned and answer these questions:

1. How do I tend to behave when faced with a dispute?

2. How can I best use my tendencies as strengths when resolving disputes?

3. How might my tendencies work as weaknesses when resolving disputes?

4. What will I do to maximize my strengths and minimize my weaknesses?

Chapter 4

UNDERSTANDING THE NEGOTIATION PROCESS

When people prepare for bargaining encounters, they spend hours on the factual issues, the legal issues, the economic issues, and the political issues. How much time do they spend on their actual negotiation strategy? Usually no more than ten to fifteen minutes. When they begin an interaction, most negotiators have only three things in mind relating to their bargaining strategy: (1) where they plan to begin; (2) where they hope to end up; and (3) their bottom line. Between their opening offer and the conclusion of their encounter, most individuals "wing it," thinking of the interaction as wholly unstructured. If they only understood how structured bargaining transactions are, they would know what to do during each stage of the process!

In this chapter, we will explore the six distinct stages of the negotiation process: (1) Preparation; (2) Preliminary; (3) Information; (4) Distributive; (5) Closing; and (6) Cooperative. We will discuss the purpose of each stage and the most effective ways to accomplish the objectives underling each.[1] We encourage you to read this in conjunction with the **LexisNexis Webcourse** for this chapter where you will find video examples and other supplemental materials.

A. PREPARATION STAGE: ESTABLISHING LIMITS AND GOALS

> If you know the enemy and know yourself, you need not fear the result of a hundred battles. If you know yourself but not the enemy, for every victory gained you will also suffer a defeat. If you know neither the enemy nor yourself, you will succumb in every battle.[2]

Persons who thoroughly prepare for bargaining encounters generally achieve more beneficial results than those who do not, because knowledge constitutes power at the bargaining table.[3] As noted in Chapter 2, well prepared negotiators possess the knowledge they need to value their impending interactions, and they exude a greater confidence in their positions than their adversaries. Their confidence undermines the conviction of less prepared opponents and causes those persons to question their own positions. As less prepared advocates subconsciously defer to the greater certainty exhibited by their more knowledgeable adversaries, these less prepared participants tend to make more frequent and greater concessions.

---

[1] The phases of negotiation are given different names by different authors. Whatever they are called, it is important to understand what they are and when they occur.

[2] SUN TZU, THE ART OF WAR 43 (J. Clavell ed., Delta 1983).

[3] *See* ORAN R. YOUNG, ED., BARGAINING: FORMAL THEORIES OF NEGOTIATION 10-11 (Univ. of Illinois Press 1975).

1. Client Preparation

When attorneys are asked to negotiate on behalf of clients, those legal representatives must elicit all of the relevant factual information possessed by their clients. They must also determine what those clients hope to achieve through legal representation. Clients frequently fail to disclose their real underlying interests and objectives when they talk with lawyers, because they only consider options they think attorneys can obtain for them. It is thus critical for lawyers to carefully probe client interests and goals, and to listen intently to client responses.[4]

Persons who say they wish to purchase or lease specific commercial property may suggest that they are only interested in that location. When these people are asked probing questions regarding their intended use, it may become apparent that alternative locations may be acceptable. Knowledge about alternatives enhances bargaining power by providing viable options if the current discussions do not progress satisfactorily. Clients contemplating the investment of resources in other enterprises should be asked about their ultimate objectives. Are they willing to invest their assets in a single venture, or would they prefer to diversify their holdings? Are they willing to risk their capital to achieve a higher return or would they prefer a less generous return on an investment that is likely to preserve their initial investment? Is a business seller willing to accept future cash payments, shares of stock in the purchasing firm, or in-kind payments in goods or services provided by the purchasing company? The lawyer who fully explores the client's interests and objectives will better understand what "value" is for the client, can better plan the negotiation and acquire more of what the client is really seeking.

Clients who initially ask for monetary relief through the litigation process may have failed to consider alternative interests. Someone contemplating a defamation action may prefer a retraction and a public apology to protracted litigation. A person who thinks she was wrongfully discharged from employment may actually prefer reinstatement and a transfer to another department instead of a substantial monetary sum. A victim of alleged sexual harassment may prefer an apology and stay-away promise from the harasser to monetary compensation and likely future difficulties. If attorneys do not ascertain the real underlying interests of their clients, they may ignore options that could enhance their bargaining positions and help them achieve optimal agreements.[5]

As lawyers explore client interests and objectives, they must try to determine the degree to which the clients want the different items to be exchanged. Most legal representatives formally or informally divide client goals into three categories: (1) essential; (2) important; and (3) desirable. *Essential* items include terms clients must obtain if agreements are to be successfully achieved. *Important* goals concern things clients want to acquire, but which they would be willing to exchange for essential or other important items. *Desirable* needs involve items of secondary value which clients

---

[4] *See* Leonard L. Riskin, *The Contemplative Lawyer: On the Potential Contributions of Mindfulness Meditation to Law Students, Lawyers, and Their Clients*, 7 Harv. Negot. L. Rev. 601, 649-650 (2002); Abraham P. Ordover & Andrea Doneff, Alternatives to Litigation 32-33 (NITA 2002).

[5] *See* Roger Fisher & William Ury, Getting to Yes 101-11 (Houghton Mifflin 1981).

would be pleased to obtain, but which they would exchange for "essential" or "important" terms.

For each item to be negotiated, attorneys should try to determine how much clients value different levels of attainment.[6] For example, money may be an "essential" issue for a person who has sustained serious injuries in an automobile accident. The client may consider the first $200,000 critical, both to make up for lost earnings and to enable her to pay off unpaid medical bills and increased credit card debt. While the client would like to obtain more than $200,000, she may only consider amounts above $200,000 "important," rather than "essential." As a result, the client may not consider $400,000 to be twice as beneficial as the initial $200,000. Her lawyer may have to obtain $500,000 or even $600,000 before the client would consider the sum achieved twice as good as the first $200,000. Lawyers preparing for bargaining encounters must make these calculations for *each item* to be negotiated. Only by appreciating the degree to which the client values different amounts of particular commodities can they hope to obtain results that will most effectively satisfy the client's underlying interests.

Attorneys must similarly ascertain the relative values of the various items to be negotiated within each broad category. Does the client value Item A twice as much as Item B or two-thirds as much? How does Item C compare to Items A and B? It helps to mentally assign point values to the various items to enable legal representatives to understand how they can maximize overall client satisfaction. Legal advocates can use this relative value information to decide which items to seek and which items to trade for other terms the client values more highly. In most of the negotiation exercises set forth in this book, point values have been assigned to the different items to be exchanged. Negotiators should recognize that these assigned points represent their *clients'* value systems. Negotiators should strive to maximize the degree of satisfaction they obtain for their assigned clients. These assigned point values also make it easy for negotiators to determine how well they did vis-a-vis other negotiators and how efficiently they and their opponents divided the items involved.

When determining client objectives, *lawyers should avoid the substitution of their own values for those of their clients*, realizing that client interests must guide their negotiation strategy. Negotiating lawyers should not be constrained by judicial authority or usual business practices. Negotiators can agree to any terms that are legal. Clients often prefer results that could not be achieved through adjudications (*e.g.*, retractions in defamation actions or apologies in harassment cases) or which might not be consistent with usual business arrangements (*e.g.*, in-kind payments). Lawyers should not ignore these possibilities merely because courts could not award them or many business leaders would not approve them. To the contrary, acquiring a result that cannot be reached in court or in normal business channels is often what makes a negotiated settlement that much more valuable.

---

[6] *See* Howard Raiffa, Negotiation Analysis: The Science and Art of Collaborative Decision Making 129-147 (Belknap/Harvard Univ. Press 2003).

2. Lawyer Preparation

Once lawyers have ascertained the relevant factual information and the underlying interests and goals of their clients, they must become thoroughly familiar with the relevant legal doctrines, economic factors, and, where pertinent, political agendas that drive the conflict. They must develop cogent legal theories to support their positions, and anticipate the counter-arguments they expect opposing counsel to make. Negotiators confronted with positions they have anticipated are unlikely to have their confidence undermined and can respond most effectively.

a. *Calculating Own and Opposing Side's Bottom Lines*

After attorneys become familiar with the relevant factual and legal matters affecting their own side, they must determine their bottom line — i.e., their Best Alternative to a Negotiated Agreement (BATNA).[7] What are the best results they could realistically hope to obtain through other channels? It is critical for negotiators to have a set bottom line to be certain they will not enter into agreements that would be worse than what would happen if no accords were obtained.[8]

Negotiators who are initially unable to evaluate the results of non-settlements must take the time to develop alternatives. This is especially important for transactional experts. Their client may be seeking a buy-sell agreement with a single firm or a licensing arrangement with one party. Are there other potential purchasers or sellers they should contact? Other potential license partners? As alternatives become numerous, lawyers and their clients may wish to create decision trees that graphically depict the strengths and weaknesses associated with each option.[9] Each limb represents a different alternative, with the advantages and disadvantages of each option being listed with the likelihood of obtaining those results. This visual approach makes it easier for many individuals to appreciate the comparative values of the different options.

When the alternative to a negotiated agreement is an administrative, arbitral, or judicial proceeding, lawyers must carefully assess the likely outcome of the adjudication process. They must review the pertinent factual circumstances and legal doctrines, and then evaluate such subjective factors as witness credibility and the sympathetic nature of the parties involved. When attorneys attempt to assess the probable trial result, they must not only predict which party is likely to prevail and with what degree of probability (*e.g.*, 50% or 70% likelihood), but also the expected amount of such an award.[10]

---

[7] *See* FISHER & URY, *supra* note 5, at 101-111. Some litigators, especially defendants, use the term WATNA (Worst Alternative to a Negotiated Agreement) to establish their bottom line. Economic game theorists often use the terms "reservation point" or "resistance point."

[8] *See* Russell Korobkin, *A Positive Theory of Legal Negotiation*, 88 GEO. L.J. 1789, 1797 (2000); SAMFRITS LEPOOLE, NEVER TAKE NO FOR AN ANSWER 60-61 (Kogan Page 2d ed. 1991).

[9] *See generally* JOHN S. HAMMOND, RAL. KEENEY & HOWARD RAIFFA, SMART CHOICES: A PRACTICAL GUIDE TO MAKING BETTER DECISIONS (Harvard Bus. School Press 1999).

[10] *See* LEIGH THOMPSON, THE MIND AND HEART OF THE NEGOTIATOR 24-28 (Prentice Hall 3d ed. 2005).

Suppose the plaintiff has a 20 percent chance of obtaining a $500,000 verdict, a 30 percent chance of obtaining a $400,000 verdict, a 30 percent chance of obtaining a $300,000 and a 20 percent chance of a verdict for the defendant. The expected law suit value would be:

0.20 (20%) × $500,000	$100,000
0.30 (30%) × $400,000	$120,000
0.30 (30%) × $300,000	$90,000
0.2 (20%) × $0	$0
Expected Value:	$310.000

The monetary and nonmonetary transactional costs associated with settlement and non-settlement must also be considered by all parties. Litigants must recognize that the monetary and psychological costs[11] of trial must be *subtracted from* the anticipated plaintiff's outcome, because these costs would diminish the net expected value of any plaintiff judgment.[12] Also, since the defendant would have to incur the cost of defense no matter who prevails at trial, these defense costs have to be *added to* the defendant's expected value.

A similar expected-value analysis should be performed by persons preparing for transactional encounters. Suppose the owner of a firm is deciding how much she should expect to obtain from the sale of the corporation. Let's assume the owner believes there is a 10 percent chance the business will sell for $50 million, a 30 percent chance it will sell for at least $45 million, a 60 percent chance it will sell for at least $40 million, a 90 percent chance it will sell for at least $35 million, and a 100 percent chance it will sell for at least $30 million. What would be the expected value of the firm?

0.10 (10%) × $50,000,000	$5,000,000
0.20 (30% − 10%) × $45,000,000	$9,000,000
0.30 (60% − 30%) × $40,000,000	$12,000,000
0.30 (90% − 60%) × $35,000,000	$10,500,000
0.10 (100% − 90%) × $30,000,000	$3,000,000
Expected Value:	$39,500,000

The client must now be asked how much money she really has to obtain to sell her business. She may have to have at least $35 million, and would not accept anything below that figure. How willing is she to hold out for the possibility of a higher amount? The attorney and client must determine how risk averse or risk tolerant the client is. A risk taker may be willing to hold out for $45 million, while a risk averse seller may not be able to tolerate holding out much past $40 million.

---

[11] Note that the psychological and financial cost for plaintiff and defendant are not always the same. For example, in a personal injury case, a big corporation or insurance company may be easily able to absorb a loss, where loss would be financially and emotionally devastating to the plaintiff.

[12] Even if the plaintiff is suing under a fee-shifting statute that authorizes awards of attorney fees to prevailing plaintiffs (*e.g.*, Title VII of the Civil Rights Act of 1964, 42 U.S.C. § 2000e-5(k) (2000)), they may have other monetary costs and will have definite nonmonetary costs that still have to be considered.

Once attorneys have determined their own side's expected value, they often think they have completed this part of the evaluative process. The many lawyers who come to this conclusion ignore an equally critical part of the preliminary equation: their *opponent's expected value*.[13] Legal representatives should employ formal and informal discovery techniques to obtain the relevant information possessed by the opposing party. They must ascertain, to the degree they can before they begin to directly negotiate, the needs and interests of their adversaries. This will allow them to predict the items they want that are of minimal importance to the other side, and which terms the other side wants that are not valued by their own client. They must also attempt to determine the alternatives available to the other side if no agreement is achieved through the current negotiations. If Side B's nonsettlement (BATNA) options are worse than Side A's BATNA options, then Side A has greater bargaining power. The cost of nonsettlement to Side A is less onerous than to Side B. An appreciation of Side B's nonsettlement alternatives allows Side A to prepare a negotiation strategy that will culminate in an offer that Side B should prefer to its nonsettlement options.

b. *Establishing Elevated Aspiration Levels*

Attorneys preparing for bargaining encounters must recognize that persons who begin their interactions with elevated goals routinely obtain more beneficial results than individuals who begin with modest objectives.[14] These goals should always be well above their bottom lines if negotiators hope to obtain optimal results.[15] Bargainers should not establish modest objectives merely to avoid the possibility they might not obtain everything they want.[16] While high aspiration bargainers might not achieve their ultimate goals, they usually obtain better results than negotiators with lower objectives. Persons who always get what they want when they negotiate should realize that their successes may reflect their unduly modest objectives. They should thus raise their goals for future encounters by five to ten percent. If these persons continue to obtain everything they want, they should continue to raise their goals. They should continue this incremental process until they begin to obtain less than they hoped to get. At this point, these individuals have probably learned to establish appropriately elevated objectives.[17]

Consistently successful negotiators establish elevated aspiration levels before they begin interactions with opponents. They ascertain the pertinent factual, legal, and economic issues, and estimate the most generous results they could reasonably hope to obtain. They then increase their objectives and work diligently to formulate arguments that make their seemingly excessive goals seem reasonable. Less certain

---

[13] *See* Korobkin, *supra* note 8, at 1797-99.

[14] *See* Russell Korobkin, *Aspirations and Settlement*, 88 CORNELL L. REV. 1, 4, 20-30 (2002); ROGER DAWSON, SECRETS OF POWER NEGOTIATING 16-17 (Career Press 2d ed. 2001); MAX H. BAZERMAN & MARGARET A. NEALE, NEGOTIATING RATIONALLY 28 (Free Press 1992).

[15] *See* LePoole, *supra* note 8, at 62-63.

[16] *See* RICHARD SHELL, BARGAINING FOR ADVANTAGE 32-33 (Viking 1999).

[17] This approach applies to standard negotiating technique and is distinguished from the approach used by lawyers practicing collaborative law, which we will discuss in Part Three.

adversaries tend to defer to the overt confidence exuded by these more thoroughly prepared participants.[18]

Proficient negotiators focus primarily on their **aspiration levels** when they bargain. They only rely upon their **bottom lines** when they have to decide whether to continue interactions that appear to be unproductive. Less skilled bargainers tend to focus excessively on their bottom lines throughout their interactions. Once they attain these minimal objectives, they relax knowing that some agreement will be achieved, and they no longer work hard to surpass their bottom lines. Observant opponents can discern their relaxed states and become less generous with respect to subsequent concessions. These bottom line oriented negotiators thus settle for less generous terms than their cohorts who continue to focus on their aspiration levels throughout their bargaining interactions.[19]

There is an important limitation on setting one's aspiration levels. When individuals prepare for negotiation encounters, they should establish ambitious — but **realistically attainable** — objectives. If their goals are entirely unreasonable, they may discourage opponents and induce those persons to think that mutually acceptable agreements are unattainable.[20] Unusually elevated aspiration bargainers may encounter an additional problem. Once they get into the negotiation and realize that their objectives are not achievable, they may lose this important touchstone and move quickly toward their bottom lines.

c. *Formulating Elevated but Principled Opening Offers*

Advocates who commence bargaining interactions with raised expectations recognize that it is impossible for even skilled negotiators to accurately calculate the value of impending encounters solely from their own side's perspective. Until they begin to interact with their opponents, they are not certain regarding the degree to which those individuals want or need the prospective deal.

Many persons are hesitant to formulate excessive opening positions for fear of offending their opponents. Nonetheless, proficient negotiators attempt to develop the most beneficial positions they can rationally defend.[21] They realize that if their initial offers are wholly unrealistic, they will feel awkward when they try to justify their positions and undermine their credibility. On the other hand, they understand that if they begin with modest offers, they immediately place themselves at a disadvantage.

Some individuals commence bargaining encounters with modest proposals hoping to generate reciprocal behavior by their opponents. Opening offers that are overly generous to adversaries are likely to have the opposite effect due to the impact of a phenomenon known as *"anchoring."*[22] When people receive better offers than they anticipated, they question their own preliminary assessments and *increase* their own

---

[18] *See* Jennifer Gerarda Brown, *The Role of Hope in Negotiation*, 44 U.C.L.A. L. Rev. 1661, 1675 (1997).

[19] *See* Shell, *supra* note 16, at 24-32.

[20] *See* Korobkin, *supra* note 14, at 62-63.

[21] *See* Shell, *supra* note 16, at 160-61.

[22] *See* Korobkin, *supra* note 14, at 30-36; Shell, *supra* note 16, at 161-62; Russell Korobkin & Chris

aspiration levels. They expect to obtain more beneficial results than they initially thought possible, and they make initial offers more favorable to their own side.

When negotiators formulate their initial offers, they should develop principled rationales they can use to explain how they arrived at their stated positions.[23] Litigators should thus carefully explain the exact basis for their offers. How have they valued the past and expected future medical expenses and compensation loses? How have they valued the pain and suffering? Transactional bargainers should do the same thing. How have they valued the real property, building and equipment, accounts receivable, patents and trademarks, good will, etc.? The development of specific values for each of the components to be discussed supported by logical explanations demonstrates a firm commitment to the overall positions being articulated.[24] It also makes it more difficult for opponents to dismiss such positions without careful consideration of the supporting rationales.[25] A principled opening offer often allows the initiating party to accomplish one other important objective - it may enable that party to define the bargaining agenda.

d. *Choreographing the Impending Interaction*

Once legal representatives have determined their bottom lines, aspiration levels, and opening offers, they must plan their bargaining strategies. How do they envision moving from where they begin to where they would like to conclude their encounter? Do they anticipate a number of small concessions or a few large position changes? What bargaining techniques do they think would most effectively move their opponents toward their objectives? At what point during their interaction do they plan to take a firm stand, hoping to generate beneficial final terms? The more negotiators visualize a successful transition from their opening positions to their desired results, the more likely they are to be successful.

Proficient negotiators appreciate the importance of planning to reach ultimate offers that will be considered attractive by reasonably risk averse opponents. If their offers are wholly unacceptable, it is easy for adversaries to accept the less onerous consequences associated with nonsettlements. On the other hand, most people find it difficult to reject definitive offers that are at least as good as what they think they might achieve through their nonsettlement alternatives.

When individuals prepare for bargaining encounters, the following Negotiation Preparation Form may be helpful. As you can see, it guides you through an intentional Preparation Stage in anticipation of the following 5 stages which are described below. For your convenience, this is available for download at the **LexisNexis Webcourse**, Chapter 4, along with a Post-Negotiation Evaluation Checklist.

Guthrie, *Psychological Barriers to Litigation Settlement: An Experimental Approach*, 93 MICH. L. REV. 107, 138-42 (1994).

[23] *See* JAMES C. FREUND, SMART NEGOTIATING 122-23 (Simon & Schuster 1992); JOHN ILICH, DEAL-BREAKERS & BREAK-THROUGHS 112 (John Wiley & Sons 1992).

[24] *See* STEFAN H. KREIGER, RICHARD K. NEUMANN, JR., KATHLEEN H. MCMANUS & STEVEN D. JAMAR, ESSENTIAL LAWYERING SKILLS 282-83 (Aspen Law & Bus. 1999).

[25] *See* ANTHONY R. PRATKANIS & ELLIOT ARONSON, AGE OF PROPAGANDA 26-27 (W.H. Freeman 1991).

NEGOTIATION PREPARATION FORM

TO BE COMPLETED DURING PREPARATION STAGE

Most of these questions are applicable in every negotiation. Sometimes, the answers are longer and more complex than other times. Asking these questions during the Preparation Stage before you really commence the negotiation is critical to developing an intentional negotiating strategy that will maximize results for your client. As you get more proficient, you may find that you can condense the outline. However, you should be thinking about all of these questions whenever you prepare for a negotiation.

INITIAL CONSIDERATIONS FOR THE PREPARATION STAGE:

1.   What items are *essential* to your client?

2.   What items are *important* to your client?

3.   What items are *desirable* to your client?

4.   What are your client's *alternatives* to a negotiated agreement?

5.   Given your answers to 1-4, above, what is your client's *minimum settlement point [BATNA]?* (Include in the analysis *transaction costs* associated with both settlement and nonsettlement. In other words, when comparing settlement to non-settlement, focus on the expected *net* to client.)

6.   What is your client's *aspiration level [target point]* — What is the best result your client might achieve? Is your *aspiration level* high enough? Never commence a negotiation until you have mentally solidified your ultimate goal with respect to *each item* to be negotiated.

7.   What items do you think are *essential* to your opponent?

8.   What items do you think are *important* to your opponent?

9.   What items do you think are *desirable* to your opponent?

10. What do you think are your opponent's *alternatives* to a negotiated agreement?

11. Given your answers to 7-10, above, what do you think is your opponent's *minimum settlement point [BATNA]?* (Include in the analysis *transaction costs* associated with both settlement and nonsettlement. In other words, when comparing settlement to non-settlement, focus on the expected *net* to opponent.)

12. Given your answers to 7-10, above, what do you think is your opponent's *aspiration level [target point]* with respect to *each item* to be negotiated?

PLANNING FOR THE PRELIMINARY STAGE:

13. What do you (and your client) have in common with your opponents?

     A.   Are you from the same city, state, region, etc.? Do you root for the same sports teams? Enjoy the same music? Did you attend the same schools? Do you have children attending the same schools?

     B.   What personal connections can you make during the Preliminary Stage, when negotiator identities are being established and the tone for the negotiation is being set?

     C.   Are there any cultural, gender, race, class, or other matters that might affect communication and interaction?

14. What do you know about your opponent's negotiating style?

    A.   If you have not previously negotiated with your opponent, who has? If you can speak to others who have negotiated without losing a tactical advantage, do it. What do they say?

    B.   Based upon what you know, what do you anticipate in the way of conduct? Can you expect candor? Dissembling?

    C.   Based upon what you know, what is your planned approach during this stage?

PLANNING FOR THE INFORMATIONAL STAGE:

15. What **information** do you want to elicit to determine your opponent's underlying needs, interests, and objectives?

16. What specific **questions** do you anticipate asking in order to obtain the desired information? (Start with broad, open-ended questions.)

17. What **information** are you **willing to disclose** and how do you plan to divulge it? (It's best to disclose important information in response to the opponent's questions)

18. How do you plan to prevent disclosure of sensitive information?

    A.   What **blocking techniques** do you anticipate using and how?

19. What will be your **principled opening offer** and how did you determine it? Make sure it leaves you a chance to negotiate down to the **aspiration level** that you identified in 6, above.

20. What do you anticipate will be your opponent's **principled opening offer** and how will it be determined?

21. Based on your current knowledge, what **facts** are there in your client's favor that give you **leverage** during the negotiation?

    A.   How do you plan to use these facts during the explanation of your **principled opening offer** and throughout the negotiation?

    B.   What do you anticipate that your opponent will say in response in an attempt to minimize the significance of these facts?

    C.   What do you plan to say and/or do in response to your opponent's anticipated comments?

22. Based on your current knowledge, what **facts** are there in your opponent's favor that give your opponent **leverage** during the negotiation?

    A.   How do anticipate that your opponent will use these facts during the explanation of a **principled opening offer** and throughout the negotiation?

    B.   What do you anticipate that you will say in response in an attempt to minimize the significance of these facts?

    C.   What do you anticipate that your opponent will say and/or do in response to your anticipated comments?

23. What **law** is there in your client's favor that gives you **leverage** during the negotiation?

    A.   How do you plan to use this law during the explanation of your *principled opening offer* and throughout the negotiation?

     B.   What do you anticipate that your opponent will say in response in an attempt to minimize the significance of this law?

     C.   What do you plan to say and/or do in response to your opponent's anticipated comments?

24.   What *law* is there in your opponent's favor that gives your opponent *leverage* during the negotiation?

     A.   How do you anticipate that your opponent will use this law during the explanation of a *principled opening offer* and throughout the negotiation?

     B.   What do you anticipate that you will say in response in an attempt to minimize the significance of this law?

     C.   What do you anticipate that your opponent will say and/or do in response to your anticipated comments?

PLANNING FOR THE DISTRIBUTIVE STAGE:

25.   What is your overall negotiation strategy?

     A.   Based upon what you currently know, what *principled concessions* do you plan to make?

     B.   What will be your *explanation* for the *principled concessions*?

     C.   In what order do you currently plan to make the *principled concessions* and why?

     D.   What negotiation tactics do you plan to employ? (Be prepared to vary them for the particular facts and parties and so you do not become totally predictable.)

          1.   In what order or combination?

          2.   What are you hoping to achieve by the use of these tactics?

          3.   What counter-measures do you expect your opponent to use to neutralize your tactics?

          4.   What do you plan to say/do in response?

26.   What do you anticipate will be your opponent's overall negotiation strategy?

     A.   Based upon what you currently know, what *principled concessions* do you anticipate your opponent will make?

     B.   What do you anticipate will be your opponent's *explanation* for the *principled concessions*?

     C.   In what order do you anticipate your opponent will make the *principled concessions* and why?

     D.   What negotiation tactics do you anticipate your opponent plans to employ?

          1.   In what order or combination?

          2.   What do you believe your opponent will be hoping to achieve by the use of these tactics?

          3.   What counter-measures do you plan to use to neutralize your opponent's tactics?

PLANNING FOR THE CLOSING STAGE:

27. Is there anything about your personality or your client's personality that will make it difficult for you to be patient during this stage?
    A. If yes, what is it?
    B. How will you handle it to avoid having it be a problem?

28. Is there anything about your opponent's personality that will make it difficult for them to be patient during this stage?
    A. If yes, what is it?
    B. What is your strategy for using this to your client's greatest advantage?

PLANNING FOR THE COOPERATIVE STAGE:

29. Based upon what you currently know, is there anything that can maximize the value for both parties without costing your client? In other words, are there any opportunities to make the pie bigger?
    A. If yes, what is your strategy/timing for introducing this?
    B. Whether yes or no, what is your strategy if you discover opportunities during the negotiation?

B.   PRELIMINARY STAGE: ESTABLISHING NEGOTIATOR IDENTITIES AND THE TONE FOR THE INTERACTION

In the Preparation Stage, you worked with your client to understand the conflict and to identify what the client considers to be essential, important and desirable. You then looked at the conflict from the *opponent's* perspective and did your best to identify what the *opponent* considers to be essential, important and desirable. With that information, you and your client developed an aspiration level and a bottom line (BATNA). You did your best to estimate the opponent's bottom line. You completed the outline shown above, or something similar, that set out the information and your strategy in an intentional way. You are now ready to enter the Preliminary Phase of negotiation, where you establish negotiator identities and tones for the interaction.

The beginning of the Preliminary Stage is somewhat like two dogs meeting each other on a path. They establish their identities (you know how . . .) and give visual signals as to whether they are friendly, submissive, aggressive, etc. We do not recommend that you copy their behavior in polite society, but it is an instructive simile.

Lawyers who have previously interacted at the bargaining table are usually familiar with each other's negotiating styles. They are generally able to commence new negotiations without having to formally establish preliminary ground rules. Nonetheless, they should still take the time to reestablish cordial environments that will contribute positively to their impending discussions. Individuals who have not had extensive prior dealings with one another should expect to spend the initial portion of their interaction establishing their personal and professional identities and the tone for their subsequent discussions.

During the preliminary portion of bargaining interactions, lawyers should look for common interests they share with opponents. They may be from the same city or state, they attended the same college or law school, their children attend the same schools, they enjoy the same music or sports, etc. Persons who can identify and share such common interests enhance the probability they will like each other and develop mutually beneficial relationships.[26]

Attorneys who are unfamiliar with the negotiating styles of opposing counsel should try to obtain pre-negotiation information from other people in their own offices and from other lawyers they know. Can they expect their opponents to behave in an open and cooperative manner in which they seek to achieve mutually beneficial results or in a closed and adversarial fashion in which they try to maximize their own side's results?[27] Can they anticipate candor or dissembling from those persons? What types of bargaining techniques can they expect the other side to employ?[28]

Attorneys who encounter seemingly cooperative opponents should try to determine whether those people's apparent predisposition toward cooperative interactions is

---

[26] *See* CHRISTOPHER W. MOORE, THE MEDIATION PROCESS 184-85 (Jossey-Bass 3d ed. 2003).

[27] *See* Charles B. Craver, *Negotiation Styles: The Impact on Bargaining Transactions*, DISP. RES. J. 48 (Feb.-Apr. 2003). These are discussed in Chapter 5, *infra*.

[28] *See generally* Charles B. Craver, *Frequently Employed Negotiation Techniques*, 4 CORP. COUNSEL'S Q. 66 (1988).

consistent with their actual behavior. Is their own openness being reciprocated by opponent candor? Until they verify this fact, they should not disclose excessive amounts of critical information regarding their own situations. They might otherwise permit manipulative adversaries to create false impressions of cooperation, so they can take advantage of one-sided disclosures by this side.[29] If lawyers find that their preliminary openness is not being reciprocated by their opponents, they should be less forthcoming with their own important information to avoid exploitation by opportunist adversaries.

As lawyers begin the Preliminary Stage, they should take the time to develop some rapport with opposing counsel. Through warm eye contact and a pleasant demeanor, they can establish a mutually supportable environment. This reduces the unproductive anxiety created by adversarial conduct. Negotiators should recognize that they can be forceful advocates without resorting to disagreeable tactics.[30] Individuals who equate offensive behavior with effective negotiating strategy will be doubly disappointed — their professional interactions will be increasingly unpleasant and they will find it more difficult to obtain optimal results for their clients.

The preliminary portion of bargaining encounters is critical, because the participants create the atmosphere that affects their entire bargaining transaction. Studies have found that persons who commence interactions in positive moods negotiate more cooperatively and are more likely to use problem-solving efforts designed to maximize the joint returns achieved by the participants.[31] On the other hand, people who begin their encounters in negative moods negotiate more adversarially and tend to generate less efficient results. In addition, negative mood participants are more likely to resort to deceptive tactics than others, while positive mood actors are more likely to honor the agreements reached than their negative mood cohorts.[32]

Attorneys who encounter overtly competitive "win-lose" opponents should recognize that while they may not be able to convert those individuals into cooperative "win-win" negotiators, they may be able to diminish the competitive tendencies of those persons. Through friendly introductions, sincere smiles, and warm handshakes, they can try to establish more personal relationships. They can use a prolonged Preliminary Stage to enhance the negotiating atmosphere. They can attempt to sit in cooperative, rather than competitive, configurations. They can ask these opponents about their families or their colleagues, while making similar disclosures about

---

[29] *See* Gary T. Lowenthal, *A General Theory of Negotiation Process, Strategy, and Behavior*, 31 KAN. L. REV. 69, 82 (1982).

[30] *See* BOB WOOLF, FRIENDLY PERSUASION 34-35 (G.P. Putnam(s Sons 1990). *See generally* RONALD M. SHAPIRO & MARK A. JANKOWSKI, THE POWER OF NICE (John Wiley & Sons rev. ed. 2001).

[31] *See* Clark Freshman, Adele Hayes & Greg Feldman, *The Lawyer-Negotiator as Mood Scientist: What We Know and Don't Know About How Mood Relates to Successful Negotiation*, 2002 J. DISP. RES. 13, 15 (2002); Leigh L. Thompson, Janice Nadler & Peter H. Kim, *Some Like It Hot: The Case for the Emotional Negotiator, in* SHARED COGNITION IN ORGANIZATIONS: THE MANAGEMENT OF KNOWLEDGE 142-44 (Leigh L. Thompson, John M. Levine & David M. Messick, eds.) (Lawrence Erlbaum 1999); Joseph P. Forgas, *On Feeling Good and Getting Your Way: Mood Effects on Negotiator Cognition and Bargaining Strategies*, 74 J. PERSONALITY & SOC. PSYCH. 565, 566-74 (1999).

[32] *See* Freshman, Hayes & Feldman, *supra* note 31, at 22-24; Thompson, Nadler & Kim, *supra* note 31, at 142-44.

themselves. If they can establish first-name relationships, they can accentuate the personal nature of the impending interactions.

If their preliminary efforts do not diminish the competitive behavior of opponents, lawyers may employ *"attitudinal bargaining"* to encourage more pleasant conduct.[33] They may indicate their unwillingness to view the bargaining process as a combative exercise, and suggest the need to establish some preliminary ground rules for the interaction.[34] Litigators can suggest that if the other side prefers open hostility, a trial setting would be the appropriate forum due to the presence of a presiding official. Transactional negotiators may indicate that their clients are looking for mutually beneficial, on-going relationships that cannot be created and maintained through untrusting adversarial behavior. The best negotiators remain firm, fair and friendly, regardless of how the adversary behaves.

When attitudinal bargaining fails to generate appropriate conduct, individuals who must interact with unpleasant opponents should try to control their encounters in ways that diminish the ability of offensive participants to bother them. For example, against a sarcastic and belittling opponent, they could use the telephone to conduct their discussions. When the other side's behavior begins to bother them, they can indicate that they have another call and break off talks. They can call back their adversary once they have calmed down.

C.   INFORMATIONAL STAGE: EXCHANGE OF INFORMATION AND VALUE CREATION

Once the negotiators have established their identities and the tone for their interaction, the third stage of the negotiation process begins. This is the Informational Stage, where the negotiators actually begin to exchange information. Lawyers can easily observe the commencement of this stage, because this point coincides with a shift from small talk to questions regarding the other side's needs and interests. During this part of the process, the participants work to determine the items available for joint distribution. They hope to discern the underlying interests and objectives of the other party. Proficient bargainers look for ways to create value — to expand the overall pie to be divided, recognizing that in most situations, the parties do not value each of the items identically and oppositely. The more effectively the participants can expand the pie, the more efficiently they should be able to conclude their interaction.[35]

---

[33] *See* RAIFFA, *supra* note 6, at 300-01.

[34] *See* HENRY S. KRAMER, GAME, SET, MATCH: WINNING THE NEGOTIATIONS GAME 264-65 (ALM Pub. 2001); LEIGH STEINBERG, WINNING WITH INTEGRITY 144-49 (Random House 1998). *See generally* WILLIAM URY, THE POWER OF A POSITIVE NO (Bantam 2007); WILLIAM URY, GETTING PAST NO (Bantam 1991).

[35] *See* ROBERT H. MNOOKIN, SCOTT R. PEPPET & ANDREW TULUMELLO, BEYOND WINNING: NEGOTIATING TO CREATE VALUE IN DEALS AND DISPUTES 11-43 (Harvard Univ. Press/Belknap 2000).

1. Use of Information-Seeking Questions

The optimal way to elicit information from opponents is to ***ask questions***.[36] During the preliminary part of the Informational Stage, many parties make the mistake of asking narrow questions that can be answered with brief responses. As a result, they merely confirm what they already know. It is more effective to ask broad, open-ended information-seeking questions that induce opponents to speak.[37] The more the opponents talk, the more information they directly and indirectly disclose. Lawyers who suspect something about a particular area should formulate several expansive inquiries pertaining to that area. The people being questioned usually assume that the askers know more about their side's circumstances than they actually do, and they tend to answer the questions being asked, providing more information than they would have in response to specific questions. Only after negotiators have obtained a significant amount of information should they begin to narrow their inquiries to confirm what they think they have heard.[38] If opponents attempt to avoid direct responses to these questions, to prevent the disclosure of particular information, the questioners should reframe their inquiries in a way that compels definitive replies.[39]

Skilled negotiators actively listen and carefully observe opponents during the Informational Stage.[40] They maintain supportive eye contact to encourage further opponent disclosures and to discern verbal leaks and nonverbal clues. They use smiles and occasional head nods to encourage additional responses from adversaries who feel they are being heard. Active listeners not only hear what is being said, but recognize what is not being discussed, since they understand that omitted topics may suggest weaknesses opponents do not wish to address.[41]

Questioners should listen carefully for ***verbal leaks*** that inadvertently disclose important valuation information. For example, an opponent might say: "I ***have to have*** Item A, I ***really want*** Item B, and I would ***like to get*** Item C." Item A is ***essential*** — she has to have it. Item B is ***important*** — she really wants it, but does not have to have it. Item C is ***desirable*** — she would like to get it, but would be willing to give it up for anything better. These leaks disclose the true priorities of the items being discussed.

Advocates should proceed slowly during the Informational Stage, because it takes time for the persons being questioned to decide what should be disclosed and when it should be divulged. Patient questioning and active listening are usually rewarded with the attainment of greater knowledge. Too many negotiators rush through the Informational Stage, because they can hardly wait to begin the distributive portion of

---

[36] *See* Jeswald W. Salacuse, The Global Negotiator 48-52 (Palgrave 2003); Leigh Thompson, The Mind and Heart of The Negotiator 60-61 (Prentice Hall 1998).

[37] *See* Russell Korobkin, Negotiation Theory and Practice 12-13 (Aspen Law & Bus. 2002); Abraham P. Ordover & Andrea Doneff, Alternatives to Litigation 20-22 (NITA 2002); Ilich, *supra* note 23, at 68.

[38] *See* Thomas F. Guernsey, A Practical Guide to Negotiation 62-63 (NITA 1996).

[39] *See* Donald D. Gifford, Legal Negotiation: Theory and Applications 123 (West 1989).

[40] *See* Ordover & Doneff, *supra* note 37, at 23-26; Shapiro & Jankowsli, *supra* note 30, at 76-77; Daniel Goleman, Working with Emotional Intelligence 178-80 (Bantam 1998).

[41] *See* Kramer, *supra* note 34, at 234.

interactions.[42] When impatient bargainers conduct an abbreviated Informational Stage, they usually miss important pieces of information and achieve agreements that are less beneficial than the accords they might have obtained through a more deliberate questioning process.

Since negotiators cannot impose their will on opponents, they must ascertain the underlying needs and interests of those parties and seek to at least minimally satisfy the basic goals of those participants. Through patient and strategically planned questioning, they can try to learn as much as possible about opponent interests, objectives, and relative preferences. What issues would the other side like to have addressed, and which terms are essential, important, and desirable? Which items do both sides consider essential or important, and which are complementary terms that can be exchanged in ways that simultaneously advance the goals of both parties?

2.   Exploring Underlying Needs and Interests of Parties

When expansive settlement range (overlap) exists between the bottom lines of the two sides, the participants should be able to achieve accords. Their resulting agreement, however, will probably not be a Pareto superior solution — which is where neither party could further enhance its circumstances without simultaneously worsening the other side's situation. When one side's gain is the other side's loss, this is also called a "zero sum game." But if the parties can thoughtfully explore their respective underlying interests and rely upon objective standards to guide their discussions, they are often able to expand the overall pie and enhance the benefits to both sides.[43]

Although many legal practitioners consider the negotiation process an inherently adversarial endeavor, they should appreciate the benefits that may be derived during the Informational Stage from the use of nonadversarial questioning techniques. Too many bargainers make the mistake of assuming that the parties have a fixed amount of goods to be divided — i.e., identical value systems and analogous utility functions that generate zero-sum transactions.[44] If they replaced leading questions, intended to challenge the positions being taken by opponents, with more neutral questions designed to elicit the underlying needs and interests of the other side, negotiators could more easily look for areas that would allow joint gains.[45]

---

[42] *See* MARK MCCORMACK, WHAT THEY DON'T TEACH YOU AT HARVARD BUSINESS SCHOOL 152 (Bantam 1984).

[43] The use of integrative bargaining techniques to maximize the joint returns achieved by the negotiating parties will be discussed in connection with the Cooperative Stage, *infra*. If the parties fail to explore their underlying interests and needs during the Information Stage, it makes it less likely that they will be able to make the exchanges during the subsequent Cooperative Stage that will generate efficient results.

[44] *See* Richard Birke & Craig R. Fox, *Psychological Principles in Negotiating Civil Settlements*, 4 HARV. NEGOT. L. REV. 1, 30-31 (1999); James J. Gillespie, Leigh L. Thompson, Jeffrey Loewenstein & Dedre Gentner, *Lessons from Analogical Reasoning in the Teaching of Negotiation*, 15 NEGOT. J. 363, 367 (1999).

[45] *See* RAIFFA, *supra* note 6, at 198-201; MNOOKIN, PEPPET & TULUMELLO, *supra* note 35, at 11-44; Carrie Menkel-Meadow, *Toward Another View of Legal Negotiation: The Structure of Problem Solving*, 31 U.C.L.A. L. REV. 754, 813 (1984); FISHER & URY, *supra* note 5, at 41-57.

Even entirely monetary transactions do not have to be regarded as zero-sum endeavors. The two sides may have quite different preference curves with respect to the value of money. In addition, through the use of in-kind payments consisting of goods or services, the parties may convert their interaction into a non-zero-sum transaction. A purchaser of a company may agree to provide $50 million in cash and $15 million in goods or services. The seller believes she just sold her firm for $65 million, while the purchaser thinks he only paid $59 million, because it only cost $9 million to generate the goods and services valued by the seller for $15 million. The parties may alternatively provide for some future payments that may be considered beneficial by both sides.

People involved with multi-item negotiations must appreciate the fact that the parties probably value the various items quite differently. This enables them to look for exchanges that can simultaneously benefit both sides.[46] For example, individuals negotiating the terms for a marital dissolution may be discussing their primary residence and vacation home, their SUV and sports car, custody of their two young children, child support payments, and possible alimony. They may be arguing over joint custody, when only one spouse really wants primary parenting responsibilities. If the spouse who does not strongly desire primary parenting obligations is provided with adequate visitation rights, he or she may provide the other person with the primary residence in which to continue living with the children and the SUV needed to transport the children, in exchange for the vacation home and the sports car. They can then talk about child support payments and possible alimony.

If negotiators hope to expand the overall pie and ultimately explore beneficial exchanges that may simultaneously benefit both sides, they must initially, during the client preparation stage, classify the goals sought by their client as "essential," "important," and "desirable." They must then endeavor to determine during the information exchanges the degree to which their own side's goals conflict with the objectives of the other side.[47] In some instances, both parties may actually desire the identical distribution of the items in question ("shared needs"), allowing them to enhance their respective interests at the same time. In other situations, each may wish to attain independent objectives that do not conflict with the interests of their opponent ("independent needs"). In only some areas do both parties wish to claim the identical items for themselves. Even with respect to these "conflicting needs," the two sides must ascertain the degree to which each prefers the terms in question. One may consider them "essential," while the other may only regard them as "important" or "desirable." The party with a higher preference should be willing to trade terms of lesser value to obtain the items they prefer to get. Only when the parties both value conflicting needs identically are both going to vie for them. In these areas, even trades of similarly valued terms can move the parties toward final accords.

---

[46] *See* SHAPIRO & JANKOWSLI, *supra* note 30, at 101-03; Michael Watkins, *Principles of Persuasion*, 17 NEGOT. J. 115, 124 (2001).

[47] *See* RAIFFA, *supra* note 6, at 199-201; Watkins, *supra* note 46, at 22-23; Carrie Menkel-Meadow, *Aha? Is Creativity Possible in Legal Problem Solving and Teachable in Legal Education?* 6 HARV. NEGOT. L. REV. 97, 109-111 (2001).

3. Multiple Item Negotiations

When numerous terms have to be negotiated, the participants have to ascertain the degree to which each side values each item. They often obtain this information from the way in which the serious discussions commence. It is unwieldy to bargain over twenty-five or fifty items simultaneously. As a result, most negotiators begin the real talks with a group of four or five terms. They generally begin with a group of either important or unimportant items. Anxious bargainers tend to start with a group of important items, thinking that if agreement can be reached on these terms, the remaining issues should be resolvable. While this is true, it is also risky. When parties begin the substantive talks by focusing on the more important items, they often reach a quick impasse. The gap between the stated positions may seem immense, and the participants may conclude that no accord is possible. On the other hand, if parties begin with a discussion of the less significant terms, they can quickly achieve tentative agreements with respect to many of the issues to be addressed. As they reach agreement on twenty then forty and even sixty percent of the items to be covered, they emphasize the areas for joint gain and become psychologically committed to settlement.[48] As they approach the more controverted terms, they remember the success they have already achieved and do not want to allow the remaining items to prevent an overall accord.[49] In addition, the final items no longer seem as insurmountable as they would have if the parties had begun their discussions with those terms.

4. How to Disclose and Withhold Important Information

While individuals prepare for a negotiation, they must decide several things regarding their own side's information. What information are they willing to disclose, and how do they plan to divulge it? What sensitive information do they wish to withhold, and how do they plan to avoid the disclosure of these facts? People who resolve these crucial issues *before* they begin to interact with their opponents are more likely to have successful Informational Stages than those persons who do not think about these issues until they are forced to do so during the actual negotiations.

Negotiators who readily volunteer their critical information may encounter difficulties. As they naively disclose their interests and objectives, their statements may not be heard by opponents who are not listening intently to such statements. In addition, when adversaries do hear the information being disclosed, they tend to discredit it because of "*reactive devaluation*."[50] That is, they assume the disclosures are manipulative and self-serving, and they discount much of what they hear.

Bargainers who want their important information to be heard and respected should disclose that information slowly in response to opponent questions. When they answer opponent inquiries with such disclosures, their adversaries hear more of what

---

[48] *See* Michael Watkins & Susan Rosegrant, Breakthrough International Negotiation 21-22 (Jossey-Bass 2001).

[49] *See* Chester Karrass, The Negotiating Game 72-73 (Crowell 1970).

[50] *See* Mnookin, Peppet & Tulumello, *supra* note 35, at 165.

they are saying, because people listen more intently to the answers to their own questions. In addition, opponents attribute these disclosures to their questioning capabilities and accord what they hear greater respect.

What should negotiators do when opponents ask them about areas they would prefer not to address? They should appreciate the fact that it is much easier to avoid the disclosure of important information if their adversaries are unaware of the fact that knowledge is being withheld. The most effective way to accomplish this objective is through the use of *"blocking techniques."*[51] These tactics are regularly employed by politicians who do not wish to provide answers to sensitive questions that may cost them votes no matter how they respond. People who listen carefully to such politicians will be amazed by the number of inquiries that go unanswered.[52]

The first blocking technique involves *non-focus*, by ignoring the question being asked. Negotiators who do not like a particular inquiry should continue the current conversation or change the discussion to other topics they would prefer to explore as if they never heard the question that was propounded. The opponent will often get caught up in the continued talks and forget to restate their initial inquiry.

The second blocking technique involves *selective focus*, by intentionally answering only part of the question. For example, someone being asked a three or four part question can focus on the part she likes and ignore the rest. If she can induce her opponent to focus on the part being addressed, he may never return to the other parts of the initial inquiry.

The third blocking technique involves *refocus*, by answering the question in a way that changes the scope of the inquiry. For example, a person being asked a delicate question may over or under answer it. If he is asked a specific question, he can provide a general response. If asked a general inquiry, he can give a narrow response. He might alternatively misinterpret the question being asked. An opponent asks about a particular topic, and he responds by indicating that the opponent must be concerned about a different subject. He then steers the discussion in the direction he would like to see it progress. If he can induce his adversary to focus on the new area being discussed, the opponent may fail to restate the original inquiry.

Finally, negotiators should be vigilant when it comes to questions that seek information of a confidential or privileged nature. The person asking these questions often hopes to catch the respondent off guard or may be testing the opponent's level of sophistication. Before negotiators commence bargaining interactions, they should determine what information they are not willing to disclose. What information concerns confidential lawyer-client communications? What information is privileged (*e.g.*, attorney work product)? They should be prepared to respond to opponent inquiries pertaining to these areas by indicating that they concern confidential or privileged matters that will not be discussed. Once adversaries realize these areas are

---

[51] *See* Robert M. Bastress & Joseph D. Harbaugh, Interviewing, Counseling, and Negotiating 422-28 (Little Brown 1990); Freund, *supra* note 23, at 64-65. Of course, these blocking techniques are less effective on negotiators who properly prepare and carefully listen!

[52] While this is a standard negotiating tactic, we caution new advocates that this is *not* an appropriate tactic with judges and persons in similar roles.

off limits, they will move on to other areas.

D. DISTRIBUTIVE STAGE: EXCHANGING ITEMS TO BE DIVIDED — VALUE CLAIMING

The transition from the Informational Stage to the Distributive Stage is usually visible. When parties are still exchanging information, the focus is primarily upon *opponents*, as the negotiators try to ascertain what is available for distribution and determine the degree to which the other party values the items to be exchanged. When parties begin to exchange items during the discussions, the focus is on the negotiator's own side, as both sides begin to claim the items they discovered during the previous stage. The participants cease asking each other what they want and why they want it, and begin to talk about what they have to have or are willing to give up.

No matter how much altruistic negotiators try to create win-win bargaining environments, there will always be items both sides wish to obtain. Most proficient legal representatives hope to claim more of the conflicted terms for their own clients. In their book *The Power of Nice*, Ron Shapiro and Mark Jankowski unambiguously articulate this philosophy: "[W]e're out to achieve *all* (or most) of *our* goals, to make *our most desirable deal.* But the best way to do so is to let the other side achieve *some* of *their* goals, to make their acceptable deal. That's **WIN-win**: big win for your side, little win for theirs."[53] Throughout the Distributive Stage, the parties compete for these mutually desired terms.

1. Benefits of Inducing Opponents to Make First Offers

Which side should make the initial offer, and does it make any difference who goes first? Some negotiators prefer to make the first offer because they think this approach allows them to define the bargaining range and discourage wholly unrealistic opponent offers.[54] Even individuals who often go first recognize the risks of making the initial offer if they are not certain of the value of the items being exchanged. The use of preemptive first offers can be an effective technique when both sides have a realistic understanding of the items involved and have established a trusting relationship. When such factors are not present, however, we prefer to elicit first offers from our opponents for three reasons.

First, if one or both sides have miscalculated the value of the interaction, whoever goes first will disclose the misunderstanding and place their side at a disadvantage. Even though proficient bargainers can frequently predict accurately the areas in which their adversaries will commence the process, they can never be certain. Opponents may have estimated their side's strengths or weaknesses, and their preliminary offer is likely to disclose this error.

A second reason to elicit first offers from the other side concerns a phenomenon known as *"**bracketing**."* If negotiators can induce their opponents to make the initial

---

[53] Shapiro & Jankowski, *supra* note 30, at 5 (emphasis in original).

[54] *See* Steinberg, *supra* note 34, at 52-53; Freund, *supra* note 23, at 114-15.

offer, they can *bracket* their goals by adjusting their own opening offers to keep their objectives near the mid-point between their respective opening positions.[55] For example, if plaintiff's attorney hopes to obtain $500,000 and defense counsel initially offers $250,000, plaintiff's counsel can begin with a demand of $750,000 to keep the $500,000 target in the middle. Since parties tend to move toward the center of their opening positions, due to the accepted obligation of bargaining parties to make reciprocal concessions, the people who go second can manipulate the central point and place their adversaries at a psychological disadvantage.

The third reason to induce opponents to make the initial offer is because negotiators who make the first concessions tend to do less well than their adversaries.[56] People who make the first concessions tend to be anxious negotiators who make more and larger concessions than their opponents. Individuals who induce their adversaries to make the first offers have a good chance of persuading them to also make the first concessions. After A makes the initial offer, B's opening position looks like a counter-offer. It appears to be in "response" to A's opening offer. Now A must respond — presumably by making some kind of concession as the parties move closer. It is thus easy for B to look to A for the first concession.

It is not always easy to induce opponents to make the opening offers. In some situations, usual practices suggest that the party initiating the bargaining encounter should begin the substantive discussions. For example, someone who has decided to sell her business may be expected to propose a price, and a person initiating a lawsuit may be expected to indicate what he wishes to obtain.[57] Despite this factor, skilled bargainers who might otherwise be expected to initiate the process may be able to induce less proficient opponents to do so. They may prolong the Preliminary Stage discussions and the early portions of the Informational Stage until a less patient adversary simply articulates the first offer to get the substantive talks moving. These persons might alternatively begin the Informational Stage by asking the opponent a number of questions that lead to a request for an opening position statement.

2.   Carefully Planned Concession Patterns

Persuasive bargainers begin the Distributive Stage with the articulation of "principled" positions that rationally explain why they deserve what they are offering or seeking. This bolsters their confidence in their own positions, and undermines the confidence of less prepared opponents in their own positions. Proficient negotiators also begin with carefully prepared concession patterns.[58] They know how they plan to move from their opening offers to their final objectives. They may intend to make several deliberate, but expansive, concessions, or prefer to employ a series of incremental position changes. They know that this aspect of their strategy must be thoughtfully choreographed to maximize their bargaining effectiveness. They try to

---

[55] *See* DAWSON, *supra* note 14, at 18-20; Birke & Fox, *supra* note 44, at 41.

[56] *See* BASTRESS & HARBAUGH, *supra* note 51, at 493; HERBERT KRITZER, LET'S MAKE A DEAL 68 (Univ. of Wisc. Press 1991).

[57] *See* ILICH, *supra* note 37, at 169.

[58] *See* FREUND, *supra* note 23, at 130-41.

make only *"**principled concessions**"* that they can rationally explain to their adversaries. This lets others know why they are making the precise position change being articulated, and indicates why a greater modification is not presently warranted. This approach also helps them to remain at their new position until they obtain a reciprocal concession from the other side.

The timing of concessions is important. Many anxious negotiators find it difficult to cope with the uncertainty indigenous to the bargaining process, and they often make rapid — and occasionally unreciprocated — concessions in a desperate effort to generate accords.[59] They ignore the fact that 80 percent of position changes tend to occur during the last 20 percent of interactions.[60] People who attempt to expedite transactions in an artificial manner usually pay a high price for their impatience.[61]

Concessions must be carefully formulated and tactically announced. If properly used, a position change can signal a cooperative attitude; it can also communicate the need for a counteroffer if the opponent intends to continue the bargaining process. If carelessly issued, however, a concession can signal anxiety and a loss of control. This may occur when a position change is announced in a tentative and unprincipled manner by an individual who continues to talk nervously and defensively after the concession has been articulated. Such behavior suggests that the speaker does not expect immediate reciprocity from the other side. When one encounters such individuals, they should subtly encourage them to keep talking, since this approach may generate additional, unanswered concessions.[62] To avoid this problem, proficient negotiators announce their position changes with appropriate explanations, then shift the focus to their opponents. By exuding a patient silence at this point, they indicate that reciprocal behavior must be forthcoming if the interaction is to continue.

The exact amount and precise timing of each position change are critical. Each successive concession should be smaller than the preceding one, and each should normally be made in response to an appropriate counteroffer from the opponent. If a subsequent change is greater than the prior ones, this may signal that the conceding party is adrift. If successive concessions are made too quickly, this may similarly indicate a lack of control. Following each change, the focus should be shifted to the other side. Patient silence will let the other party know that they must reciprocate to keep the process moving.[63]

Although negotiators should carefully plan their concession patterns in advance, they must remain flexible in recognition of the fact that opponents do not always react to position changes as initially expected. Participants must thus be prepared to change their planned behavior as new information regarding adversary strengths,

---

[59] Go back to your personality inventory from Exercise 2.2. Do your personality traits suggest that you will need to be particularly vigilant to avoid this trap in your own negotiating? Self-knowledge is critical.

[60] *See* DAWSON, *supra* note 14, at 171.

[61] *See* LEPOOLE, *supra* note 8, at 72.

[62] *See* John C. Harsanyi, *Bargaining and Conflict Situations in Light of a New Approach to Game Theory, in* BARGAINING: FORMAL THEORIES OF NEGOTIATION 74, 80-81 (Oran R. Young, ed.) (Univ. of Illinois Press 1975).

[63] *See* PRATKANIS & ARONSON, *supra* note 25, at 180-81.

weaknesses, and preferences is obtained.[64] They should not only be prepared to adjust their aspiration level, when appropriate, but also be ready to alter their concession strategy based upon mutually acknowledged objective criteria.[65] They must be patient, recognizing that a particular interaction may take longer to complete than they originally anticipated. When concessions are small and the issues are numerous and/or complex, negotiators must allow the process to develop deliberately. If they try to hasten the transaction in an unnatural way, they may place themselves at a tactical disadvantage.[66]

Negotiators should always remember their nonsettlement options and preliminarily established resistance points as they approach their bottom lines during bargaining interactions. They must recognize the fact that it would be irrational to accept proposed terms that are less beneficial than their external alternatives (BATNA). As the Distributive Stage unfolds and they approach their resistance points, many advocates feel greater pressure to settle, when they should actually feel less pressure to achieve accords. When the terms being offered by opponents are not much better than their nonsettlement options, participants approaching their bottom lines possess more — not less — bargaining power than the offerors. Assuming they have correctly identified their BATNA, such persons have little to lose if no agreements are achieved, thus they should not be afraid to reject the disadvantageous proposals on the table. Instead of exuding weakness, as many negotiators do in these circumstances, they should project strength. Since their opponents are likely to lose more than they lose from nonsettlements, they can confidently demand further concessions as a prerequisite to any final accord.

As the Distributive Stage develops, the parties frequently encounter temporary impasses. The participants are attempting to obtain optimal terms for their respective clients, and each is hoping to induce the other to make the next position change. Individuals who have viable external options should not hesitate to disclose — at least minimally — this critical fact. The more their adversaries know about these alternatives, the more likely they are to appreciate the need for more accommodating behavior. It is usually most effective to convey this information in a calm and non-confrontational manner.[67] Bargainers who refuse to divulge the scope of their nonsettlement options at critical points often fail to achieve accords that may have been attainable had their adversaries been fully aware of their actual circumstances.

Despite the competitive nature of distributive bargaining, a cooperative/problem-solving approach which is firm, fair and friendly is more likely to produce beneficial results than a competitive/adversarial strategy.[68] The former style permits the participants to explore the opportunity for mutual gain in a relatively objective and

---

[64] *See* P. Gulliver, Disputes and Negotiations: A Cross-Cultural Perspective 100 (Academic Press 1979).

[65] *See* Fisher & Ury, *supra* note 5, at 88-89.

[66] *See* Jeffrey Rubin & Bert Brown, The Social Psychology of Bargaining and Negotiation 145 (Academic Press 1975).

[67] *See* Freund, *supra* note 23, at 47.

[68] *See generally* Andrea Kupfer Schneider, *Shattering Negotiation Myths: Empirical Evidence on the Effectiveness of Negotiation Style*, 7 Harv. Negot. L. Rev. 143 (2002). In her empirical study of attorneys in Milwaukee and Chicago, Professor Schneider found that while 54 percent of cooperative/problem-solving

detached manner.[69] The latter approach, however, is more likely to generate mistrust and an unwillingness of the negotiators to share sensitive information.

When specific offers are met with unreceptive responses, negotiators can employ their questioning skills to direct the attention of opponents toward the areas that may generate joint gains. This may enable them to elicit information from their adversaries regarding their underlying interests and goals.[70] As they obtain helpful insights pertaining to the other side's value system, they should divulge information concerning their own side's objectives. This approach may permit the parties to generate a degree of trust and encourage the participants to employ a problem-solving approach.

During this part of the negotiation process, participants should listen carefully for *verbal leaks* that subtly indicate that the other side is actually willing to modify its current position. For example, she might say "I *don't want* to go higher" or "I'm *not inclined* to go higher." The verbal leaks "don't want" and "not inclined" strongly suggest that if her opponent is patient, the speaker will increase her offer.

No matter how effectively negotiators have been interacting, they occasionally find themselves moving toward an impasse. Before they permit an impending stalemate to preclude further talks, they should consider other options that may enable them to keep the process moving.[71] They may reframe especially emotional issues in an effort to find more neutral language that may be more acceptable to both sides. They may temporarily change the focus of their discussions, ceasing to talk about the issues on which they have been concentrating and moving to other issues that may regenerate stalled discussions. They may briefly talk about recent political events, sports, weather, mutual acquaintances, or similar topics, hoping to relieve their bargaining tension. It can be helpful to recount a humorous story that will humanize the participants and remind them not to take the current circumstances too seriously.

When the bargaining atmosphere becomes unusually tense, it may be beneficial for the parties to take a break to allow themselves to cool off and reconsider their positions. They should carefully review their nonsettlement alternatives and contemplate unexplored bargaining options that may enable them to expand the pie and generate better joint agreements. Before they recess the talks, however, they should set a firm date for their next session. If they fail to do this, each may be hesitant to contact the other lest they appear weak.

---

lawyers were considered by their peers to be effective negotiators, only 9 percent of competitive/adversarial bargainers were viewed as effective. *Id.* at 167. On the other hand, while only 3.6 percent of cooperative/problem-solving negotiators were rated ineffective, 53.3 percent of competitive/adversarial bargainers were.

[69] *See* Gifford, *supra* note 39, at 16-18.

[70] *See* Max H. Bazerman & Margaret A. Neal, Negotiating Rationally 90-95 (Free Press 1992).

[71] *See* Dawson, *supra* note 14, at 66-71.

3. Power Bargaining

The Distributive Stage generally involves some degree of power bargaining, as the participants attempt to obtain optimal results for their respective clients concerning the items both sides value.[72] The purpose of this approach is to induce opponents to think they have to provide more generous terms than they actually have to provide. This objective may be accomplished by inducing those persons to reassess their own situations. Have operative weaknesses been ignored or inappropriately minimized? Have their strengths been estimated? Negotiators may expand their own power by convincing adversaries that they possess greater strength or less vulnerability than their opponents think they do.[73] They may casually mention possible nonsettlement options their opponents may not think are available to them, or suggest ways they can avoid negative consequences the other side thinks they will suffer if accords are not achieved.

Self assurance is one of the most important attributes possessed by successful negotiators. They exude an inner confidence in their positions, and always appear to be in control of the situation. They do not appear to fear the possibility of nonsettlements, suggesting to opponents that they have developed alternatives that will protect their clients if the current negotiations are unproductive. These factors cause less certain adversaries to accord these persons more power and respect than they objectively deserve.

Proficient bargainers always commence their interactions with high and well supported aspiration levels, while less skilled negotiators often begin with deflated goals, fearing that their initial demands may engender hostility if they are not modest. The confidence exhibited by the more prepared negotiators with higher aspirations frequently causes less prepared bargainers with lower goals to doubt the propriety of their minimal objectives. They assume the high goal participants possess beneficial nonsettlement alternatives, and accord them greater respect than they deserve.

During the Distributive Stage, the participants employ various power bargaining techniques to advance their interests. Some are used in isolation, while others are employed simultaneously. These tactics are generally designed to keep opponents off balance and to induce them to think they have to make greater concessions if the bargaining process is to continue. Negotiators should carefully plan their own techniques, and anticipate and prepare for the tactics they think the other side will use. Here are some of the most common:

---

[72] *See generally* Gerald B. Wetlaufer, *The Limits of Integrative Bargaining*, 85 Geo. L.J. 369 (1996).

[73] *See* Samuel B. Bachrach & Edward J. Lawler, Bargaining: Power, Tactics and Outcomes 60-63 (Jossey-Bass 1981).

a. Argument

The negotiating tactic employed most frequently by lawyers involves legal and nonlegal argument.[74] When the facts support their positions, they emphasize the factual aspects of the transaction. When legal doctrines support their claim, they cite statutes, regulations, judicial decisions, and scholarly publications. Public policy may be cited when it advances client positions. When appropriate, economic and/or political considerations will be used.

Negotiators do not really use arguments to elucidate, but rather to convince opponents to give them what they wish to achieve.[75] Persuasive advocates are persons who are able to provide adversaries with seemingly valid reasons to provide them with their objectives. They employ apparently objective standards to bolster their claims. They also frame the issues to be resolved in ways that lend moral support to their own positions.[76] Individuals with greater bargaining power tend to argue in favor of equitable distributions that favor their own side, while persons with less power tend to argue for egalitarian distributions.[77]

Persuasive arguments have to be presented in a relatively even-handed and objective manner if they are to appeal to opposing parties.[78] They are most effective when presented in a logical and orderly sequence that will have a cumulative impact upon the recipients. Instead of merely restating arguments, speakers should restate them in different forms that are designed to enhance their persuasiveness.

Proficient bargainers work to develop innovative arguments they hope have not been anticipated by opponents. Once adversaries are forced to internally question their previously developed rationales supporting their own positions, they begin to suffer a loss of bargaining confidence. The weakening of their underlying positional foundations causes them to seriously consider the legal and factual interpretations being offered by their adversaries.

Lawyers should not ignore the potential persuasiveness of well-crafted emotional appeals.[79] While most attorneys are intelligent people who can easily counter logical assertions, they often find it difficult to ignore emotional presentations that generate guilt or compassion. Advocates should thus formulate arguments that are designed to elicit emotional responses, because these appeals may produce beneficial results.

---

[74] *See* GERALD WILLIAMS, LEGAL NEGOTIATION AND SETTLEMENT 79-81 (West 1983).

[75] *See* Robert Condlin, *Cases on Both Sides: Patterns of Argument in Legal Dispute-Negotiation*, 44 MD. L. REV. 65, 73 (1985).

[76] *See* SHELL, *supra* note 16, at 104-05.

[77] *See* Birke & Fox, *supra* note 44, at 34-35.

[78] *See* BASTRESS & HARBAUGH, *supra* note 51, at 437-38.

[79] *See id.* at 439-40.

b. Threats, Warnings, and Promises

Almost all legal negotiations involve the use of overt or implicit threats. Transactional negotiators indicate that they will deal with other parties if this side does not sweeten its offer, while litigators suggest that they will resort to adjudications if they do not get what they want at the bargaining table. Threats are employed to convince opponents that the cost of disagreeing with proposed offers transcends the cost of acquiescence.[80]

Less confrontational negotiators try to avoid the use of direct *"threats,"* preferring to use less challenging *"warnings."* Instead of threatening to personally impose negative consequences on their opponents if they do not change their positions, these people caution their adversaries about the consequences that will naturally result from their failure to accept mutual accords.[81] These "warnings" do not concern action that the declarants plan to take, but events that will independently evolve if no settlements are achieved. The negative effects may be imposed by absent clients, judges, or the market place.

When adverse consequences are likely to occur, it is usually beneficial to articulate the negative possibilities as "warnings" rather than "threats."[82] Threats are direct affronts to opponents and often induce reciprocal behavior; warnings are more indirect, based on what a third party will do, making such warnings more palatable to listeners.[83] In addition, the warning device enhances the credibility of the negative consequences being discussed, since the speakers are suggesting that the adverse effects will result from the actions of third parties over whom they exert minimal or no control.

At the opposite end of the spectrum from negative threats and warnings are affirmative *"promises."*[84] A "promise" does not involve the suggestion of negative consequences, but rather consists of "an expressed intention to behave in a way that appears beneficial to the interests of another."[85] For example, instead of threatening legal action if an opponent does not alter her current position, a negotiator indicates that if the other side provides a more generous offer, he will respond with a better offer of his own. The affirmative promise provides a face-saving way for opposing sides to move jointly toward each other, because it promises reciprocal action in response to a change by the other party.

---

[80] *See* Thomas C. Schelling, *An Essay on Bargaining, in* BARGAINING: FORMAL THEORIES OF NEGOTIATION 319, 329-34 (Oran R. Young, ed.) (Univ. of Illinois Press 1975).

[81] *See* FREUND, *supra* note 23, at 212-13; FRED C. IKLE, HOW NATIONS NEGOTIATE 62-63 (Harper & Row 1964).

[82] *See* Jon Elster, *Strategic Uses of Argument, in* BARRIERS TO CONFLICT RESOLUTION 236, 252-53 (Kenneth Arrow, Robert H. Mnookin, Lee Ross, Amos Tversky & Robert Wilson, eds.) (W.W. Norton 1995).

[83] *See* ROBERT MAYER, POWER PLAYS 4-65 (Times Bus. 1996).

[84] *See* DEAN G. PRUITT & JEFFREY Z. RUBIN, SOCIAL CONFLICT 51-55 (Random House 1986); Schelling, *supra* note 80, at 335-37.

[85] RUBIN & BROWN, *supra* note 66, at 278.

Threats, warnings, and promises convey significant information concerning the transmitter's perception of the opponent's circumstances. Threats and warnings disclose what the threatening side thinks the listener fears, while promises indicate what the promisor believes the recipient hopes to obtain. People receiving threats, warnings, or promises may be able to use these tactics to their own advantage. If, for example, A suggests through a threat or warning that A believes that B would lose more from a nonsettlement than B would actually lose, it may be beneficial for B to disabuse A of this misperception to prevent A from estimating B's need to reach an agreement. Conversely, if A's threat or warning suggests that A desires a particular item that is not valued by B, B can try to extract some other meaningful term in exchange for this item.

Proficient negotiators tend to transmit affirmative promises more frequently than they do negative threats or warnings.[86] This surprises many bargainers, because most people remember disruptive threats and warnings more than face-saving promises, causing them to estimate the number of threats and warnings they encountered. The use of promises increases the likelihood of mutual accords, while the use of threats and warnings reduces this probability.[87]

Negotiators who plan to employ threats to advance their agendas should appreciate the characteristics of effective threats. The proposed negative consequences must be carefully communicated to opponents, and the threatened result must be proportionate to the action the user is seeking. Insignificant threats are ignored as irrelevant, while excessive threats are dismissed as irrational.[88] In addition, bargainers should never issue ultimatums they are not prepared to effectuate, because if their bluffs are called and they back down, their credibility is lost.[89]

Negotiators who are threatened with negative consequences if they do not change their current positions must always consider a critical factor. What is likely to happen to their side if no agreement is reached with the other side? If their external alternatives are preferable to what would be the result if they acceded to their opponent's threat, these persons should not be afraid to maintain their present positions. If they wish to preserve a positive bargaining atmosphere, hoping that continued discussions will cause their adversaries to move in their direction, they can simply ignore the threat.[90] If threatened parties behave as if no ultimatum has been issued, the other side may be able to withdraw the threat without suffering a loss of face.

---

[86] *See id.* at 282.

[87] *See id.* at 286.

[88] *See* RICHARD NED LEBOW, THE ART OF BARGAINING 92-93 (Johns Hopkins Univ. Press 1996); Gary T. Lowenthal, *A General Theory of Negotiaiton Process, Strategy, and Behavior*, 31 KAN. L. REV. 69, 86 (1982).

[89] *See* LEBOW, *supra* note 88, at 107; MAYER, *supra* note 83, at 64.

[90] *See* BASTRESS & HARBAUGH, *supra* note 51, at 461-62.

c. Ridicule and Humor

Humor can be used by people during the Preliminary Stage of the bargaining process to help them create more positive environments. Studies indicate that the use of humor can increase the likability of the communicators.[91] This approach can help negotiators develop more open and trusting relationships with opponents. Humor may also be employed during the Distributive Stage to induce adversaries to accept proposals they might otherwise be hesitant to accept.[92] When negotiations become unusually tense, a one-liner can remind the other side that the parties should not be taking the situation so seriously.

Ridicule and humor can be employed by negotiators to indicate negative responses to poor proposals. For example, a derisive smile or sarcastic laughter may be used in response to an especially one-sided offer to demonstrate how unacceptable it is. If employed skillfully, this approach may embarrass an opponent and induce that person to make another more reasonable offer. If used less proficiently, such behavior may anger the other side and create an unproductive environment.

d. Silence

Silence is an extremely effective bargaining tactic often overlooked by negotiators.[93] Less competent negotiators fear silence. They are afraid that if they stop talking, they will lose control of the interaction. They remember the awkwardness they have experienced in social settings during prolonged pauses, and they feel compelled to speak. When they prattle on, they tend to disclose, both verbally and nonverbally, information they did not intend to divulge, and they frequently make unintended concessions.[94] When confronted by further silence from adversaries, they continue their verbal leakage and concomitant loss of control.

When negotiators have something important to convey, they should succinctly say what they have to say and become silent. There is no need to emphasize the point with unnecessary reiteration. They need to give their listener the chance to absorb what has been said.[95] This approach is especially critical when concessions are being exchanged. Bargainers should articulate their new positions and quietly and patiently await responses from the receiving parties. If the prolonged silence makes them feel uncomfortable, they should review their notes or look out the window. Their calm patience indicates to the other side that they expect a response before they continue the discussions.

Negotiators who encounter impatient opponents who exhibit an inability to remain silent should use extended pauses to their own advantage. After talkative adversaries make position changes, they may become disconcerted if they receive no responses. As their anxiety increases, they may be induced to say more and even bid against

---

[91] *See* K. O'Quin & J. Aronoff, *Humor as a Technique of Social Influence*, 44 Soc. Psych. Q. 349 (1981).

[92] *See id.* at 354.

[93] *See* Steinberg, *supra* note 34, at 171.

[94] *See* Mark Mccormack, What They Don't Teach You at Harvard Business School 108-11 (Bantam 1984).

[95] *See* Mayer, *supra* note 83, at 30.

themselves through the articulation of unreciprocated concessions.

e.   Patience

Persons involved in bargaining interactions must appreciate the fact the process takes time to unfold. Individuals who seek to accelerate developments usually obtain less favorable and less efficient results than they would have attained had they been more patient. Offers that would have been acceptable if conveyed during the latter stages of a negotiation may not be attractive when conveyed prematurely. The participants have not had sufficient time to appreciate the fact that a negotiated deal is preferable to their external alternatives.

All negotiators experience some anxiety created by the uncertainty that is inherent in bargaining encounters. Individuals who can control the tension they experience and exude a quiet confidence are generally able to achieve better deals than less patient persons. They exhibit a stamina that indicates that they are prepared to take as long as necessary to attain their objectives. Less patient opponents often give in, because they are unwilling to take the time they have to expend to generate better results for their own side.

Negotiators who hope to use their own stamina to wear down less patient adversaries should develop pleasant styles that help them keep the process going when circumstances become difficult. If the bargaining environment becomes unusually tense, they might use short breaks to alleviate the tension. If they can convince their opponents that they will continue the process until they achieve their goals, they will frequently obtain capitulations from less committed adversaries.

f.   Guilt, Embarrassment, and Indebtedness

Some negotiators seek to create feelings of guilt or embarrassment in opponents for the purpose of inducing those persons to accede to their demands. They cite insignificant transgressions, such as someone showing up late for a meeting or forgetting to bring an unimportant document, hoping to disconcert adversaries. These persons wish to make the others feel so uncomfortable that they will try to regain social acceptability by doing something nice for them. When someone tries to place a bargaining participant at a disadvantage over a small oversight, they should simply apologize and move on without feeling the need to give up something of substance.

g.   Voice and Language

Some negotiators are afraid to raise their voices during interactions for fear of offending opponents. They fail to appreciate the beneficial impact that can be achieved through the strategic use of loudness. Controlled voice volume can be a characteristic of persuasiveness. When individuals talk in a louder voice, others tend to listen. So long as the raised voice is not viewed as inappropriately aggressive or offensive, it does not hurt to speak more loudly when someone really wants to be heard.

Many persons think they will be more persuasive negotiators if they use more intense language during their interactions. Studies show, however, that low intensity discussions are likely to be more persuasive than high intensity presentations.[96] This seeming anomaly is due to the negative reaction most negotiators have toward high intensity persuasive efforts. High intensity speakers seem manipulative and offensive, while low intensity presenters tend to induce opponents to be less suspicious of and more receptive to their entreaties.

4.   Negotiators must Remember Their Nonsettlement Options

Throughout the Distributive Stage, negotiators should always remember their *current nonsettlement alternatives* (**BATNA**). It is no longer relevant what they were six months or a year ago, when these individuals began to prepare for the present interaction. The passage of time has generally affected the options that were previously available. The discovery process may have strengthened or weakened the case of litigators, while changes in the business market may have influenced the value of the transaction being discussed. Has the market improved the situation of the firm being purchased or sold? Are the technology rights being licensed worth more or less than they were a year ago?

If bargainers fail to appreciate changes in the value of the present interactions, they may enter into arrangements that are not better than what they would have had with no agreement. They must always remember that bad deals are worse than no deals. When nonsettlement alternatives are presently more beneficial than the terms being offered at the bargaining table, they should not hesitate to walk away from the current discussions. They should do this as pleasantly as possible, for two reasons. First, when their opponents realize that these persons are really willing to end the interaction, their adversaries may reconsider their positions and offer them more beneficial terms. Second, even if the current negotiations fail to regenerate and no accord is achieved, the parties may see each other in the future. If both parties remember these talks favorably, even if they were not successful, future negotiations are likely to progress more smoothly than if these talks ended on an unpleasant note.

E.   CLOSING STAGE: MAKING THE DEAL AND VALUE SOLIDIFYING

Near the end of the Distributive Stage, after the parties have tentatively exchanged a lot of items and moved substantially from their original positions, the participants realize that a mutual accord is likely to be achieved. They feel a sense of relief, because the anxiety generated by the uncertainty of the negotiation process is about to be alleviated by the attainment of a definitive agreement. Careful observers can often see signs of relief around the mouths of the negotiators, and they may exhibit more relaxed postures. As the bargainers become psychologically committed to settlement, they may move too quickly toward the conclusion of the transaction.

---

[96] *See* Roy J. Lewicki, Joseph A. Litterer, John W. Minton & David M. Saunders, Negotiation 214 (Irwin 2d ed. 1994).

The Closing Stage represents a critical part of the bargaining process. The majority of concessions tend to be made during the concluding portion of negotiations,[97] and overly anxious participants may forfeit much of what they obtained during the Distributive Stage if they are not careful. They must remain patient and allow this stage to develop in a deliberate fashion.

By the conclusion of the Distributive Stage, *both sides* have become psychologically committed to a joint resolution. Neither wants their prior bargaining efforts to culminate in failure. Less proficient negotiators focus almost entirely on their own side's desire for an agreement, completely disregarding the settlement pressure affecting their opponents. As the Closing Stage commences, *both sides* want an agreement. It is thus appropriate for both parties to expect joint movement toward final terms. Negotiators should be careful not to make unreciprocated concessions, and to avoid excessive position changes. They should only contemplate larger concessions than their adversaries when their opponents have been more accommodating during the earlier exchanges and the verbal and nonverbal signals emanating from those participants indicate that they are approaching their resistance points.

The Closing Stage is not a time for swift action; it is a time for **patient perseverance**. Negotiators should continue to employ the tactics that got them to this point, and they should be well aware of their prior and present concession patterns. They should endeavor to make smaller, and, if possible, less frequent position changes than their opponents. If they fail to heed this warning and move too quickly toward a conclusion, they are likely to close most of the gap remaining between the parties.

Patience and silence are two of the most effective techniques during the Closing Stage. Negotiators should employ "principled" concessions to explain the reasons for their exact moves. Following each announced position change, they should become silent and patiently await the other side's response. They should not prattle on and disclose their anxiety, and they should not contemplate further movement without reciprocity from the other side. They must remember that their adversaries are as anxious to achieve final terms as they are.

Skilled bargainers are often able to obtain a significant advantage during the Closing Stage by exhibiting a calm indifference. If negotiators can persuade their anxious opponents that they really do not care whether final terms are achieved, their adversaries may be induced to close most of the distance remaining between the parties.[98] As anxious participants make more expansive and more frequent concessions in an effort to guarantee an agreement, they significantly enhance the terms achieved by the other side.

The Closing Stage can be a highly competitive portion of the negotiation process. It often involves a substantial number of position changes and a significant amount of participant movement. Negotiators who think that this part of the interaction consists primarily of cooperative behavior are likely to obtain less beneficial results than strategic opponents who use this stage to induce naive adversaries to close more of the

---

[97] *See* DAWSON, *supra* note 14, at 171.

[98] *See id.* at 173-76.

outstanding distance between the two sides. As they plan their closing strategies, negotiators must remember that their adversaries also wish to attain final accords. Their opponents may be even more anxious in this regard than they are. If negotiators carefully and deliberately move toward agreement, they may induce their more anxious opponents to give them better deals than they would otherwise obtain.

Negotiators who think their opponents are approaching their bottom lines should listen carefully for *verbal leaks* indicating that they are not. Their opponent may say "that's *about as far* as I can go" or "I don't have *much more room*" — both of which indicate that the speaker has more room. When bargainers get to their true bottom lines, they say something like "that's as far as I can go," and they tend to have an open, palms-up posture supporting their representation that they are really at their reservation point.

F. COOPERATIVE STAGE: VALUE MAXIMIZING

1. Carefully Working Together to Make the Pie as Big as Possible

Once the Closing Stage has been successfully completed through the attainment of a mutually acceptable agreement, many persons consider the negotiation process finished. While this conclusion may be correct with respect to zero sum problems, such as the immediate exchange of money, where neither party could improve its results without a corresponding loss to the other side,[99] it is certainly not true for multi-issue encounters. Nonetheless, many participants in multi-issue bargaining assume a fixed pie that cannot be expanded.[100] This is rarely correct, due to the different client preference curves involved.[101] As a result, it is frequently possible for the negotiators to formulate proposals that may expand the pie and simultaneously advance their respective interests.

Once a tentative accord has been reached through the distributive process, the negotiators should contemplate alternative trade-offs that might concurrently enhance the interests of both parties. The bargainers may be mentally, and even physically, exhausted from their prior discussions, but they should at least briefly explore alternative formulations that may prove to be mutually advantageous. During the Information Stage, the parties often overstate or understate the actual value of different items for strategic reasons. During the Distributive and Closing Stages, they tend to be cautious and opportunistic. Both sides are likely to employ power bargaining tactics designed to achieve results favorable to their own circumstances. Because of the tension created by these distributive techniques, Pareto superior

---

[99] Even when the only issue to be negotiated concerns the payment of money by one party to another, there may be room for cooperative bargaining. If the parties can agree upon in-kind payments (*e.g.*, the provision of goods or services) or future payments, the receiving party may still obtain what it wants but at less cost to the other side. It thus behooves even money traders to contemplate alternative payment schemes that might prove mutually beneficial.

[100] *See* Birke & Fox, *supra* note 44, at 30-31.

[101] *See* MNOOKIN, PEPPET & TULUMELLO, *supra* note 35, at 14-16.

arrangements are rarely attained by this point in the negotiation process. The participants are likely to have only achieved "acceptable" terms. If they conclude their interaction at this point, they may leave a substantial amount of untapped joint satisfaction on the bargaining table.

In simulation exercises, it is easy to determine the extent to which negotiators have successfully used the Cooperative Stage. By comparing the aggregate point totals attained by the two sides, one may assess the degree to which they maximized their joint results. For example, where two opponents might potentially divide 800 points between themselves, some participants with proficient cooperative skills may reach agreements giving them combined totals of 750 to 800 points. On the other hand, less cooperative groups may end up with joint totals of 550 to 600 points. These results graphically demonstrate to the participants the benefits to be derived from cooperative bargaining. Had the latter negotiators been able to discover the 200 to 250 points they missed, both would have left the table with more generous terms.

If the Cooperative Stage is to develop successfully, several prerequisites must be established. First, the parties must achieve a tentative accord. Second, at the conclusion of the Closing Stage, one or both parties should suggest movement into the Cooperative Stage. If one side is concerned that the other will be reluctant to progress in this direction until a provisional agreement has been attained, it can suggest that both parties initial the terms they have already agreed upon. Although proficient negotiators may occasionally merge the latter part of the Closing Stage with the introductory portion of the Cooperative Stage, most bargainers only move into the Cooperative Stage after they have reached a mutually acceptable distribution of the pertinent items.[102]

It is crucial that both sides recognize their movement from the Closing to the Cooperative Stage. If one party attempts to move into the Cooperative Stage without the understanding of the other, problems may arise. The alternative proposals articulated may be less advantageous to the other participant than the prior offers. If the recipient of these new positions does not view them as beginning cooperative overtures, she might suspect disingenuous competitive tactics. It is thus imperative that a party contemplating movement toward cooperative bargaining be sure her opponent understands the intended transition. When such a move might not be apparent, this fact should be explicitly communicated.

Once the participants enter the Cooperative Stage, they should seek to discover the presence of previously unfound alternatives that might be mutually beneficial. They must work to expand the overall pie to be divided between them.[103] They may have failed to consider options that would equally or even more effectively satisfy the underlying needs and interests of one side with less cost to the other party.[104] To accomplish this objective, the participants must be willing to candidly disclose the underlying interests of their respective clients. Although they should have explored many of these factors during the Informational, Distributive, and Closing Stages, they

---

[102] *See* DAWSON, *supra* note 14, at 172-73.

[103] *See* MNOOKIN, PEPPET & TULUMELLO, *supra* note 35, at 11-43; FISHER & URY, *supra* note 5 at 58-83.

[104] *See* KARRASS, *supra* note 49, at 145.

may not have done so with complete candor for strategic reasons. Each may have overstated or understated the value of different items to advance their competitive interests. Once a tentative accord has been achieved, the parties should no longer be afraid of more open discussions.

Both sides must be quite open during the Cooperative Stage if the process is to function effectively. Through the use of objective and relatively neutral inquiries, the participants should explore their respective needs. Negotiators should use brainstorming techniques to develop options not previously considered. They should not be constrained by traditional legal doctrines or conventional business practices, recognizing that they can agree to anything that is lawful. They should not hesitate to think outside the box.[105] When one side asks the other if another resolution would be as good or better for it than what has already been agreed upon, the respondent must be forthright. It is only where the parties have effectively explored all of the possible alternatives that they can truly determine whether their initial agreement optimally satisfies their fundamental needs.

As the participants enter the Cooperative Stage, they must be careful to preserve their credibility. Consistent with ethical limitations discussed in Chapter 5, they may have been somewhat deceptive during the Informational, Distributive, and Closing Stages with respect to actual client needs and interests. In the Cooperative Stage, they hope to correct the inefficiencies that may have been generated by their prior dissembling. If they are too open regarding their previous misrepresentations, however, their opponents may begin to question the accuracy of all their prior representations and seek to renegotiate the entire accord.[106] This would be a disaster. It is thus imperative that negotiators not overtly undermine their credibility while they seek to improve their respective positions during the Cooperative Stage.

It is important for persons participating in cooperative bargaining to appreciate the competitive undercurrent that is present even during these seemingly win-win discussions. While participants are using cooperative techniques to expand the overall pie and improve the results achieved by both sides, some may also employ competitive tactics to enable them to claim more than their share of the newly discovered areas for mutual gain. For example, if the participants discover an additional "250 points"[107] of client satisfaction that can be divided between them, there is nothing that requires them to allocate 125 points to each side. If one party realizes that a proposed modification of the existing agreement could increase her client's situation by 150 or even 200 points, she might disingenuously indicate that the new proposal would be a "slight improvement" to allow her to make her opponent think the new proposal would

---

[105] *See generally* Tom Kelley, The Art of Innovation (Doubleday 2001).

[106] *See* Robert Condlin, *Bargaining in the Dark: The Normative Incoherence of Lawyer Dispute Bargaining Role*, 51 Md. L. Rev. 1, 44-45 (1992).

[107] In our Legal Negotiation courses, we assign point values for each item to be negotiated to apprise students of the relative values placed on the different terms from their respective client perspectives. When representing real clients, attorneys should mentally do the same thing, as they probe underlying client needs and interests. The "essential" terms should have a higher value than the "important" terms, which should be valued more than merely "desirable" issues. While lawyers may not assign exact point values for each item, they should have a good idea of the comparative value of the different terms.

only expand the overall pie by 75 or 100 points. She would then give her adversary 35 to 50 points, and retain the other 100 to 150 points for her own side.

2. Committing it to Writing

Once final agreements have been achieved, the parties often hang up the phones or depart for home, thinking that they are finished. As a result, they may fail to ensure a complete meeting of the minds. Before they conclude their interaction, participants should briefly review the specific terms they think have been agreed upon. They may occasionally find misunderstandings. Since they are psychologically committed to agreements, they are likely to resolve their disagreements amicably. If they do not discover the misunderstandings until one side has drafted the accord, there may be claims of dishonesty and recriminations. It is thus preferable to confirm the basic terms with a Memorandum of Agreement — a document which sets forth the basic terms of the agreement — before the parties conclude their encounter. This minimizes the chance of a misunderstanding when the final documents are later prepared. It also minimizes the chance that either side will need to resort to a motion to enforce the settlement agreement or an action for breach of contract.

EXERCISES

EXERCISE 4.1
PRACTICING THE NEGOTIATION STAGES

GENERAL DESCRIPTION OF EXERCISE: Negotiation of a sexual harassment claim by a law student against her professor

SKILLS INVOLVED: Negotiation.

PARTICIPANTS NEEDED: You will be divided into pairs.

ESTIMATED TIME REQUIRED:

75 minutes: 45 minutes for negotiation and 30 minutes for discussion

LEVEL OF DIFFICULTY (1-5):

"SEXUAL HARASSMENT"

Now it's time to put your new knowledge to use! You will be divided into pairs. Your professor will assign one person to represent the plaintiff and the other person to represent the defendant. Start by reading the General Information below. After that, read the Confidential Information and the instructions that will be provided.

GENERAL INFORMATION

Last year, Jane Doe was a first year law student at the Yalebridge Law School, which is part of Yalebridge University, a private, non-sectarian institution. Ms. Doe was a student in Professor Alexander Palsgraf's Tort Law class.

During the first semester, Professor Palsgraf made sexually suggestive comments to Ms. Doe on several occasions. These comments were always made outside of the classroom and when no other individuals were present. Ms. Doe unequivocally indicated her personal revulsion toward Professor Palsgraf's remarks and informed him that they were entirely improper and unappreciated.

During the latter part of the second semester, Professor Palsgraf suggested to Ms. Doe in his private office that she have sexual relations with him. Ms. Doe immediately rejected his suggestion and told Professor Palsgraf that he was "a degenerate and disgusting old man who was a disgrace to the teaching profession."

Last June, Ms. Doe received her first year law school grades. She received one "A", two "A-", one "B+", and one "D", the latter grade pertaining to her Tort Law class. She immediately went to see Professor Palsgraf to ask him about her low grade. He said that he was sorry about her "D", but indicated that the result might well have been different had she only acquiesced in his request for sexual favors.

Ms. Doe then had Professor Irving Prosser, who also teaches Tort Law at Yalebridge, review her exam. He said that it was a "most respectable paper" which should certainly have earned her an "A-" or "B+", and possibly even an "A".

Ms. Doe has threatened to sue Professor Palsgraf in state court for $250,000 based upon three separate causes of action: (1) sexual harassment in violation of Title IX of the Education Amendments of 1972; (2) intentional infliction of emotional distress; and (3) fraud. Professor Palsgraf has a net worth of $450,000, including the $350,000 equity in his house and a $50,000 library of ancient Gilbert's outlines.

EXERCISE 4.1
PRACTICING THE NEGOTIATION STAGES

REFLECTION

Ask yourself what you learned from this exercise and to what extent you accomplished the following:

1. Preparation Stage:

A. Identified and distinguished between the client's **essential, important and desirable** goals.

B. Developed cogent legal theories to support your client's position and anticipated the counter-arguments of opposing counsel.

C. Calculated your client's and the opposing side's **bottom lines** (**BATNA**)

D. Established sufficiently elevated **aspiration levels**.

E. Formulated an elevated but principled opening offer.

F. Effectively choreographed the expected interaction by using the Negotiation Preparation Form or something similar.

2. Preliminary Stage:

A. Established rapport with opposing counsel through warm eye contact and pleasant demeanor.

B. Attempted to identify and establish common backgrounds and/or interests.

3. Informational Stage:

A. Used broad, open-ended "what" and "why" information seeking questions to ascertain other side's **needs** and **interests**.

B. Listened for **verbal leaks** like "really want," "would like to get," "important," "desirable," etc.

C. Disclosed information in strategic manner, and used **blocking techniques** where appropriate.

4. Distributive Stage:

A. Strategically considered who would make first offer and its potential effect on the outcome.

B. Employed a carefully planned "*principled*" concession pattern.

C. Listened for **verbal leaks** like "really want," "would like to get," "important," "desirable," etc.

D. Established a tone and attitude of confidence.

E. Commenced negotiations with a view toward your *elevated aspiration levels* and a strong justification for your position.

F. Carefully planned for and used appropriate *power bargaining* techniques.

G. Identified and appropriately deflected opponent's use of *power bargaining* techniques.

H. Kept track of your BATNA during the negotiations and included it in your analysis as a viable alternative to settlement, e.g., no "settlement at all costs."

5. Closing Stage:

A. Remained *patiently perseverant* even though settlement appeared imminent.

B. Continued to listen for *verbal leaks*.

6. Cooperative Stage:

A. After reaching an accord, continued to work with opponent to explore unfound *alternatives* that might be mutually beneficial and that could *maximize joint results*.

B. Reached a settlement that was *efficient* compared to the other settlements arrived at by your fellow students.

———

Going forward, we encourage you to look back at these questions after each exercise until you incorporate them into your thought process. Also going forward, you should complete the following outline after each negotiation. For your convenience, it is available for download at the **LexisNexis Webcourse**, Chapter 4, along with the Negotiation Preparation Form.

POST NEGOTIATION EVALUATION CHECKLIST

1. Was your **pre-negotiation preparation** sufficiently thorough? Did you effectively choreograph the expected interaction by using the Negotiation Preparation Form or something similar? Were you completely familiar with operative facts and law? Did you fully understand your client's value system? Did you develop cogent legal theories to support your client's position and anticipate the counter-arguments of opposing counsel.

2. Did you carefully determine your side's **bottom line**? Did you also attempt to estimate the **bottom line** of the **other side**?

3. Was your **initial aspiration level** high enough? Did you have a firm goal for **each issue** to be addressed? If you obtained everything you sought, was this due to fact you did not establish sufficiently high objectives? Was your aspiration level so unrealistic that it provided no meaningful guidance to you?

4. Did you prepare an elevated but **principled opening offer** that explained the bases for the positions you were taking?

5. Did your **pre-bargaining prognostications** prove to be accurate? If not, what caused your miscalculations?

6. Which party dictated the **contextual factors** such as time and location? Did these factors influence the negotiations?

7. Did you use the **Preliminary Stage** to establish rapport with your opponent and to create a positive negotiating environment, such as using warm eye contact and a pleasant demeanor, identifying common backgrounds, interests, etc.? Did you employ **Attitudinal Bargaining** to modify inappropriate opponent behavior?

8. Did the **Information Stage** develop sufficiently to provide participants with the knowledge they needed to understand their respective needs and interests and to enable them to consummate an optimal agreement? Did you ask **broad, open-ended questions** to get the other side talking and **"what" and "why" questions** to determine what the other side wanted and the interests underlying those positions? Did you listen for verbal leaks, such as "really want," "would like to get," "important," "desirable," etc.?

9. Were any unintended **verbal or nonverbal disclosures** made by either side? What precipitated such revelations? Were you able to use **Blocking Techniques** to prevent the disclosure of sensitive information?

10. Who made the **first offer**? The first **"real"** offer? Was a **"principled" initial offer** made by you? By your opponent? Was yours sufficiently high to allow you a chance to obtain your aspiration level? How did your **opponent react** to **your initial proposal**? How did **you react** to your **opponent's opening offer**?

11. Did you establish an attitude and tone of confidence? If so, what did you do to accomplish that? If not, what will you do next time? What did your opponent do?

12. Were *consecutive opening offers* made by one party before the other side disclosed its initial position?

13. What specific *bargaining techniques* were employed by your *opponent* and how were these tactics countered by you? What else might you have done to counter these tactics?

14. What particular *bargaining techniques* were employed *by you* to advance your position? Did the *opponent* appear to *recognize* the various negotiating techniques you used, and, if so, how did he/she endeavor to minimize their impact? What *other tactics* might you have used to advance your position?

15. Which party made the *first concession* and how was it precipitated? Were *subsequent concessions* made on an alternating basis? You should keep a record of each concession made by you and by your opponent throughout the transaction.

16. Were *"principled" concessions* articulated by you? By your opponent? Did *successive position changes* involve decreasing increments and were those increments relatively reciprocal to the other side's concomitant movement?

17. How did the parties *close the deal* once they realized that they had overlapping needs and interests? Did either side appear to make greater concessions during closing phase? Did you continue to listen for *verbal leaks*?

18. Did the parties resort to *cooperative/integrative bargaining* to maximize their aggregate return?

19. How close to the *mid-point* between the initial *real* offers was the final settlement?

20. How did *time pressures* influence the parties and their respective concession patterns? Try not to ignore the time pressures that affected your opponent.

21. Did either party resort to *deceitful tactics* or deliberate misrepresentations to enhance its situation? Did these pertain to material law or fact, or only to value system or settlement intentions?

22. What finally induced you *to accept* the terms agreed upon or *to reject* the final offer made by the other party? Did you keep track of your BATNA during the negotiations and include it in your analysis as a viable alternative, e.g., no "settlement at all costs"? Did you remain patiently perseverant even though settlement appeared imminent?

23. Did *either party* appear to obtain *more favorable terms* than the other side? If so, how was this result accomplished? What could the *less successful* participant have *done differently* to improve its situation?

24. If *no settlement* was achieved, what might have been done differently with respect to client preparation and/or bargaining developments to produce a different result?

25. What did you do that you *wish* you had *not done*? Do you think your opponent was aware of your mistake? How could you avoid such a mistake in

the future?

26. What did you *not do* that you *wish you had done*? If you encountered a new technique, how could you most effectively counter this approach in the future?

27. Did you reach a settlement that was efficient and *maximized joint results* as compared to the settlements arrived at by your fellow students? If yes, how did you accomplish this? If no, what could you do differently next time to create a more efficient settlement?

EXERCISE 4.2
PRACTICING THE NEGOTIATION STAGES
ONE MORE TIME NOW WITH FEELING

GENERAL DESCRIPTION OF EXERCISE: Negotiation of a medical malpractice claim.

SKILLS INVOLVED: Negotiation.

PARTICIPANTS NEEDED: You will be divided into pairs.

ESTIMATED TIME REQUIRED:

90 minutes: 60 minutes for negotiation and 30 minutes for discussion

LEVEL OF DIFFICULTY (1-5):

"MEDICAL MALPRACTICE"

Now that you have reflected on Exercise 4.1, it's time to try it again. Think about what you learned. What worked well? What do you want to do differently? You will be divided into pairs. Your professor will assign one person to represent the plaintiff and the other person to represent the defendant. Start by reading the General Information below. After that, read the Confidential Information and the instructions that will be provided.

GENERAL INFORMATION

This case involves a claim of medical negligence, also known as "malpractice." The claim is made by Susan Smith, as mother and next friend of her infant son, Adam Smith. Susan Smith is the 28 year-old single mother of Adam Smith. Susan is a widow. Her husband, Robert, was killed in a factory accident only two weeks after Adam was born.

Adam suffers from cerebral palsy. The claim is that the defendant, Stoneydale Hospital, negligently handled the labor and delivery of Adam, thus causing a lack of oxygen during delivery resulting in brain damage.

This was Susan's third pregnancy. Her medical history included two prior vaginal deliveries at Stoneydale of healthy babies. She was in good health and had no known family history of labor complications. She did not drink or smoke. She exercised regularly and followed her doctor's instructions regarding prenatal care. There is no evidence that anything in her history made this a high risk pregnancy. Her due date for the pregnancy was April 26.

On April 12, Susan was seen at Stoneydale for a possible spontaneous rupture of membranes. This would suggest the possible onset of labor, but she had no contractions. She was placed on an electronic fetal monitor for a non-stress test, which provides information on the baby's well-being by recording information on heart beat patterns and speed. The test was reactive, with accelerations, a normal baseline, an absence of decelerations and good variability. This was reassuring to the hospital staff responsible for her care, and she was discharged from the hospital shortly before midnight.

On April 13, at 5:29 p.m., Susan again went to Stoneydale. At this point, she had contractions every ten minutes. Her vaginal exam showed that she was 100% effaced and 5 centimeters dilated. This was evidence that she was clearly in labor. The medical records show that she was admitted for "routine labor management." She was placed on an external electronic fetal monitor which showed a baseline fetal heart rate in the normal range of approximately 130 beats per minute with average fetal heart rate variability (6 to 25 beats per minute). Jane Gray, RN, a Stoneydale employee, was on duty in the labor and delivery suite and monitored Susan throughout the night.

Jane Gray has been deposed, and testified that she was reassured by everything she saw on the Fetal Heart Monitor (FHM). She saw no reason to treat this as anything but routine labor. Dr. Simon Franks, the treating obstetrician who is also a Stoneydale employee, has testified that he also treated this as routine labor and was reassured by the FHM. Dr. Franks made no entries in Susan's chart throughout the entire labor and delivery. Both Nurse Gray and Dr. Franks acknowledge, in retrospect, that there were instances when the FHM showed short term abnormalities in heart beat to beat variability, beats per minute and number of contractions per minute. But they both say that short term abnormalities are actually common and are not a reason for intervention through emergency C-section or other means.

Shortly after midnight on April 14, the heart beat recorded on the FHM exceeded the normal range of 160 beats per minute. This is called "tachycardia." The monitor also recorded some prolonged contractions (contractions in excess of 60-90 seconds) and several instances of more than 5 contractions in a 10 minute period (tachysystole). Nurse Gray and Dr. Franks admit that these conditions may all be evidence of fetal distress, which can sometimes result in oxygen deprivation leading to brain damage if longstanding and untreated. However, given the overall picture on the night in question, none of the signs appeared ominous or even troubling.

Adam was delivered vaginally at 1:15 a.m. His Apgar scores were 0, 2 and 4 at 1, 5 and 10 minutes, respectively, which suggests that he was born in a state of distress. The medical records refer to Adam as suffering from hypoxic ischemic encephalopathy (HIE) — a condition in which the brain does not receive enough oxygen. This is not in dispute. What is in dispute is when and why the HIE occurred.

Adam has profound disabilities. According to his medical records, he is cortically blind and deaf. It is uncertain whether he can see some light. He failed a hearing exam but does open his eyes to the voice of his mother. He has cerebral palsy and global development delay. He has spastic quadriparesis with spasticity in his extremities (arms and legs) and low tone in his trunk and neck. He wears ankle foot orthotics on both lower limbs. He moves his arms and legs in a non-purposeful manner and is unable to turn himself. He loves to be touched and enjoys warm water. He is unable to suck and has no gag reflex. He does not smile, make sounds, or cry. He does not blink to threat and his eyes do not fix, focus or track. He shows recognition of familiar people by turning towards them. He shows preferences by stiffening when excited or tickled. He shows pain and discomfort by tears and a reddened face. He will never walk or talk. He is totally dependent on others for his needs.

In his three years of life, Adam has had twenty-one admissions to the hospital for his various needs. In addition to his hospitalizations, he has ongoing outpatient follow up at various clinics. His medical bills to date total $2,200,000. His ongoing health care costs are projected by plaintiff's expert to be approximately $75,000 per year. The Life Care Plan produced by plaintiff's expert shows projected home care costs of over $9,000,000 if Adam lives twenty more years and over $12,500,000 if he lives thirty more years. In the event he is institutionalized, the estimated cost of care is $4,100,000 for twenty years and $5,900,000 for thirty years. His parents did not graduate from college but graduated from high school. His father attended community college on a part-time basis and had nearly earned an associate's degree when he died. Assuming Adam graduated from high school, his lost earning capacity is estimated by the plaintiff's expert at $1,100,000. If he received an associate's degree, his lost earning capacity is estimated at $1,500,000.

EXERCISE 4.2
PRACTICING THE NEGOTIATION STAGES

REFLECTION

Ask yourself what you learned from this exercise. To what extent did you change your approach from Exercise 4.1, based upon experience and reflection? To what extent did you accomplish the following:

1. **Preparation Stage**:

A. Identified and distinguished between the client's **essential, important and desirable** goals.

B. Developed cogent legal theories to support your client's position and anticipated the counter-arguments of opposing counsel.

C. Calculated your client's and the opposing side's **bottom lines** (**BATNA**)

D. Established sufficiently elevated **aspiration levels**.

E. Formulated an elevated but principled opening offer.

F. Effectively choreographed the expected interaction by using the Negotiation Preparation Form or something similar.

2. **Preliminary Stage**:

A. Established rapport with opposing counsel through warm eye contact and pleasant demeanor.

B. Attempted to identify and establish common backgrounds and/or interests.

3. **Informational Stage**:

A. Used broad, open-ended "what" and "why" information seeking questions to ascertain other side's **needs** and **interests**.

B. Listened for **verbal leaks** like "really want," "would like to get," "important," "desirable," etc.

C. Disclosed information in strategic manner, and used **blocking techniques** where appropriate.

4. **Distributive Stage**:

A. Strategically considered who would make first offer and its potential effect on the outcome.

B. Employed a carefully planned "***principled***" concession pattern.

C. Listened for **verbal leaks** like "really want," "would like to get," "important," "desirable," etc.

D. Established a tone and attitude of confidence.

E. Commenced negotiations with a view toward your *elevated aspiration levels* and a strong justification for your position.

F. Carefully planned for and used appropriate *power bargaining* techniques.

G. Identified and appropriately deflected opponent's use of *power bargaining* techniques.

H. Kept track of your BATNA during the negotiations and included it in your analysis as a viable alternative to settlement, e.g., no "settlement at all costs."

5. **Closing Stage**:

A. Remained *patiently perseverant* even though settlement appeared imminent.

B. Continued to listen for *verbal leaks*.

6. **Cooperative Stage**:

A. After reaching an accord, continued to work with opponent to explore unfound *alternatives* that might be mutually beneficial and that could *maximize joint results*.

B. Reached a settlement that was *efficient* compared to the other settlements arrived at by your fellow students.

––––––––––

Complete the Post Negotiation Evaluation Checklist following Exercise 4.1 and available for download at the **LexisNexis Webcourse**, Chapter 4.

Chapter 5

ETHICAL BOUNDARIES AND DILEMMAS

A. TRUST ME, I'M A LAWYER

In Chapter 4, we identified some common negotiation "tactics" or "techniques" used during the Distributive Stage of a negotiation. Of course, various tactics are used throughout every stage of every negotiation process. There are only so many variations on a theme, and we will discuss more tactics in Chapter 6. But now that you have a flavor of the negotiation process, and before we arm you with more techniques, we want you to carefully consider the ethical rules that apply to your conduct in any negotiation setting.

As a lawyer, you will be bound by the rules of professional conduct in the jurisdiction(s) in which you practice. All tactics and strategies must be subject to those rules and limitations. This is not only required, but is smart practice. You will find during your career that a lawyer's reputation for honesty can be her biggest asset or liability. You want yours to be an asset. So how do you square this with Section 2, below?

B. HOW DO YOU TELL WHEN A LAWYER'S LYING? HIS LIPS ARE MOVING!

So you want your reputation for honesty to be an asset, yet you will be involved in very few negotiations where you can effectively negotiate by being totally honest! There will often be times when it is not advisable to tell the truth. In fact, you will lie. Likewise, there are times when you absolutely must tell the truth. To make it even more confusing, there are times when you do not have to say anything, but must tell the whole truth if you speak.

1. Lying Without Being Dishonest

How can negotiators lie without being dishonest? ***By misrepresenting matters they are not expected to discuss truthfully***. This reality causes real discomfort for many new negotiators, and it is important to know where the lines are.

Two people get together to negotiate. One is authorized to accept any amount over $100,000, while the other is authorized to pay up to $130,000. They thus have a $30,000 settlement range between their respective bottom lines. They initially exchange small talk, then begin to explore the substantive issues of their exchange. The person who hopes to obtain money states that he cannot accept anything below $150,000, while the person willing to pay money indicates that she cannot go a penny over $75,000. They are pleased to have begun their interaction successfully, yet both have begun with overt misrepresentations. Have they committed ethical violations?

Model Rule 4.1 provides that an attorney "shall not knowingly: (a) make a false statement of material fact or law to a third person." This unequivocally indicates that lawyers may not lie. But when is a lie not a lie? When it's by a lawyer! When this rule was being drafted, people who teach negotiation skills pointed out that if all misrepresentations were forbidden, when attorneys negotiated, most would be subject to discipline because of what is euphemistically characterized as "puffing" or "embellishment." As a result, Reporter's Comment 2 was included with Rule 4.1 indicating that different expectations are involved when attorneys are negotiating:

> Whether a particular statement should be regarded as one of fact can depend on the circumstances. Under generally accepted conventions in negotiation, certain types of statements ordinarily are not taken as statements of material fact. Estimates of price or value placed on the subject of a transaction and a party's intentions as to an acceptable settlement of a claim are in this category.

As a result, if one party offered to pay the other $115,000, the recipient of the offer could ethically indicate that this sum was unacceptable to his side even though he knew it was perfectly acceptable.[1]

Comment 2 not only permits attorneys to misrepresent their side's settlement intentions, but also to misrepresent the way in which they subjectively value the items being exchanged. For example, if the other side requested a non-admission provision indicating that her side wished to disclaim any admission of legal responsibility for what was being resolved, the first party could oppose such a provision even though he knows that his client does not care about such a provision. He may do this in an effort to obtain more money for his client in exchange for the non-admission clause the other side values. Both of these statements are considered "puffing" since they pertain to nonmaterial information.

Most lawyers have no difficulty with the Reporter's Comment indicating that statements concerning one's actual settlement intentions and the subjective value placed on items being exchanged do not have to be truthful. They pertain to "puffing" and "embellishment," and do not involve matters one expects to be discussed with complete candor.[2] On the other hand, it is strange to suggest that these matters do not concern "material fact." When lawyers negotiate, the factual, legal, economic, and political issues underlying the instant transaction are really secondary. What parties have to determine through the negotiation process is how the other side values the items being exchanged and how much of each must be offered to induce the other side to enter into an agreement. Nonetheless, attorneys generally expect such "puffing" and are not offended by persons who over- or under- state the value of items for

---

[1] Under Rule 1.4, he would have an ethical duty to convey such an offer to his client, unless it was already clear that the amount in question is unacceptable to the client. Under Rule 1.2, the attorney would also be obliged to abide by his client's decision whether to accept or reject the offer in question.

[2] See Charles B. Craver, *Negotiation Ethics for Real World Interactions*, 25 Ohio St. J. Disp. Res. 299 (2010).

strategic purposes or who are not entirely forthright regarding their true settlement intentions.

The principal difficulty professional organizations have regulating the behavior of negotiators concerns the unique circumstances in which most bargaining interactions are conducted. They are usually done on a one-on-one basis in person or over the telephone. If one person is a lying scoundrel and they are accused of dishonesty by another party, they lie to the disciplinary authority. It is extremely difficult for such a body to determine which side is telling the truth. These lawyers are the minority who form the basis for the lawyer jokes we have all heard.

What really regulates this area is the market place. If persons behave in a questionable manner, their reputations will be quickly tarnished. When someone encounters others who lie about what they have the right to know, they usually tell their friends and associates. Those deceivers begin to encounter difficulties when they negotiate. Individuals do not trust them. Their statements have to be independently verified. We have seen instances where other lawyers insist that all communications from the deceiving lawyer be in writing. Deceiving lawyers' negotiations become more cumbersome and less efficient. If they try to regain reputations for honesty, they discover how difficult it is to overcome stories about their past. Any negotiator who contemplates improper behavior during bargaining interactions should appreciate the substantial risks involved. A short-term gain may easily become a long-term stumbling block to future deals.

2.   Three Basic Areas of Factual Misrepresentation

The three basic areas of misrepresentation concern: 1) affirmative factual misrepresentations; 2) truthful statements that are incomplete and misleading; and 3) the failure to disclose information necessary to prevent misunderstandings by the other side.

a.   Affirmative Factual Misrepresentations

Suppose a client is thinking of selling her company and another party has approached her attorney to discuss their possible purchase of this firm. Assume that the corporate owner has told her negotiator that she would like to get at least $50 million, but might go as low as $45 million, if necessary. The prospective buyer asks how much it would take to buy this firm. Can her lawyer ethically suggest $60 million? Clearly the answer is yes, because this pertains to non-material information — their settlement intentions — and is considered acceptable "puffing." The prospective buyer then offers $35 million, and the seller's representative asks if they would consider going higher. Could the prospective buyer's attorney ethically suggest an unwillingness to increase his offer even if he knows his client would be willing to do so? Again yes, since this is still "puffing."

If no one else has indicated an interest in the seller's business, could the seller's representative ethically indicate that other parties have made offers? Although some attorneys would contend that this type of statement is mere "puffing," we do not agree. This is highly material fact information that must be discussed honestly if it is mentioned at all. As a result, if the seller's attorney states that other prospective buyers have tendered offers, that person has to convey truthful information. If another party has expressed an interest in the same firm and has offered $40 million, could the seller's attorney ethically state that she has been offered $50 million? Since we consider this to be material fact information that this possible buyer has the right to rely upon, we do not believe she can make such a misrepresentation. She might, however, be able to avoid the ethical dilemma by indicating that other parties are interested in this firm and by stating that someone will have to pay $50 million if they wish to purchase the company. She is not disclosing what offers have actually been received, but is only indicating — truthfully — that some offers have been tendered. Without disclosing the actual amounts involved, she is merely stating that it will take $50 million to buy the company. Even if her client is willing to sell for less, this is nonmaterial "puffing."

To what degree may attorneys overstate the true value of the company their client is selling? May they suggest it has a rosy future, even if that is not entirely clear? May they say the firm is on the verge of an important product development when that is incorrect? May they indicate that the firm has accounts receivable of $540,000, when those accounts total only $150,000? The first statement of a wholly subjective nature is probably acceptable if they do not embellish too greatly. The other two would be improper, because they concern material fact information the other party has the right to rely upon. While they may have no affirmative obligation to disclose these facts, if they choose to discuss them, they must do so honestly.

b. Partially Truthful Factual Statements

Some seemingly truthful statements can be misleading. Suppose someone is thinking of purchasing a house that suffered substantial damage in a hurricane but seems to have been restored. What if the prospective purchaser asks if the storm damage has been repaired? Could the seller truthfully indicate that the roof has been completely replaced, but say nothing about the fact that the eaves under the roof still leak when it rains? Since it should be apparent that the person hearing this representation would be likely to assume that the storm damage has been entirely repaired, the seller should either have to remain silent or include information indicating that additional leaks exist. In many states requiring house sellers to disclose known defects of a serious nature, the seller would be obliged to disclose the leaking eaves even if they are not specifically asked about this issue. Comment 1 to Rule 4.1 expressly recognizes that a "misrepresentation can also occur by partially true but misleading statements or omissions that are the equivalent of affirmative false statements." Ethical opinions have thus held that truthful statements may constitute actionable misrepresentations when they are made under circumstances in which the person making the statements knows the other party is misinterpreting what is being conveyed.

When negotiators are asked about delicate issues or decide to raise those matters on their own, their statements should be phrased in a manner that conveys — both explicitly and implicitly — truthful information. They should not use half-truths they know are likely to induce listeners to misunderstand the actual circumstances. If they are not sure what to say, they may remain silent. If they choose to speak, however, they must do so in a way that is not misleading.

c.   Impermissible Factual Omissions

In many business and legal interactions, the basic rule is caveat emptor — buyer beware. If the buyer does not ask the right questions and the seller makes no affirmative misrepresentations, the buyer has no recourse if he subsequently discovers problems. When might seller silence give rise to legal liability? Whenever the law imposes an affirmative duty to disclose. As noted above, the laws in many states require home sellers to disclose known defects of a serious nature. Sellers who fail to satisfy this duty may be sued for the damages caused by the undisclosed defects.

Similar affirmative duties are imposed upon stock and bond sellers by securities laws. Before selling stocks or bonds to buyers, owners are required to provide prospectuses that include detailed financial information. If they fail to include relevant positive and negative information, they can be held liable for their omissions.

3.   Legal Misrepresentations and Omissions

When negotiators interact in the legal arena, they almost always discuss relevant statutes, regulations, and judicial decisions. Side A emphasizes the doctrines supportive of its position, while Side B cites the rules supporting its position. It is clear that neither side may knowingly make a false statement of material law without violating the proscription set forth in Rule 4.1.[3] On the other hand, Rule 4.1 does not require attorneys to provide opposing counsel with citations supportive of that side's situation. If Side B's representatives fail to discover applicable code provisions or case law supporting their circumstances, almost no lawyers feel obliged to provide them with the missing citations. They maintain that it is the duty of the other side's lawyers to locate these references, and if they fail to do so, these attorneys feel no need to assist them. They must merely refrain from any representations that would be contrary to the legal doctrines they know about. On the other hand, if they are litigators and the matter in dispute ends up in court, Rule 3.3(a)(2) provides that "A lawyer shall not knowingly: . . . (2) fail to disclose to the tribunal[4] legal authority in the controlling jurisdiction known to the lawyer to be directly adverse to the position of the client and not disclosed by opposing counsel." In this circumstance, they must thus apprise the court of the citations supporting the position of their adversary.

---

[3] Litigators are under a similar obligation under Rule 3.3(a)(1) to refrain from making **any** false statement of law (or fact) — material or otherwise — to a tribunal.

[4] "Tribunal" is defined in Rule 1.0(m): " 'Tribunal' denotes a court, an arbitrator in a binding arbitration proceeding or a legislative body, administrative agency or other body acting in an adjudicative capacity. A legislative body, administrative agency or other body acts in an adjudicative capacity when a neutral official, after the presentation of evidence or legal argument by a party or parties, will render a binding legal judgment directly affecting a party's interests in a particular matter."

C. UNCONSCIONABLE NEGOTIATING TACTICS

Some lawyers — especially in larger urban areas[5] — employ highly offensive tactics to advance client interests. They are often rude or nasty. These persons erroneously equate discourteous actions with effective advocacy. Such inappropriate tactics are actually a substitute for proficient lawyering skill. Competent practitioners realize that impolite behavior is the antithesis of effective representation. Although Model Rule 1.3 provides that "[a] lawyer shall act with reasonable diligence and promptness in representing a client," Comment 1 specifically states that "[t]he lawyer's duty to act with reasonable diligence does not require the use of offensive tactics or preclude the treating of all persons involved in the legal process with courtesy and respect."

Legal representatives should eschew tactics that are merely designed to humiliate or harass opponents. Model Rule 4.4 expressly states that "a lawyer shall not use means that have no substantial purpose other than to embarrass, delay, or burden a third person . . . ." The ABA Section of Litigation Guidelines for Conduct, "Lawyers' Duties to Other Counsel," states, "We will not, even when called upon by a client to do so, abuse or indulge in offensive conduct directed to other counsel, parties, or witnesses. We will abstain from disparaging personal remarks or acrimony toward other counsel, parties, or witnesses. We will treat adverse witnesses and parties with fair consideration."[6]

Win-lose negotiators may endeavor to achieve total annihilation of adversaries through the degradation of opposing counsel. Not only is such behavior morally reprehensible, but it needlessly exposes the offensive perpetrators to future recriminations that could easily be avoided through common courtesy. In litigation situations, it might also expose the offensive actors to judicial sanctions.[7] This approach guarantees the offensive actors far more nonsettlements than would be experienced by their more cooperative cohorts.

D. INTERACTIONS WITH NEUTRAL FACILITATORS

Part One of this book focuses on negotiation between the parties, where both parties are advocates. But we will soon be considering the advocate's role in mediations and arbitrations, where the recipient of the representation may be a neutral. So while we are discussing ethical considerations, we want to alert you to the particular issues that apply with respect to representations before neutral facilitators.

When lawyers representing clients interact with judicial settlement facilitators or private mediators, may they puff and embellish as they can with opposing attorneys pursuant to Comment 2 to Rule 4.1? *ABA Formal Opin. 93-370* (1993) indicated that

---

[5] In our experience, the smaller the bar, the more collegial the behavior. People who work and socialize with each other all the time cannot afford to soil their own nest.

[6] http://www.americanbar.org/groups/litigation/policy/conduct_guidelines/lawyers_duties.html, site last visited 5-21-12.

[7] A number of courts have adopted litigation guidelines and commonly make them part of the rules of behavior. *See* http://www.nhd.uscourts.gov/pdf/litguide.pdf, site last visited 5-21-12; http://www.lacba.org/Files/Main%20Folder/Services/FaxOnDemand/files/LitigationGuidelines.pdf, site last visited 5-21-12.

knowing misrepresentations to judicial mediators regarding client settlement intentions and subjective values would be impermissible, based upon the view that the Comment 2 exception only applies to bargaining interactions with *opposing counsel*. Since such misstatements to judicial officials would not be confined to adversarial communications, they would contravene Rule 4.1.

In *ABA Formal Opin. 06-439* (2006),[8] the ABA had to decide whether the logic of *Formal Opin. 93-370* (1993) barred puffing and embellishment to nonjudicial mediators. If it followed the reasoning of the 1993 Opinion, lawyers could not misrepresent client settlement intentions and values to all neutral parties, but the ABA felt uncomfortable with such an expansive prohibition. As a result, it decided to limit the coverage of the prior Opinion to judicial officers. It held that: 1) conversations with judicial settlement facilitators are governed by Model Rule 3.3(a)(1) which forbids lawyers from knowingly making ***any*** false statements of fact to tribunals; and 2) Comment 2 to Rule 4.1 applies to communications between advocates and ***nonjudicial*** mediators in separate caucus sessions, allowing the use of traditional puffing and embellishment. Because many mediators are selected through various court panels and programs, the difficult question is whether a private mediator who is on a court panel is judicial or nonjudicial. In our experience as mediators, we expect "puffing" and "embellishment" as part of the mediation process, but you should be aware of this issue and find out what the custom is in your practice locale.

E. CONCLUSION

Although some misrepresentations are considered acceptable "puffing," others are clearly inappropriate. It is not always easy to draw the line between statements the other side does not have the right to rely upon and those they may consider sacrosanct. As you work through the exercises in this course, ask yourself how you would feel if your opponent were to make the misrepresentation you are contemplating. If you would consider them dishonest, then you should refrain from such conduct yourself.

---

[8] Available online at: http://www.illinoislegalmal.com/archives/06-439.pdf, site last visited 5-21-12.

EXERCISES

EXERCISE 5.1
PRACTICING THE NEGOTIATION PROCESS

GENERAL DESCRIPTION OF EXERCISE: Negotiation of a personal injury claim.

SKILLS INVOLVED: Negotiation.

PARTICIPANTS NEEDED: You will be divided into pairs.

ESTIMATED TIME REQUIRED:

75 minutes: 45 minutes for negotiation, 30 minutes for discussion

LEVEL OF DIFFICULTY (1-5):

"PARKER v. DAVIDSON"

You will be divided into pairs. Your professor will assign one person to represent the plaintiff and the other person to represent the defendant. Start by reading the General Information below. After that, read the Confidential Information pertaining to your assigned side and follow the instructions that are provided.

GENERAL INFORMATION

Last September 1, at 2:35 p.m., twenty-seven year old Harry Parker was driving south in his three-year old Honda Accord on Wisconsin Avenue in Washington, D.C. This is a four-lane street that carries a substantial amount of traffic between Georgetown and the Maryland suburbs. It was a clear, sunny day, and the pavement was dry. Although the speed limit on that part of Wisconsin Avenue is 25 mph, Mr. Parker was driving 35 mph. As Mr. Parker approached the stop light at R Street, N.W., he observed a green light for southbound traffic and he continued to travel at 35 mph.

John Davidson was driving west on R Street in his new Ford Taurus. He was then employed by the District of Columbia Department of Public Works as a civil engineer. At 1:30 p.m., Mr. Davidson had become embroiled in a disagreement with his immediate supervisor concerning Mr. Davidson's dissatisfaction with the 2 percent salary increase he had recently received. Their discussion had taken more time than he had anticipated. Mr. Davidson was thus late for an important job interview he had scheduled with a private engineering firm. He was hoping to obtain a new position that would pay him almost $10,000 more per year than the $47,500 he was currently earning.

As Mr. Davidson approached Wisconsin Avenue, he was driving 37 mph in a 25 mph zone. When he arrived at the Wisconsin Avenue-R Street intersection, Mr. Davidson noticed that the light for traffic in his direction was red. Mr. Davidson reduced his speed to 25 mph and endeavored to make a right turn onto Wisconsin Avenue. His rate of speed was excessive, and his car swerved into the outer lane of southbound traffic. His car struck the left front portion of Mr. Parker's vehicle, causing that car to veer into a light pole located just below the south-west corner of the intersection. When Mr. Parker's car struck the light pole, it stopped abruptly.

Mr. Davidson was wearing his seat belt, and his air bag opened as soon as the two vehicles collided. As a result, he suffered no serious injuries. Mr. Parker was also wearing a seat belt, but the air bag in his car did not deploy until it struck the light pole. When his automobile first collided with the Davidson car (and before the air bag opened), his upper chest struck the steering wheel. He sustained a crushing blow to the chest that caused a cracked sternum and multiple rib fractures. Mr. Parker was taken to the Georgetown University Hospital where he was thoroughly examined. They discovered the cracked sternum and the fractured ribs. They taped Mr. Parker's upper body and provided him with medication to reduce his discomfort. Although Mr. Parker's upper body was severely contused, there was no evidence of additional injury. The Emergency Room treatment cost Mr. Parker $1,425. His subsequent examinations by Dr. Joan Bannon, an orthopedic specialist, cost an additional $475. He was out of work for two weeks. Mr. Parker is a self-employed electrician, and these two weeks of missed work cost him $2,200. Mr. Parker continued to experience some pain for an eight-week period, but he was able to perform his usual job duties after the second week. On October 28, Dr. Bannon examined Mr. Parker and declared him recovered. Mr. Parker's Honda Accord was totally wrecked, at a loss of approximately $12,400.

Last month, Mr. Parker filed a civil action against Mr. Davidson alleging that his negligent driving caused their accident. His complaint requested $100,000. Defendant Davidson carries liability insurance providing $100,000 coverage per accident. The District of Columbia is still a contributory negligence jurisdiction.

Your professor will provide further instructions and confidential information for each side.

EXERCISE 5.1
PRACTICING THE NEGOTIATION PROCESS

"PARKER v. DAVIDSON"

REFLECTION

Ask yourself what you learned from this exercise. Regardless of who you represented, consider the questions raised by your professor when you debrief the exercise and include that information as part of your reflection.[9]

Look again at the reflective questions you first reviewed following Exercise 4.1. To what extent were you able to improve on your ability to understand and observe the stages of negotiation? In what ways do you need to improve? What steps are you going to take during the next exercise to improve? What effect, if any, did ethical considerations/limitations play in your conduct? In your opponent's conduct?

1. **Preparatory Stage**:

A. Identified and distinguished between the client's **essential, important and desirable** goals.

B. Developed cogent legal theories to support your client's position and anticipated the counter-arguments of opposing counsel.

C. Calculated your client's and the opposing side's **bottom lines** (**BATNA**)

D. Established sufficiently elevated **aspiration levels**.

E. Formulated an elevated but principled opening offer.

F. Effectively choreographed the expected interaction by using the Negotiation Preparation Form or something similar.

2. **Preliminary Stage**:

A. Established rapport with opposing counsel through warm eye contact and pleasant demeanor.

B. Attempted to identify and establish common backgrounds and/or interests.

3. **Informational Stage**:

A. Used broad, open-ended "what" and "why" information seeking questions to ascertain other side's **needs** and **interests**.

B. Listened for **verbal leaks** like "really want," "would like to get," "important," "desirable," etc.

---

[9] *See generally* Timothy W. Floyd & John Gallagher, *Legal Ethics, Narrative, and Professional Identity: The Story of David Spaulding*, 59 MERCER L. REV. 941 (2008), available at: http://www2.law.mercer.edu/lawreview/getfile.cfm?file=59302.pdf (last visited 10-27-12).

C. Disclosed information in strategic manner, and used **blocking techniques** where appropriate.

4. **Distributive Stage**:

A. Strategically considered who would make first offer and its potential effect on the outcome.

B. Employed a carefully planned "**principled**" concession pattern.

C. Listened for **verbal leaks** like "really want," "would like to get," "important," "desirable," etc.

D. Established a tone and attitude of confidence.

E. Commenced negotiations with a view toward your **elevated aspiration levels** and a strong justification for your position.

F. Carefully planned for and used appropriate **power bargaining** techniques.

G. Identified and appropriately deflected opponent's use of **power bargaining** techniques.

H. Kept track of your BATNA during the negotiations and included it in your analysis as a viable alternative to settlement, e.g., no "settlement at all costs."

5. **Closing Stage**:

A. Remained **patiently perseverant** even though settlement appeared imminent.

B. Continued to listen for **verbal leaks**.

6. **Cooperative Stage**:

A. After reaching an accord, continued to work with opponent to explore unfound **alternatives** that might be mutually beneficial and that could **maximize joint results**.

B. Reached a settlement that was **efficient** compared to the other settlements arrived at by your fellow students.

Complete the Post Negotiation Evaluation Checklist following Exercise 4.1 and available for download at the **LexisNexis Webcourse**, Chapter 4.

Chapter 6

ADDITIONAL NEGOTIATION TECHNIQUES

At this point, you should know just enough about negotiation to make you dangerous! In Chapter 4, you considered the 6 stages of negotiation and had a chance to practice and observe them. In Chapter 5, you learned that lawyers have ethical boundaries that can create a real tension in the give and take of the negotiation process.

When individuals negotiate, there are a relatively finite number of techniques they can employ to advance their interests. It is beneficial for negotiators to understand the different techniques both to enable them to decide which ones they should use and to allow them to recognize and counteract the tactics being used by their opponents. We will focus on the most common and interesting ones.

In Chapter 4 we already introduced you to some of the most common negotiation techniques. In this chapter, we will discuss some additional tactics that you will see in your practice. We encourage you to read this in conjunction with the **LexisNexis Webcourse** for this chapter, where you will find video examples and other supplemental materials. You will find some of them offensive and even lame, but you need to be aware of the tactics so you can name them if they are used on you in a negotiation. If you can silently name a tactic when it's being used, it makes it much less likely that you will get "hooked" by it. Also, to a limited extent, the concept behind some of these tactics is sound, and you may want to include them in your tool kit. After you become familiar with all of them, you will see that negotiators use them in various ways. Like a good composer, they create a theme and variations, using the instruments to their advantage.

A. EXTREME INITIAL DEMANDS/OFFERS

Some negotiators like to commence bargaining interactions with extreme opening positions. They hope to use this technique to anchor the preliminary discussions. If their adversaries are not thoroughly prepared, they may begin to bargain up or down from these extreme positions instead of ignoring these openings and articulating rational offers or demands of their own. If negotiators hope to enhance the credibility of one-sided opening positions, they should prepare detailed and logical explanations to support their seemingly unreasonable demands or offers. Such an approach creates an aura of legitimacy, and it usually induces opponents to treat such extreme positions more seriously than positions not supported by rational explanations.

People confronted by extreme opening positions should not casually dismiss them, because this approach may lead opponents to believe their wholly one-sided demands or offers are more realistic than they initially thought. Recipients of such offers should politely but firmly indicate that they are completely unreasonable and unworthy of serious discussion. Such communications can induce the original offerors to moderate both their internal objectives and their external position statements in the other side's direction.

An effective way to counteract extreme opening positions involves the use of *probing questions*. Offerees can ask offerors a series of questions requiring those persons to explain the rationales supporting each aspect of their opening positions. The questioners should begin with the most finite components where there is little room for significant puffing and then move on to the less finite aspects. If the unreasonable offerors are forced to explain each component, they begin to falter, because it is difficult to defend unrealistic positions with respect to such finite items as lost wages or the value of real estate.

B. BOULWAREISM — BEST OFFER FIRST BARGAINING

People who dislike the give-and-take of traditional bargaining encounters occasionally seek to shortcut the process by beginning with firm and unyielding opening offers. This was the approach taken by Lemuel Boulware, the former labor negotiator for the General Electric Company, who wished to make it clear to workers that they were getting their wage and benefit increases due to corporate generosity rather than union demands. Parties wishing to employ this device must possess a substantial amount of bargaining power, because, if they do not, opponents will simply ignore their offers and do business with someone else. This approach is an affront to opponents who expect to participate meaningfully in the bargaining process and feel they influenced the final terms agreed upon. It is basically a parent-child interaction, with the "parent" offerors telling the "child" offerees what they must accept.

The visceral reaction to Boulwareism is to call the offerors' bluff. This may cause a work stoppage or a failed interaction. Some persons deal with this tactic by ignoring the promise of the offerors not to alter their initial positions and by articulating realistic offers of their own. They hope to generate typical adult-to-adult discussions that will allow the initial offerors to begin to retreat from their seemingly resolute positions.

Although Boulwareism may work against less competent negotiators, it will rarely intimidate proficient bargainers. It is likely to turn them off and cause them to contemplate their nonsettlement options. Persons considering the use of best-offer-first tactics should realize the offensive impact such an approach has on opponents. It is more effective for bargainers to begin the discussions with lower offers or higher demands and allow the other side to talk them up or down to where they initially thought the parties would conclude their interactions. This approach is much more likely to satisfy opponents who wish to feel they were respected and allowed to influence the final terms agreed upon. Also, most negotiators such as labor negotiators and insurance adjusters report to a higher authority who will document the course of the negotiations. A negotiator who reports to someone else is unlikely to agree to a settlement if she has to report that the other side would not concede so she accepted the demand. Negotiators tend to be more satisfied with objectively less beneficial results when they feel the bargaining process was fair than with objectively more beneficial results when they feel the process was not fair.

C. LIMITED CLIENT AUTHORITY

Many negotiators like to indicate when they commence bargaining encounters that they lack authority to bind their principals. Some persons who actually possess real authority make such representations to avoid being bound before they have the time to consider terms tentatively agreed upon or to use the Nibble Technique that will be discussed next.[1] Others make such representations based upon the fact they must actually obtain the approval of absent clients before terms can become final.

The advantage of limited authority concerns the ability of such negotiators to bind their opponents without binding themselves. Once their opponents have become psychologically committed to agreements, they are likely to make additional post-"agreement" concessions to preserve the arrangements they think have been achieved.

Negotiators who are told by opponents that such persons lack the authority to bind their principals may wish to indicate a similar constraint on their own side.[2] This means that no agreement can become binding until the principals on *both sides* have had the opportunity to review the tentative terms already reached. Another way to deal with such opponents is to let them know when terms have been preliminarily achieved that this side has absolutely no additional room to move. They can indicate that if the other side demands further changes, the agreement will be lost.

Negotiators who tell opponents that they possess limited authority even when they have a good idea what their clients would accept should never make the mistake of telling someone who has provided them with an unexpectedly generous offer that they will get back to that person in a couple of days after they check with their absent clients. By then, the other side may realize that they have made a mistake and withdraw their offer. The recipients of such an offer should excuse themselves to allow them to contact their client to see if the client would be willing to accept the proffered terms. They can then solidify the deal before the other side can reconsider its offer.

Negotiators should be careful not to interact seriously with opponents who possess *no client authority*. Such persons contact people to find out what they expect to achieve. Once these individuals obtain opening position statements, they indicate that the offers are wholly unacceptable, hoping to induce careless negotiators to bid against themselves with new offers. Negotiators who encounter such adversaries should not succumb to this tactic. They should immediately ask such persons to state their own opening positions. When they indicate a lack of client authority, they should be told to

---

[1] With respect to lawyers, we believe that this would be an impermissible false representation of a material fact, in violation of Model Rule 4.1. But many lawyers will get around this by telling their clients not to give them final authority to bind or by simply saying that they will not bind the deal without first running it by their clients.

[2] In this instance it would not be an affirmative misrepresentation to say, "In that case, I will not agree to bind my clients without first running it past them."

get some authority so they can put their own offer on the table so both sides will be on an equal footing.

Finally this tactic can often be avoided or greatly minimized by setting the ground rules in advance of the negotiation session. It is common for parties to demand that the negotiation take place in the presence of people with full settlement authority.

D. NIBBLE TECHNIQUE

A few negotiators agree to "final" terms with apparent client approval. Their opponents are pleased with the agreements and inform their clients of the good news. Several days later, these bargainers contact their opponents with seeming embarrassment and explain that their clients have to have several "slight changes" before the agreements can become final. Since their unsuspecting opponents are psychologically committed to final agreements and do not wish to allow these modifications to negate their prior efforts, they give in to the requested changes. This allows the nibblers to obtain post-agreement concessions that are not reciprocated by them.

The individuals being nibbled usually ask themselves the incorrect question — "are *we* going to let the whole deal fall through over these slight changes?" They need to refocus their attention on the other side and ask: "Are *they* going to let the whole deal fall through over these slight changes?" When they examine the circumstances from the perspective of both sides, they realize that the other side is as interested in a final accord as they are. Those persons are thus not likely to walk away from the deal the parties have already achieved simply because they have been unable to extract post-agreement unilateral concessions from this side.

Individuals confronted by nibbler opponents need to be "provocable" if they wish to avoid exploitation. When their opponents inform them of the necessity for modifications, they should demand reciprocity. They should indicate that their clients have some qualms of their own and suggest that they can accommodate the changes being requested if their concerns can be simultaneously satisfied.

If the persons demanding post-agreement changes are actually sincere and their clients really have to have several changes, they will recognize the principle of reciprocity and make concessions in exchange for the modifications they are seeking. If they are disingenuously employing the nibble technique to extract unreciprocated, post-agreement concessions and they are confronted with demands for reciprocity, they will most likely realize that they are better off accepting the original terms agreed upon. They will withdraw their demands for post-agreement modifications.

So long as persons employing the Nibble Technique expressly indicate that they have limited authority and have to obtain client consent before terms can become final, use of the Nibble Technique is considered ethical. On the other hand, if a negotiator indicated that she possessed final authority to bind her side and used this device to obtain one-sided, post-agreement concessions from the other side, we believe it would be a material misrepresentation of fact, and would contravene Model Rule 4.1. In addition, the law in many jurisdictions is that lawyers have apparent authority to bind their clients, so this tactic could result in a breach of contract action or, in a litigated matter, a motion to enforce a settlement. Lawyers thinking of using this tactic should thus be careful to indicate that any terms preliminarily agreed upon will still be subject to final client review.

E. LIMITED TIME OFFERS/DECREASING OFFERS OR INCREASING DEMANDS

During the preliminary stages of some negotiations, a few attorneys make fairly realistic offers or demands they say must be accepted by specific dates. They make it clear that if their offers are not accepted by those dates, they will either withdraw those offers entirely *or* begin to reduce the amounts being offered or increase the amounts being demanded. They employ this tactic hoping to intimidate less proficient opponents to cave in to their positions.

It can be entirely appropriate for negotiators to establish firm dates by which time their offers must be accepted or are withdrawn — especially where their principals have other options they may decide to explore or where litigation is ongoing and will increase costs. The major risk associated with this tactic concerns the fact their adversaries may not yet be prepared to make binding determinations on such a limited time line. As a result, deals that might have been consummated may be lost.

Occasionally, people making opening offers not only set time limits, but also indicate that if their offers are not accepted they will *demand more* or *offer less*. It can be a justified position if time is truly of the essence and delay changes the benefits of the bargain. For example, if trial is scheduled to take place in two weeks and final trial preparation (with its attendant economic and diverted human resource costs) is about to begin, or if a statute granting favorable tax treatment for the negotiated exchange is about to expire, the current settlement offer could become unattractive to the offeror. In the absence of a legitimate, articulable reason, this is an extremely risky approach to bargaining. When other parties begin to move *away from* their starting positions, this will induce most opponents to move toward their nonsettlement alternatives (BATNA). They either prepare for trial in matters involving litigation or look for other business deals.

F. ANGER/AGGRESSIVE BEHAVIOR

Negotiators sometimes resort to anger or aggressive tactics to convince their opponents of the seriousness of the circumstances involved. They raise their voice, pound the table, and occasionally walk out. They hope to intimidate less confident opponents to give in to their demands. Proficient negotiators almost never lose their tempers, since they recognize that such behavior would likely have a negative impact on their interactions. They thus employ this device in a carefully controlled manner.

When opponents seem to become angry, most persons respond in kind. This often causes problems as the battle escalates. The best way to respond to strategic "anger" is the opposite of what is expected. If opponents stand over someone and shout, those victims should remain calm and silent. Like a parent to a child, they should remain firm, fair and friendly. They should listen carefully for verbal leaks that may inadvertently disclose important information. It is difficult to have a one-way harangue for long without becoming embarrassed. As the demonstrative parties feel ashamed of their behavior, they tend to make concessions in an effort to regain social acceptability.

G. WALKING OUT/HANGING UP TELEPHONE

Some especially demonstrative negotiators like to walk out of in-person talks or slam down their telephone receivers. This approach is used to intimidate timid opponents into unplanned concessions. If others walk out or hang up rudely, negotiators should not follow them out the door or call them right back. Such behavior would only embolden them. Such demonstrative bargainers should instead be allowed to leave or to hang up without further interaction. They have to be taught that such tactics will not be rewarded. Once they realize that this approach is not working, they are unlikely to employ it again. Again, it is best to remain firm, fair and friendly.

H. IRRATIONAL BEHAVIOR

Some individuals behave as if they are unstable in an effort to intimidate their opponents. It would be extremely rare for professional negotiators to encounter truly irrational opponents, because it is virtually impossible for such persons to survive in the competitive business world. Most persons who appear to be irrational are behaving like foxes. Their conduct is carefully controlled. Adversaries should ignore their strange demeanors and make their planned presentations. When the parties part company, their strangely behaving opponents will evaluate the offers they have received as logically as other negotiators.

I. UPROAR

Negotiators occasionally threaten dire consequences if their demands are not met. They hope to convince opponents that they must give in or face total destruction. When someone threatens such extreme consequences, the person being threatened should ask two critical questions. First, is the threatened result likely to result? When they step back and look at the situation objectively, it may become clear that this is an idle threat the other side cannot possibly effectuate. Second, if the threatened consequence may result, how would that situation affect the other side? When someone threatens mutual annihilation, the key word is "*mutual.*" Is the other side really willing to destroy itself to get at this side? When they realize that the threat is not having the hoped for impact, they will usually move on to other less drastic techniques.

J. BRER RABBIT

Joel Chandler Harris created the unforgettable character named Brer Rabbit. When he was caught by the fox, he asked to be skinned or to have his eyeballs ripped out, as long as he was not flung in the briar patch. The fox tossed him in the briar patch, and he escaped. This technique is based on reverse psychology. People employing this technique indicate a preference for Items 1 and 2, but suggest a willingness to accept Items 3 and 4 if they cannot have what they prefer to obtain. Items 3 and 4 are their real objective. Win-lose opponents will force upon them the items they think they least prefer. They should play the game to the end by suggesting that if this is all they obtain, their client will be disappointed. Their Brer Rabbit adversaries will be relieved to think they have put them in a negative position.

This tactic can be especially effective against highly competitive win-lose opponents who are only satisfied when they think their counterparts have completely lost. They thus try to give others what they think those persons least wish to obtain. If the Brer Rabbit approach is used effectively against them, they will force the other side to accept Items 3 and 4 instead of the other two things that side professes to want, causing their counterparts to leave with exactly what they wanted.

K.   TOM SAWYER AND THE FENCE

This tactic is similar to the Brer Rabbit reverse psychology gambit, but appeals to a somewhat different emotion. Also, instead of making something appear ***undesirable***, the tactic involves making something appear ***more desirable***. In Mark Twain's *The Adventures of Tom Sawyer*, Tom's Aunt Polly gives Tom the chore of whitewashing a fence that is 30 yards long and 9 feet high. At first Tom is extremely discouraged, but he suddenly has an idea. When his friend, Ben Rogers, comes up to Tom and starts to tease him for being stuck with such a lot of work, Tom acts like whitewashing the fence is an honor and that not just anyone can do it. This immediately makes Ben want to try but Tom tells him he can't. Of course, this just increases Ben's desire, and he offers Tom his apple core for the "privilege" of whitewashing the fence. Tom still says "no" but eventually relents when Ben offers the whole apple. Tom employs this same negotiating strategy on many other boys who stop by. Tom gets handsomely paid for "allowing" the boys to have a turn and gets Aunt Polly's fence whitewashed in the process.

Like the Brer Rabbit approach, Tom Sawyer's strategy can be effective against highly competitive win-lose opponents, but it can also be effective against others. Making something appear more desirable to the client often has the effect of making it appear more desirable to others.[3] Like Tom, skilled negotiators can sometimes get their opponents to pay more for the "privilege" of obtaining something that would have been freely exchanged.

L.   GOOD COP/BAD COP

The good cop/bad cop routine is one of the most common — and often effective — negotiation tactics. It has become famous in countless television police shows where two "cops" examine a suspect in an interview room. One seemingly reasonable negotiator — the "good cop" — softens up the suspect by offering him some food, a soda and a kind tone of voice. The good cop says he has to leave but will be back. In

---

[3] Bernard Madoff's infamous Ponzi scheme attracted investors, in part, by placing restrictions on who could invest. Madoff investors were made to feel that they were part of something exclusive, which served to increase investor desire. Numerous otherwise sophisticated investors placed fortunes with Madoff.

walks the "bad cop." The bad cop is tough and tries to intimidate and frighten the suspect. While the bad cop is still there abusing the suspect, the good cop returns, calms the bad cop, and again makes sure that the suspect is "all right." The suspect is so relieved to be treated like a human that he spills his guts to the good cop.

When this tactic is used in negotiations, there are various iterations, but the strategy is the same. One seemingly reasonable "good cop" negotiator softens opponent resistance by thanking them for their kind treatment and requesting seemingly modest proposals. Opponents are pleased to give him what he is seeking. As soon as they do, however, the unreasonable "bad cop" partner completely trashes these concessions and demands substantial changes. When the opponents are about to explode, good cop calms his bad cop partner and then requests additional concessions. When good cop obtains better terms, bad cop attacks the new offers being made. As obvious as this technique can be, it is amazing how often negotiators succumb to these tactics. They work so hard to please the bad cops that they fail to appreciate how effectively they have been fleeced.

Most people confronted with good cop/bad cop opponents make the mistake of arguing entirely with the bad cops. What they should do is focus on the good cops. When these seemingly reasonable persons indicate they would accept the terms if a couple of modest changes were made, they should be directly asked in the presence of the bad cop if they would agree if these modifications were made. The good cops should be forced to say "yes" or "no." Once it becomes clear that they will not say "yes" without the concurrence of their bad cop partners, the game is over and they have to change tactics.

M. PASSIVE-AGGRESSIVE BEHAVIOR

There are people who disrupt the bargaining process indirectly. They show up late or fail to bring needed papers to scheduled sessions. They promise to write up agreed upon terms, but fail to do so in a timely manner. They seem disinterested in the interaction, but they are actually very interested parties who are quite aggressive — only they are passively-aggressive. Their aggression is displayed indirectly instead of overtly.

Skilled opponents of passive-aggressive negotiators will take control of the interaction by obtaining the necessary documents and by preparing drafts of particular provisions. They want to preempt the ability of passive-aggressive individuals to disrupt the bargaining process. They will work hard to induce these persons to agree to particular terms. Passive-aggressive negotiators will usually insist upon the right to draft the final agreement. But as soon as they leave, their opponents should draft the terms. When the negotiators get back together to finalize their previous agreement, the passive-aggressive person will indicate that he did not have the time to draft the agreed upon terms and even begin to ask for changes. If the opponent has already prepared a complete draft, the passive-aggressive negotiator is likely to give up and sign the proffered documents. Once they are faced with a fait accompli, passive-aggressives usually do not have the ability to directly reject what has been placed before them, since such overt action is inconsistent with their passive-aggressive personality.

N. BELLY UP

Some sly negotiators emulate the approach of murder detective Lt. Columbo, a character made famous by Peter Falk, and act like bumbling idiots. They say that they don't know anything about these types of interactions and indicate a willingness to allow their "fair and knowledgeable" opponents to determine what would be appropriate for both sides. They hope to lull unsuspecting opponents into careless disclosures and concessions intended to help these seemingly inept bargainers. In the end, these "aw shucks" negotiators leave with everything, and their opponents are so glad they could help solve their problems. These are highly manipulative negotiators.

Negotiators should never feel sorry for seemingly incompetent adversaries. They should ignore such behavior and execute their planned negotiation strategy. They should come out with their planned opening offers/demands. When their opponents act shocked and beg them to reconsider their positions, they should ask those persons to state their own positions. Those manipulative negotiators should be forced to articulate and defend their own positions. It is the last thing they hope to do. They want the other side to make all of the concessions, without them having to meaningfully participate in the concession process. Once the belly-up participants realize that their technique is not working, they will end their charade and interact more normally.

EXERCISES

EXERCISE 6.1
PRACTICING NEGOTIATION TECHNIQUES

GENERAL DESCRIPTION OF EXERCISE: Negotiation of a personal injury claim.

SKILLS INVOLVED: Negotiation.

PARTICIPANTS NEEDED: You will be divided into pairs.

ESTIMATED TIME REQUIRED:

75 minutes: 45 minutes for negotiating, 30 minutes for discussion

LEVEL OF DIFFICULTY (1-5):

"DUBINSKI v. COWTOWN DAIRY"

You will be divided into pairs. Your professor will assign one person to represent the plaintiff and the other person to represent the defendant. Start by reading the General Information below. After that, read the Confidential Information pertaining to your assigned side and follow the instructions that are provided.

GENERAL INFORMATION AVAILABLE TO ALL STUDENTS

In the early morning hours of last June 19, Roland Dubinski was driving from Washington, D.C. to Charlottesville on Rte. 29 when he became involved in an automobile accident near Charlottesville, where Rte. 29 is a four lane highway. As a result of the accident, Mr. Dubinski, who was 27 at the time, was permanently paralyzed from the shoulders down. The accident occurred at 2:00 a.m., the highway pavement was dry, and the visibility was unrestricted.

The circumstances surrounding the accident were as follows. Mr. Dubinski had taken his fiancee, Joyce Smith, to Washington to attend a concert. Following the concert, Dubinski, who resided in Charlottesville, was driving Smith, a graduate music student at the University of Virginia, back to her Charlottesville apartment in his ten year old Volkswagen. As he approached Charlottesville, he came upon a car which was stopped in the right-hand lane of the highway. He stopped behind the car to ascertain whether he could be of assistance to the owner of the disabled vehicle. Before he could exit from his vehicle, Dubinski's car was struck in the rear, and his car and the one ahead of his were driven off the road. They had been struck by a milk truck owned by the Cowtown Dairy Company and operated by one of its employees. Although neither

Smith nor the owner of the stalled vehicle sustained any serious injuries, Dubinski received a broken neck. The driver of the milk truck reported that she did not see the stopped vehicles until just before the accident, and the police found no skid marks from that truck. The oxidation of the filaments on the light bulbs of the VW and the position of the switch on the dashboard indicated that the VW's tail lights were on at the time of the accident.

The driver of the originally stopped car had apparently run out of gas. The police officers who investigated the accident reported that they had noted the smell of alcohol when talking to that person immediately following the accident, but they had not administered any breathalyzer or blood alcohol test.

Dubinski comes from a family of exceptionally able musicians, and he was himself a professional musician. His mother is a nationally known concert pianist, his father plays the viola in the National Symphony Orchestra, and his brother is a professional rock guitarist. At the time of the accident, Dubinski was earning $42,000 per year as the first violinist for the Charlottesville Symphony Orchestra. He earned an additional $22,500 per year giving private music lessons. He was regarded as a rising star in the violin field, and it was likely that he would have received the next violin opening in the National Symphony Orchestra, a position which would have initially paid him about $100,000 per year.

At the time of the accident, Dubinski had been engaged to Smith. Three months after the collision, she terminated their relationship.

Dubinski's out-of-pocket medical expenses since the time of the accident have been $77,000. These include doctor, hospital, and rehabilitation costs. He now has very limited use of his hands and arms. With some difficulty, he can comb his hair, lift a glass, and perform very limited manual functions. He will never again play the violin. He has no bladder or bowel control and has had to have a valve installed in his bladder. It is likely that he will suffer future urinary tract infections, bed sores, and other similar maladies which commonly afflict such paralyzed individuals. Dubinski will also require someone to care for him throughout the rest of his life. This person will have to cook for him, cut his food, dress him, and assist him in the bathroom. It is likely therefore that he will have substantial continuing medical expenses as a direct result of the injuries he sustained in the accident.

One month after the accident, attorneys for Dubinski filed a suit against the Cowtown Dairy Company seeking $15,000,000 in damages. (No suit has been filed against either the driver of the milk truck or the operator of the stalled vehicle.) At the pre-trial conference which was recently conducted, plaintiff's lawyers showed a video tape. This video tape initially showed Dubinski playing the violin, with close-up shots of his finger and hand movements. It then showed him endeavoring to operate a loom at the rehabilitation center. At that center, his hands quivered and shook and finally grabbed the loom levers like hooks to pull them down. After the showing of this film, the judge, who was visibly moved, indicated that he would permit the video to be shown to the jury unless the defense could demonstrate some Virginia authority mandating its exclusion.

Note: Any settlement reached will automatically be payable immediately. Thus you may not enter into any arrangement providing for future payments.

EXERCISE 6.1
PRACTICING NEGOTIATION TECHNIQUES

"DUBINSKI v. COWTOWN DAIRY"

REFLECTION

1. Ask yourself what you learned from this exercise. Regardless of whom you represented, complete the Post Negotiation Evaluation Checklist following Exercise 4.1 and available for download at the **LexisNexis Webcourse**, Chapter 4.

2. Go back and look at the reflective questions following Exercise 4.1. To what extent were you able to improve on your ability to understand and observe the stages of negotiation? In what ways do you need to improve? What steps are you going to take during the next exercise to improve?

3. Which techniques worked best for you? Why?

4. Which techniques did not work so well? Why not?

5. Did you try any techniques that made you uncomfortable? What, if anything, did that tell you about yourself? Go back to the Assessment of Differences Inventory you completed in Chapter 2. Does it give you any clues? Is it consistent with how you feel when you negotiate?

6. What techniques will you try in the future?

EXERCISE 6.2
PRACTICING NEGOTIATION TECHNIQUES — AGAIN!

GENERAL DESCRIPTION OF EXERCISE: Negotiation of property division, custody arrangement, child support, and alimony in a divorce.

SKILLS INVOLVED: Negotiation.

PARTICIPANTS NEEDED: You will be divided into pairs.

ESTIMATED TIME REQUIRED:

75 minutes: 45 minutes for negotiating, 30 minutes for discussion

LEVEL OF DIFFICULTY (1-5):

"GOIN' THROUGH THE BIG D"

GENERAL INFORMATION
AVAILABLE TO ALL STUDENTS

Ogden, age 42, and Darshelle, age 38, had been married for twelve years when Darshelle recently filed her complaint for divorce. The marriage was the first for Ogden, but Darshelle had previously been married when she was 22. That marriage lasted for only 18 months and produced no children. Five years into the present marriage, Darshelle gave birth to twins, Tamara and Tad.

Ogden is an only child whose father died three years ago. Ogden's father was a successful salesman with an office supply company who left a substantial estate to his widow, Ogden's mom. Ogden's mother never pursued a career outside the home, preferring to be a stay-at-home mom. Ogden was her primary focus. She is now 75, but in failing health. Ogden is close to her and so are the twins. Ogden graduated from Harvard with a dual concentration in English and Literature. He then received his Master's Degree in English from Yale and completed the course work for a Ph.D.

Darshelle was the first born and only daughter of a family of six children. Her father was a carpenter, and her mother was a receptionist for a local doctor. Darshelle also attended Harvard College where she concentrated in Economics, and obtained an M.B.A. from the Wharton School at the University of Pennsylvania. After her graduation from Wharton, Darshelle obtained employment in the marketing division of a New Hampshire technology company. She advanced quickly and is currently the Vice President of Worldwide Marketing. Her current annual salary is $175,000. Last February, she received a bonus of $85,000 — the largest amount she had ever received and which is not guaranteed in future years — for her outstanding work. She regularly receives stock options which have a combined present value in excess of $300,000.

Ogden has had a different career track. After he left the Yale Ph.D. program, he secured a position at Saint Anselm's College as an Assistant Professor of English. Since he never completed his Ph.D. dissertation, he was denied tenure after four years and had to leave. He then got a teaching job at a prestigious private high school, where he is currently earning $45,000 per year. Although he has had opportunities to supplement his income by teaching summer sessions and through private tutoring, he has declined these options, preferring to spend his free time with his children.

Ogden never liked the corporate lifestyle. He reluctantly, but dutifully, attended social functions with Darshelle as she ascended the corporate ladder. After the birth of the children, Ogden spent an increasing amount of his time at home. Darshelle felt secure in this arrangement, and it enabled her to travel extensively in connection with her corporate position.

Ogden and Darshelle own a 100-year-old Victorian in Manchester which needed substantial work when it was purchased. Most of the work was done by Ogden together with Darshelle's father. This house has a current market value of $550,000 (encumbered with a $200,000 mortgage). Ogden and Darshelle also own a condominium on the Cape valued at $450,000 (encumbered with a $100,000 mortgage). They own a one-year-old Chrysler convertible and a two-year-old Ford SUV.

Ogden and Darshelle want to achieve a peaceful dissolution of their marriage. They must agree upon an arrangement with respect to the allocation of parental rights and responsibilities (formerly referred to as "custody") in the form of a "parenting plan," and a division of the two homes and the two vehicles. They must also agree upon any child support and/or alimony to be paid.

EXERCISE 6.2
PRACTICING NEGOTIATION TECHNIQUES — AGAIN!

"GOIN' THROUGH THE BIG D"

REFLECTION

1. Ask yourself what you learned from this exercise. Regardless of whom you represented, complete the Post Negotiation Evaluation Checklist following Exercise 4.1 and available for download at the **LexisNexis Webcourse**, Chapter 4.

2. Go back and look at the reflective questions following Exercise 4.1. To what extent were you able to improve on your ability to understand and observe the stages of negotiation? In what ways do you need to improve? What steps are you going to take during the next exercise to improve?

3. Which techniques worked best for you? Why?

4. Which techniques did not work so well? Why not?

5. Did you try any techniques that made you uncomfortable? What, if anything, did that tell you about yourself? Go back to the Assessment of Differences Inventory you completed in Chapter 2. Does it give you any clues? Is it consistent with how you feel when you negotiate?

6. What techniques will you try in the future?

7. In what ways, if at all, does the subject matter affect how you prepare for and handle the various negotiations?

Chapter 7

NONVERBAL COMMUNICATION — THE WORDLESS MESSAGE

When parties negotiate, they try to carefully communicate through words — either orally or in writing. But parties communicate in another way that can be extremely significant and is often overlooked. Nonverbal or **wordless** communication can be every bit as valuable as the *"verbal leaks"* discussed in Chapter 4. Sometimes nonverbal communication is intentional. A person may smile, firmly shake an opponent's hand, scowl, etc. This is all part of an intentional message sent to the other side. Negotiating parties tend to concentrate on what is being verbally communicated and what is being *intentionally* communicated nonverbally. As a result, negotiators often fail to appreciate the information being displayed through **unintentional**, nonverbal cues. This is especially true when opponents are talking, but it is also true when they are listening. Experienced poker players are familiar with this phenomenon. When people are less than forthright, they often display a kind of *"nonverbal leak,"* which poker players call a "tell."[1] People who fail to observe an opponent's nonverbal signs are likely to miss the most trustworthy messages being communicated by their adversaries. Certain nonverbal signals may also suggest that accompanying verbal messages are deceitful. While no one signal is a conclusive indication of deception, observers who look for relevant nonverbal patterns and behavioral changes can learn to spot likely prevarication.

Skilled negotiators need to appreciate the importance of nonverbal signals. They should occasionally read books on this critical subject and watch body language being communicated by others in different settings.[2] The more attuned negotiators are to these subtle messages, the more they will appreciate the actual feelings of the people with whom they interact. Recognizing that it is difficult to simultaneously speak and watch the nonverbal responses of others, many negotiators take colleagues with them to look for such signals while they are talking.[3]

It would be impossible to cover all the nonverbal signals explored in the many excellent books devoted to nonverbal communication, but we will focus on a few to

---

[1] The game of poker can teach you a lot about body language and nonverbal clues. There are many free sites on line that provide free videos and explanations.

[2] *See, e.g.*, HENRY H. CALERO, THE POWER OF NONVERBAL COMMUNICATION (2005 Silver Lake Pub.); PETER A. ANDERSON, THE COMPLETE IDIOT'S GUIDE TO BODY LANGUAGE (2004 Alpha); SUSAN QUILLIAM, BODY LANGUAGE (2004 Firefly); MIKE CARO, CARO'S BOOK OF POKER TELLS (2003 Cardoza Publishing); DESMOND MORRIS, BODYTALK (1994 Crown Trade Paperbacks); JO-ELLEN DIMITRIUS & MARK MAZZARELLA, READING PEOPLE (1998 Random House).

[3] Many experienced poker players do not look at their cards as they are dealt. They first watch the faces of their opponents as *they* look at *their* cards.

introduce you to this important subject. The first list provides "state of mind" clues and the second list provides "possibility of deception" clues. Remember that the signals described below are clues — not litmus tests. When you see these behaviors, they give you information that you must assess in conjunction with all other information available. Also, no signal is universal. People may come into the negotiation with pre-existing nervous tics, nearsightedness, acute or chronic pain, dental issues, etc. There can be more than one reason for a person's behavior. We encourage you to read this in conjunction with the **LexisNexis Webcourse** for this chapter, where you will find video examples and other supplemental materials.

A.   COMMON NONVERBAL (WORDLESS) SIGNALS (CLUES)

1.   Facial Expressions

Facial expressions are the most easily manipulated forms of nonverbal communication for most persons, yet subtle clues to the actual feelings of the signalers can often be perceived by careful observers. Taut lips or narrowed eyes may indicate frustration or anxiety. A subtle smile, often hidden quickly by a bowed head, or brief signs of relief around the corners of the offeree's mouth when new offers are made, may indicate that the offeror has approached or entered the other side's settlement range or that the offeror has otherwise made a move that pleases the offeree.

2.   Flinch

A flinch may be an uncontrolled response to an inadequate offer or concession. This may sincerely indicate the unacceptable nature of the offer being conveyed. Manipulative negotiators may employ a contrived "flinch" to silently challenge the adequacy of opponent opening offers or concessions. Negotiators who encounter what they consider to be truly reactive flinches should decide if their announced positions are clearly unacceptable. On the other hand, negotiators who think opponents are using contrived flinches to induce them to bid against themselves with consecutive position changes should: (1) recognize the manipulative nature of their opponents and (2) be careful not to change positions until they have obtained position changes from their adversaries.

3.   Wringing of Hands

This is frequently a sign of frustration or tension. Distraught individuals often twist their hands and fingers into seemingly painful contortions. This signal usually emanates from persons who are anxious regarding aggressive tactics being employed by opponents or about wholly unsatisfactory negotiation developments.

4. Rubbing Hands Together in Anticipatory Manner

This behavior is often exhibited by anxious negotiators who anticipate new and/or more beneficial offers from their opponents. Such conduct suggests an over-eagerness that may be satisfied with a minimal position change.

5. Tightly Gripping Arm Rests/Drumming Fingers on Table

Impatient or frustrated persons frequently grip the arm rests of their chairs tightly or drum their fingers on the table. Negotiators who exhibit such behavior are most likely displeased with the lack of progress they think is occurring.

6. Biting Lower Lip/Running Fingers Through Hair

These signals usually indicate stress or frustration. They emanate from persons who are disappointed by the lack of negotiation progress and/or their perceived opponent intransigence.

7. Eyes Wandering/Looking at Watch

These are signs of boredom and disinterest. Such signals would suggest a serious lack of interest in what is being said. Negotiators who encounter such signs should ask their opponents questions to force them to become more involved in the substantive discussions.

8. Opening Mouth But Not Speaking

This is usually a sign of indecision. This person would like to talk — and may even be contemplating a position change — but she is not yet sure of what to say. Opponents who encounter such a situation should remain silent and be patient. They need to give this person the time she needs to decide exactly what to say.

9. Sitting on the Edge of One's Chair

This is a definite sign of interest. When it follows a newly articulated position, it suggests real interest in what is being offered. Most people do not actually sit on the front of their chair, but only lean slightly forward. On the other hand, some individuals lean so far forward they place their elbows on the table in front of them.

10. Hands Touching Face/Stroking Chin/Playing with Glasses

These are usually signs of contemplation, although they can also be conscious or unconscious attempts to conceal emotions that would otherwise leak. Individuals feel uncomfortable sitting in silence while they consider unanticipated opponent disclosures or position changes. To cover their pregnant pauses, the actors use these devices to look as if something is actually happening while they contemplate their next moves. Such actors are likely to reject the offers that generated such nonverbal responses, but they will probably do so more positively to keep the process moving.

11. Steepling (Hands Pressed Together with Hands or Fingers Pointed Upward)

This is a sign of confidence, suggesting that the actors are pleased with developments. Negotiators who observe such signals should be careful not to concede more than they have to.

12. Leaning Back with Hands Behind Head

This particularly masculine posture is another sign of confidence. It may alternatively be an indication of contentedness. The actors are very pleased with negotiation developments. When men are interacting with women, it can also be a sign of domination. Female negotiators who observe such behavior in opponents should be cautious, because their opponents probably think things are going their way.

13. Placing One Hand Behind Head

When individuals use one hand to clasp the neck behind their ears, this is usually an indication of distress. It is as if the actors are psychologically giving themselves consoling hugs to counteract the negative consequences they are experiencing. Negotiators exhibiting this posture most likely see negative developments ahead.

14. Open/Uplifted Hands with Palms Facing Out

This posture is used to indicate the sincerity of what is being verbally communicated. It is frequently associated with "final offers" to demonstrate that the offeror has nothing more to concede. If the signal seems insincere, it is most likely a deliberate attempt to deceive opponents.

15. Crossed Arms/Crossed Legs

This may be an aggressive, adversarial posture or a defensive position, depending on the particular position of the arms and legs. If the arms are folded high on the chest and the ankle of one leg is placed on the knee of the other leg, this tends to be a combative posture. On the other hand, if the arms are folded low on the chest and one leg is draped over the other, it is a more defensive posture. In both cases, however, these tend to be unreceptive positions. If opponents begin bargaining interactions in such positions, it can be beneficial to take the time to establish sufficient rapport to induce them to become more receptive to what is being discussed. When negotiators approach impasse, one or both often exhibit this posture.

16. Covering and Rubbing One Eye

This is a nonverbal sign of disbelief. It is the nonverbal equivalent of the disbelieving expression "my eye." Negotiators who encounter this posture when they are making critical representations should recognize the possibility their statements are not being accorded much respect. They may have to restate their communications in a more credible manner.

B. COMMON NONVERBAL (WORDLESS) SIGNS OF DECEPTION

In his classic book *Telling Lies* (2009 Norton), Paul Ekman noted that people are especially inept at determining from nonverbal signals when they are being lied to. Some of this is due to the fact that dishonesty can range from mere puffing to unequivocal deceit. Despite the fact that no particular nonverbal sign is a certain indication of deception, there are some signals that should cause observers to become suspicious. Some reflect the stress usually associated with lying, while others are deliberately employed by speakers to enhance the credibility of the misrepresentations they are about to utter. No one signal should be assumed to indicate deception. Persons should look for ***changes in established behavior and patterns of behavior.***[4]

1. Increase/Decrease in Statement Specificity

When individuals tell the truth, they fill in little details as they are recalled. When people lie, however, there are no actual details to remember. As a result, they often omit the usual amplifying details, articulating the bare bones of their fabrication. Specific questions can be used to force minimal detail liars to fill in details they do not really know or to discover whether detailed statements are really accurate. On the other hand, carefully prepared liars may provide an excessive amount of information designed to make their fabrications appear more credible.

2. Increased/Decreased Gross Body Movement

When individuals interact, they move their arms, legs, and torso regularly. They rarely sit perfectly still. Under stressful situations, some persons become more fidgety and move their arms and legs at an increased rate. Deceitful people who are afraid of getting caught may exhibit similar movement. On the other hand, some fabricators deliberately minimize their body movements in an effort to appear more trustworthy. As a result, negotiators should be on guard when they evaluate the veracity of statements emanating from individuals who have clearly ***increased or decreased*** their gross body movements.

3. Placing Hand Over Mouth

Most persons believe that lying is morally wrong. Their consciences bother them when they deceive others. Psychologists have noticed that liars frequently place their hands over their mouths when they speak, as if they are subconsciously trying to hold in the lies they know are morally reprehensible.

---

[4] *See generally* Dan Crum, Is He Lying to You? (2010 Career Press); Amy R. Boyd, Alix M. McLearen, et al., Detection of Deception (2007 Professional Resource Press); Gregory Hartley & Mary Ann Karinch, How to Spot A Liar (2005 Career Press); Aldert Vrij, Detecting Lies and Deceit (2000 John Wiley & Sons); David J. Lieberman, Never Be Lied to Again (1998 St. Martin's Griffin); Charles V. Ford, Lies! Lies!! Lies!!! (1996 American Psychiatric Press).

4. Eyes Looking Up to Wrong Side

When people try to *recall past circumstances* from memory, right handed individuals tend to look up and to the left and left handed persons tend to look up and to the right. On the other hand, when individuals try to *create new images*, right handed persons tend to look up and to the right and left handed people look up and to the left. When right handed negotiators look up and to the right or left handed negotiators look up and to the left, this may suggest that they are not trying to recall actual circumstances but are instead creating false stories.

5. Dilated Pupils/More Frequent Blinking

When persons experience stress, the pupils of their eyes widen and their rate of blinking increases. Although negotiators rarely interact with others in such proximity that they can see the size of their pupils, they can easily notice increased blinking. This could be associated with other factors, such as dryness, fatigue, foreign matters, etc., but it could be due to the stress associated with deception. As with other clues, it is important to look for changes in behavior.

6. Narrowing/Tightening of Margin of Lips

Stress often causes individuals to briefly narrow and tighten the red margin of their lips just before they speak. Careful observers may be able to see the lips of prospective speakers tighten into a narrow line across their lips just before they utter false statements.

7. Elevated Voice Pitch

Persons experiencing anxiety frequently speak with an elevated voice pitch. Even though experienced prevaricators work to control their voice when they talk, listeners can often discern their higher voice pitch.

8. More Deliberate/Rapid Speech

Individuals who experience stress when they lie may inadvertently speak more rapidly. On the other hand, persons who wish to have their misrepresentations completely heard may deliberately speak more slowly.

9. Increased Speech Errors

Many persons who try to deceive others have a greater number of speech errors. They may stutter, repeat phrases, or trail off without finishing their statements. They may also include nonsubstantive modifiers like "you know" or "don't you think." It is as if their conscience is disrupting the communication between their brain and their mouth to prevent the prevarication.

10.   More Frequent Clearing of Throat

The tension associated with lying may cause speakers to engage in more throat clearing. As they prepare to utter their false statements, they nervously clear their throats. Of course, the speaker may have allergies, a cold, etc. Again, look for ***changes in established behavior and patterns of behavior***.

EXERCISES

EXERCISE 7.1
WORKING ON YOUR POWERS OF OBSERVATION

GENERAL DESCRIPTION OF EXERCISE: Observing non-verbal cues.

SKILLS INVOLVED: Observation.

PARTICIPANTS NEEDED: Individual.

ESTIMATED TIME REQUIRED:

30 minutes: 20 minutes to view videos, 5 minutes for contemplation

LEVEL OF DIFFICULTY (1-5):

SPOTTING A LIAR

Watch the video lecture of Pamela Meyers, called "How to Spot a Liar," which can be found here:

http://www.ted.com/talks/pamela_meyer_how_to_spot_a_liar.html

Then, watch Amy Cuddy's video lecture, "Your Body Language Shapes Who You Are," which can be found here:

http://www.ted.com/talks/amy_cuddy_your_body_language_shapes_who_you_are.html.

After that, watch a political speech on television with the sound on and then off. Here are a couple to choose from:

Nixon "Checkers" speech:

http://abcnews.go.com/Archives/video/sept-23-1952-nixons-checkers-speech-11378105.

Clinton "I did not have sexual relations with that woman" speech:

http://www.washingtonpost.com/wp-srv/politics/special/clinton/stories/deny012798.htm.

1. What visual clues did you see that indicated possible signs of deception?

2. Was it easier to watch for the visual clues with the sound off?

3. How will you apply this new information going forward?

Chapter 8

INFLUENCE OF NEGOTIATOR STYLES

Attorneys and businesspeople negotiate constantly. They negotiate within their own organizations with superiors, subordinates, and colleagues. They negotiate with prospective and current clients and customers, and on behalf of their clients and customers with other public and private entities. Although few people are totally one style or the other, most negotiators employ relatively "cooperative" or relatively "competitive" styles.[1] Cooperative bargainers are called *"cooperative/problem solving negotiators"*; they tend to behave more pleasantly, and strive to generate mutually beneficial agreements. Competitive bargainers are called *"competitive/ adversarial negotiators"*; they are often less pleasant, and work to obtain optimal results for their own side. Individuals look forward to interactions with cooperative opponents, but often dread their encounters with competitive adversaries.

Negotiator styles significantly affect bargaining interactions. Which style is used by more negotiators? Which style is associated with more proficient negotiators and with less effective bargainers? This chapter will discuss the two basic negotiator styles, and the impact of these styles on bargaining encounters.

A. COOPERATIVE/PROBLEM-SOLVING NEGOTIATORS

Cooperative/Problem-Solving negotiators are epitomized by the book *Getting to Yes*.[2] These persons move psychologically *toward* their opponents, try to maximize the *joint returns* achieved by the bargaining parties, begin with realistic opening positions, seek reasonable results, behave in a courteous and sincere manner, rely upon objective standards to guide discussions, rarely resort to threats, maximize the disclosure of relevant information, are open and trusting, work diligently to satisfy the underlying interests of themselves and their opponents, are willing to make unilateral concessions, and try to reason with people on the other side.

Cooperative/Problem-Solvers readily disclose their critical information, explore the underlying interests of the respective parties, and seek results that maximize the return to both sides. They often explore alternatives that may enable the bargainers to expand the overall pie through tradeoffs that simultaneously advance the interests of both sides. For example, when money is involved, they may agree to future

---

[1] *See* G. Richard Shell, Bargaining for Advantage 9-11 (Viking 1999); Donald G. Gifford, Legal Negotiation: Theory and Applications 8-11 (West 1989); Gerald R. Williams, Legal Negotiation and Settlement 18-39 (West 1983); Gerald R. Williams & Charles B. Craver, Legal Negotiating 12-73 (Thomson/West 2007).

[2] Roger R. Fisher & William W. Ury, Getting to Yes (Houghton Mifflin 1981).

payments or in-kind payments that satisfy the underlying interests of the respective participants.

B. COMPETITIVE/ADVERSARIAL NEGOTIATORS

Competitive/Adversarial negotiators are epitomized by the book *Secrets of Power Negotiating.*[3] These individuals move psychologically *against* their opponents, try to maximize their *own returns*, begin with unrealistic opening offers, seek extreme results, behave in an adversarial and insincere manner, focus primarily on their own positions rather than rely on objective standards, frequently resort to threats, minimize the disclosure of their own information, are closed and untrusting, seek to satisfy the interests of their own side, try to make minimal concessions, and manipulate opponents.[4]

Competitive/Adversarials may engage in disingenuous game-playing. They tend to conceal their negative information, and try to manipulate opponents into giving them deals that maximize the returns for themselves or their clients. They may even ignore alternative formulations that might benefit their opponents if those alternatives do not clearly advance their own interests.

C. COMPARATIVE EFFECTIVENESS OF COOPERATIVE/ PROBLEM SOLVING AND COMPETITIVE/ADVERSARIAL NEGOTIATORS

In the 1976, Gerald Williams conducted a study among attorneys in Phoenix to determine what percentage of legal negotiators behave in a Cooperative/Problem-Solving and a Competitive/Adversarial manner. He asked respondents to indicate how individuals with whom they had recently interacted conducted their interactions. He found that lawyers considered 65 percent of their colleagues to be Cooperative/Problem-Solvers, 24 percent to be Competitive/Adversarials, and 11 percent to be unclassifiable.[5]

Williams asked the respondents in his study to classify opponents as "effective," "average," and "ineffective" negotiators. They indicated that while 59 percent of Cooperative/Problem-Solvers were "effective" negotiators, only 25 percent of Competitive/Adversarials were so proficient.[6] On the other hand, while only 3 percent of Cooperative/Problem-Solvers were considered "ineffective" negotiators, 33 percent of Competitive/Adversarial bargainers were placed in that category.

---

[3] ROGER DAWSON, SECRETS OF POWER NEGOTIATING (Career Press 2d ed. 2001). *See also* JIM CAMP, START WITH No (Crown Bus. 2002).

[4] *See* HERBERT M. KRITZER, LET'S MAKE A DEAL 78-79 (Univ. of Wisconsin Press 1991).

[5] *See* WILLIAMS, *supra* note 1, at 19.

[6] *See id.*

In 1999, Andrea Kupfer Schneider replicated the Gerald Williams study using attorneys in Milwaukee and Chicago as her database.[7] Her findings reflect changes that have affected our society in general and the legal profession in particular. People are less pleasant to one another today than they were three decades ago. Many persons have become more impatient and less courteous. "The competitive negotiator described by Williams was not nearly as unpleasant and negative" as the contemporary competitive bargainer.[8]

From a detached perspective, one would expect the less courteous and more repugnant Competitive/Adversarial negotiators described in Professor Schneider's study to be less effective than the less negatively described Competitive/Adversarial bargainers in the Williams study, and this is exactly what Professor Schneider found. While Professor Williams found 25 percent of Competitive/Adversarial negotiators to be "effective," Professor Schneider found only 9 percent of such bargainers to be "effective."[9] This change should be contrasted with the relatively slight decline in the percentage of Cooperative/Problem-Solvers considered to be "effective" negotiators from 59 percent in the Williams study to 54 percent in the Schneider study.[10]

The findings with respect to persons considered "ineffective" negotiators are even starker. Professor Schneider found almost no change in the percentage of Cooperative/Problem-Solvers considered "ineffective" bargainers — an increase from 3 percent to 3.6 percent.[11] She found a profound change, however, with respect to the percentage of Competitive/Adversarials considered to be "ineffective" negotiators, rising from 33 percent in the Williams study to 53 percent in her own study. This increase in perceived ineptitude among Competitive/Adversarial negotiators would most likely be attributable to their more unpleasant demeanors. As they are perceived as more irritating, more stubborn, and more arrogant, opponents would consider them to be less effective bargainers.

In the many years we have taught various forms of negotiating courses and served as mediators, we have consistently found proficient Cooperative/Problem-Solvers to be at least as effective as proficient Competitive/Adversarials. The notion that one must be uncooperative, selfish, manipulative, and even abrasive to be successful is erroneous. To achieve beneficial negotiation results one must only possess the ability to say "no" forcefully and credibly to convince opponents they must enhance their offers if agreements are to be achieved. This can be very effectively accomplished while being firm, fair and friendly.

With respect to our student classroom negotiations, we have noticed three significant differences with respect to the outcomes achieved by different style negotiators. First, if a truly extreme agreement is reached, the prevailing party is usually a Competitive/Adversarial negotiator. Since Cooperative/Problem-Solving

---

[7] See Andrea Kupfer Schneider, *Shattering Negotiation Myths: Empirical Evidence on the Effectiveness of Negotiation Style*, 7 Harv. Neg. L. Rev. 143 (2002).

[8] See id. at 187.

[9] See id. at 167, 189.

[10] See id.

[11] See id. at 167.

bargainers tend to be more fair-minded, they generally refuse to take unconscionable advantage of inept or weak opponents. We note that this type of extreme imbalance is much less common in our actual mediation/negotiation experience, which is probably attributable to the relative lack of negotiation experience possessed by the students. Second, Competitive/Adversarial advocates generate more *nonsettlements* than their Cooperative/Problem-Solving cohorts. The extreme positions taken by Competitive/Adversarial bargainers and their frequent use of manipulative and disruptive tactics make it easier for their opponents to accept the consequences associated with nonsettlements.

The third factor concerns the fact that Cooperative/Problem-Solving negotiators usually achieve more efficient combined results than their Competitive/Adversarial colleagues — *i.e.*, they maximize the joint return to the parties. Cooperative/Problem-Solvers tend to be open and trusting individuals who seek to enhance the joint disclosure of information and maximize the overall return to the participants. They are thus more likely to attain higher joint values than more closed and untrusting Competitive/Adversarial bargainers who are primarily interested in the maximization of their own side's results.[12] Advocates who hope to achieve Pareto efficient agreements that benefit both sides must be willing to cooperate sufficiently to permit the participants to explore areas of possible joint gain. While these people may simultaneously seek to maximize their own side's returns, their attempt to enhance opponent interests increases the likelihood of agreement *and* the probability of mutually efficient terms. In addition, the more the participants can expand the pie to be divided between them, the more likely each side will obtain more satisfactory results.

D. INTERACTIONS BETWEEN PERSONS WITH THE SAME AND DIFFERENT NEGOTIATING STYLES

When Cooperative/Problem-Solving bargainers interact with other Cooperative/Problem-Solvers, their encounters are usually cooperative. The participants are relatively open with their critical information, and they seek to achieve terms that maximize the joint return of the parties. Interactions between Competitive/Adversarial negotiators are generally competitive, with minimal information disclosure and the use of manipulative tactics to advance each side's own interests. The encounter can be aggressive and unpleasant. They will often fight over little things at first to establish power and dominance. They will make ultimatums, "pack their bags" like they are about to leave, and sometimes actually break off negotiations. The negotiations are frequently characterized by brinksmanship.

When Cooperative/Problem-Solvers negotiate with Competitive/Adversarials, their transactions tend to be more competitive than cooperative. If Cooperative/Problem-Solvers are naively open with Competitive/Adversarials who are being less forthcoming, information imbalances develop which favor the more strategic Competitive/Adversarials. As a result, Cooperative/Problem-Solving participants must employ a more competitive approach to avoid the exploitation that would result if they were too

---

[12] *See* Robert H. Mnookin & Lee Ross, *Introduction, in* BARRIERS TO CONFLICT RESOLUTION 8-9 (Kenneth Arrow, Robert H. Mnookin, Lee Ross, Amos Tversky & Robert Wilson eds.) (W.W. Norton 1995).

open and accommodating with their manipulative and avaricious opponents. These cross-style interactions generate less efficient agreements than encounters involving only Cooperative/Problem-Solvers, and they increase the likelihood of nonsettlements.

When Cooperative/Problem-Solving negotiators interact with Competitive/ Adversarial bargainers, the Competitive/Adversarial participants may enjoy an advantage if their Cooperative/Problem-Solving opponents behave too cooperatively. Competitive/Adversarials feel more comfortable in openly competitive environments than Cooperative/Problem-Solvers who may feel compelled to behave in an uncharacteristically competitive fashion to avoid exploitation. Competitive/Adversarials tend to have higher client goals than Cooperative/Problem-Solving adversaries, and they are less concerned about the joint returns achieved. Less strategic Cooperative/Problem-Solvers are likely to disclose more of their critical information than their less forthcoming adversaries, providing the Competitive/Adversarial bargainers with an information-imbalance advantage.

When Cooperative/Problem-Solvers begin their interactions with persons they do not know well or with people they believe to be Competitive/Adversarial, they should release some confidential information slowly. If their openness is reciprocated, they can continue their openness. On the other hand, if they realize that their openness is not being reciprocated, they should be less forthcoming to avoid the creation of an information imbalance that would be injurious to their own interests.

E.   COMMON TRAITS FOR BOTH NEGOTIATION STYLES

In his study, Professor Williams found that certain traits are shared by both effective Cooperative/Problem-Solving negotiators and effective Competitive/ Adversarial bargainers. Successful negotiators from both groups are thoroughly prepared, behave in an honest and ethical manner, are perceptive readers of others, and are analytical, realistic, and convincing.[13] He also found that proficient negotiators from both groups endeavor to *maximize* their *own client's return.* This was the Number One objective for Competitive/Adversarial bargainers and the Number Two objective for Cooperative/Problem-Solving bargainers. In her more recent study, Professor Schneider also found that effective Cooperative/Problem-Solving negotiators *and* effective Competitive/Adversarial bargainers strive to maximize their own client results.[14] Since client maximization is the quintessential characteristic of Competitive/Adversarial negotiators, this common trait would suggest once again that Cooperative/Problem-Solving negotiators are able to accomplish competitive objectives while being perceived by others in a more favorable light than Competitive/ Adversarial negotiators.

---

[13] *See* WILLIAMS, *supra* note 1, at 20-30.

[14] *See* Schneider, *supra* note 7, at 188. This was again the Number One goal for Cooperative/Problem-Solvers and the Number Two goal for Competitive/Adversarials.

F.   BLENDED STYLES — COMPETITIVE/PROBLEM-SOLVING "BLENDED" APPROACH

Few negotiators fit neatly into one category or another. Most successful negotiators are able to **combine** the most effective traits associated with the Cooperative/Problem-Solving and the Competitive/Adversarial styles — cooperation, problem-solving and competition.[15] They are **competitive**, in that they seek to maximize client returns. But they attempt to accomplish this objective by working with the opponent to **problem-solve** in a **cooperative** and seemingly ingenuous manner.[16] Unlike less proficient negotiators who view bargaining encounters as "fixed pie" endeavors in which one side's gain is the other side's corresponding loss, effective **Competitive/Problem-Solving "Blended"** bargainers realize that in multi-item interactions, the parties generally value the various terms differently.[17]

Blended bargainers attempt to claim more of the distributive items desired by both sides,[18] but they simultaneously look for shared values. They recognize that by maximizing the joint returns, they are more likely to maximize the settlements achieved for their own clients. These Blended bargainers seek what Ronald Shapiro and Mark Jankowski characterize as WIN-win results — optimal deals for themselves while providing opponents with the best terms possible given what they have achieved for themselves.[19]

Proficient Blended (and Competitive/Adversarial) negotiators may manipulate opponent perceptions to enable them to achieve their own goals, but they rarely resort to truly deceitful tactics. They engage in "puffing" and "embellishment," but never misrepresent material information.[20] They realize that a loss of credibility would undermine their ability to achieve beneficial results for themselves. If opponents cannot believe their representations, it would be extremely difficult to induce adversaries to disclose their true underlying interests in ways that would enable the parties to expand the pie and maximize their joint returns.

Despite the fact that effective Blended bargainers generally hope to attain as much as they can for themselves, they are not "win-lose" negotiators, but rather "WIN-win." They never judge their own success by asking how poorly their opponents have done. They recognize that the imposition of bad terms on their adversaries does not necessarily benefit themselves. All other factors being equal, they hope to maximize opponent satisfaction as long as this does not necessitate significant concessions on their own part. When they conclude bargaining interactions, they do not compare their

---

[15] *See* JAMES C. FREUND, SMART NEGOTIATING 24-27 (Simon & Schuster 1992); Herbert M. Kritzer, *supra* note 4, at 78-79; BOB WOOLF, FRIENDLY PERSUASION 34-35 (G.P. Putnam's Sons 1990).

[16] *See* ROBERT MAYER, POWER PLAYS 7-8, 92 (Times Bus. 1996).

[17] *See* ROBERT H. MNOOKIN, SCOTT R. PEPPET & ANDREW S. TULUMELLO, BEYOND WINNING 14-15, 174 (Harvard Univ. Press/Belknap 2000).

[18] *See* Gary S. Goodpaster, *A Primer on Competitive Bargaining*, 1996 J. DISP. RES. 325 (1996); Gerald B. Wetlaufer, *The Limits of Integrative Bargaining*, 85 GEO. L. REV. 369 (1996).

[19] *See* RONALD M. SHAPIRO & MARK A. JANKOWSKI, THE POWER OF NICE 45-61 (John Wiley & Sons 2001).

[20] *See generally* Charles B. Craver, *Negotiation Ethics: How to Be Deceptive Without Being Dishonest/ How to Be Assertive Without Being Offensive*, 38 S. TEX. L. REV. 713 (1997).

own results with the terms achieved by their opponents. They instead ask whether they like what they got, realizing that if they attained their objectives, they had successful encounters.

Proficient Blended negotiators do not necessarily seek to maximize opponent returns for purely altruistic reasons. They understand that this approach will most effectively allow them to advance their own interests. First, they have to provide adversaries with sufficiently generous terms to induce them to accept agreements. Second, they want to be sure opponents will honor the deals agreed upon. If they experience post-agreement "buyers remorse," they may try to get out of the deal. Finally, they acknowledge the likelihood they will encounter their adversaries in the future. If those persons remember them pleasantly as courteous and professional negotiators, their future bargaining interactions are likely to be successful.

Effective Blended negotiators and effective Competitive/Adversarials realize that people tend to work most diligently to satisfy the needs of opponents they like personally.[21] Overtly Competitive/Adversarial bargainers are rarely perceived as likeable. They exude competition and manipulation, and they generate similar responses from opponents. Seemingly cooperative negotiators, however, appear to seek results that benefit both sides. Since others enjoy interacting with them, these individuals find it easier to induce unsuspecting opponents to lower their guard, behave more cooperatively, and make greater concessions.[22]

Blended negotiators really employ a composite style. They seek competitive objectives (maximum client returns), but endeavor to accomplish their goals through problem-solving strategies. This phenomenon may partially explain why Professors Williams and Schneider found more effective Cooperative/Problem-Solving negotiators than effective Competitive/Adversarial bargainers. It is likely that many effective Competitive/Problem-Solving "Blended" negotiators were so successful in their use of "problem-solving" tactics, that they induced opponents to characterize them as Cooperative/Problem-Solvers rather than as Competitive/Problem-Solvers — or as Competitive/Adversarials in the dichotomous system being employed in the Williams and Schneider studies.

Over the past several decades, legal practitioners have become less polite toward one another. Many have become more win-lose oriented. They seem to fear that if their opponents get what they want, they will be unable to achieve their own goals. These changing attitudes are adversely affecting legal practice in general and bargaining interactions in particular. Experienced attorneys regularly bemoan the decreasing civility they encounter in daily practice. Lawyers who encounter rudeness from opposing counsel should recognize that such inappropriate behavior is *not* a sign of negotiator proficiency, but just the opposite. Uncivilized behavior is an unacceptable substitute for bargaining competence. Skilled negotiators do not engage in offensive conduct. They recognize that such behavior is unlikely to induce adversaries to give them what they desire. When we like opponents, we want to satisfy their needs and

[21] *See* ROY J. LEWICKI, JOSEPH A. LITTERER, JOHN W. MINTON & DAVID M. SAUNDERS, NEGOTIATION 219-220 (Irwin 1994).

[22] *See* GIFFORD, *supra* note 1, at 15-16.

hate to say "no" to them; when we dislike opponents, we actually look for ways to deny them what they want.

Another critical reason for behaving professionally during bargaining encounters concerns recent studies indicating that people who commence negotiations in positive moods bargain more cooperatively, while individuals who begin in negative moods bargain more adversarially.[23] As a result, negotiator pairs who begin bargaining interactions with positive moods achieve larger joint gains than negotiator pairs who begin with negative moods. Persons who behave badly when they negotiate are likely to generate negative moods in their opponents, thus increasing the probability of avoidable nonsettlements. They also decrease the likelihood of Pareto efficient agreements when deals are achieved.

Legal practitioners should not take the negotiation process personally. They must recognize that their opponents have nothing against them personally - those persons are merely endeavoring to advance the interests of their own clients. Attorneys should never view adversaries as the "enemy." Those individuals are actually their best friends, because they are enabling the lawyers with whom they are interacting to earn a living. If no one was at the other end of the telephone line or sitting across the bargaining table from them, they would be unemployed. There would be no business arrangements to structure, no licensing agreements to develop, and no disputes to resolve.

G.   CONCLUSION

Most experts classify negotiators as Cooperative/Problem-Solvers or Competitive/Adversarials. The former work to achieve reasonable agreements that satisfy the underlying interests of both sides and maximize the joint returns attained, while the latter seek more one-sided arrangements favoring their own sides. More Cooperative/Problem-Solvers are considered effective negotiators than Competitive/Adversarials, and far more Competitive/Adversarials are perceived as ineffective bargainers than Cooperative/Problem-Solvers. The most effective negotiators employ a hybrid Competitive/Problem-Solving style which incorporates the optimal traits from both classifications. They competitively seek to maximize their own returns, but simultaneously seek to expand the overall pie and maximize opponent returns once they achieve their own objectives. These negotiators recognize that they are more likely to achieve their own goals if they exude a cooperative attitude and behave professionally. They also realize that their use of courteous conduct is more likely to generate positive moods in bargaining participants that increase the probability of cooperative behavior and the maximization of joint returns. They never take the process personally, acknowledging that their opponents are merely advocates for the opposing sides who are enabling them to earn a living.

---

[23] *See* Clark Freshman, Adele Hayes & Greg Feldman, *The Lawyer-Negotiator as Mood Scientist: What We Know and Don't Know About How Mood Relates to Successful Negotiation*, 2002 J. Disp. Res. 13, 15, 19, 22-23 (2002); Joseph P. Forgas, *On Feeling Good and Getting Your Way: Mood Effects on Negotiator Cognition and Bargaining Strategies*, 74 J. Personality & Soc. Psych. 565, 566-68 (1998).

EXERCISES

EXERCISE 8.1
THINKING ABOUT NEGOTIATION TECHNIQUES

GENERAL DESCRIPTION OF EXERCISE: Reflection on personal styles.

PARTICIPANTS NEEDED: The reflection is individual, with group discussion in class.

ESTIMATED TIME REQUIRED:

30 minutes for review and reflection plus class discussion

LEVEL OF DIFFICULTY (1-5):

REVIEW AND REFLECTION

Go back and read your Negotiation Preparation Outlines, reflections, and Post Negotiation Evaluation Checklists for the negotiations you have done during the course. When you have finished that, compare the outlines, reflections and checklists with the self-assessment you completed in Exercise 3.3.

1. Based upon the descriptions of negotiator styles in Chapter 8, what negotiation style(s) do you think you employ at this point?

2. If you find you use a combination of styles, which one is more dominant?

3. Does your style seem to comport with your personality inventory? If yes, in what ways is that helpful? Harmful?

4. Do you find any correlation between your negotiation style and successes in your negotiations to date?

5. Do you find any correlation between your negotiation style and less than desirable outcomes in your negotiations to date?

6. Consider the styles of your classmates. Be prepared to discuss your thoughts on negotiation styles in class.

THINKING ABOUT NEGOTIATION TECHNIQUES

REFLECTION

1. Based upon your analysis in Exercise 8.1, what changes do you think would improve your negotiating style?

2. How will you implement the desired changes described above? Give yourself a specific action plan.

Chapter 9

AN INTRODUCTION TO BRAIN SCIENCE

A. WHAT IS BRAIN SCIENCE?

Think back to Exercise 3.1, "All or Nothing." Were you first the giver or receiver of money? If you were the giver, how did you decide how much to offer? If you were the receiver, how did you decide whether to accept it or reject it? Were your decisions based entirely upon economic logic? Emotion? Some of each? What drives people to make the decisions they do? So far in this book, we have focused mainly on traditional negotiation theory. If you want to be a good negotiator, you need to learn as much as you can about how people make decisions. Is there anything you can do to increase the chances that your opponent will accurately receive your communications and decide in a certain way? Is there anything you need to know to keep you and your client from being unduly manipulated? To be most effective, this requires knowledge of how the brain works, which is what we are loosely referring to as "brain science."[1]

During the last two decades, much has been written about how the brain processes information and makes decisions. This work has been done in various disciplines, including economics, psychology, and neuroscience.[2] Economists tend to focus on precise mathematical models, which assume the operation of a single *rational* information processor.[3] Psychologists tend to focus on how decisions are made based upon cognitive constraints that involve risk and reward.[4] Neuroscientists have recently focused on brain imaging with functional magnetic resonance imaging (fMRI) by actually mapping the areas of the brain that show increased oxygen supply when various types of decisions are made. Each discipline has its own vocabulary and its own orientation.

Recently, some researchers from the various disciplines have been joining forces in an attempt to understand behavior. Rather than focusing on a single model to predict outcome, they have proposed dual models, which recognize both logic (reasoning) and emotion. In the last decade, much has been written about the combined model of neuroeconomics, which combines traditional behavioral models with discoveries from

---

[1] We use this as a generic term to describe the study of the brain, understanding that various fields have their own nomenclature. *See generally* DANIEL KAHNEMAN, THINKING, FAST AND SLOW (Farrar, Straus & Giroux 2011); DAN ARIELY, PREDICTABLY IRRATIONAL (Harper-Collins 2008).

[2] *See* Alan G. Sanfey, *Decision Neuroscience: New Directions in Studies of Judgment and Decision Making*, 16 CURRENT DIRECTIONS IN PSYCHOLOGICAL SCIENCE 151 (2007).

[3] *Id.* at 154.

[4] *Id.* at 151.

the fMRI research.[5] The literature is in a huge state of flux and much is being hypothesized and tested. While we do not propose to make you experts on brain science, we do want to expose you to it and encourage you to keep abreast of the research. In particular, we want you to be aware of the effect that emotion plays in decision making and the fact that neuroscience seems to be correlating emotional reactions with particular brain activity.

B.   THIS IS YOUR BRAIN MAKING A DECISION: INTERPRETATION, JUDGMENT, REASONING

When a person makes a decision, it is actually the end result of a brain process. Depending upon the decision being made and the circumstances surrounding it, the process may occur in an instant, a few minutes, an hour, or over the course of days or even years. Some decisions are primal survival decisions and are hard wired into our DNA. But most decisions — including the ones you and your opponents will make when negotiating — usually involve interpretation, judgment and reasoning. It is useful to consider each of these aspects of decision making separately.[6]

1.   Interpretation

Quite often, we receive information and are doubtful as to its meaning or intention. In order to make sense of the information, we interpret it. Was that facial expression a smile or sneer? Was the comment about your hair a compliment or sarcasm? Was your opponent's tone of voice when she made that last offer angry, firm, or nervous? Whether our conclusions are in fact right or wrong, we process the information and decide what it means. Interpretation is the resolution of ambiguity.[7]

We all know from personal experience that not everyone interprets the same information in the same way. This is true in daily life and in negotiation. If we are all attempting to be rational and methodical, how can this be? There are probably many reasons that science has not yet explained. But researchers have attempted to determine whether the differences in interpretation can be attributed to emotion to any substantial degree. Although the research is not conclusive, it appears that there is a definite connection. As one primary example, researchers believe that *anxiety* has a significant effect on how individuals interpret information.[8]

Studies using fMRI suggest "that anxiety modulates the output from both the amygdala and the prefrontal regions, with anxiety being associated with amygdala hyper-responsivity and prefrontal hyporesponsivity."[9] In other words, anxiety seems

---

[5] *See* Richard Burke, *Neuroscience and Settlement: An Examination of Scientific Innovations and Practical Applications*, 25 Ohio St. J. on Disp. Resol. 477 (2010).

[6] *See* Isabelle Blanchette & Anne Richards, *The Influence of Affect on Higher Level Cognition: A Review of Research on Interpretation, Judgment, Decision Making and Reasoning*, 24 Cognition and Emotion 561 (2010).

[7] *Id.* at 563.

[8] *Id.* at 568.

[9] *Id.*

to increase oxygen flow to the amygdala (which is associated with fear and aggression) and decrease oxygen flow to the prefrontal region (which is associated with decision making.) "Anxiety leads to more threatening interpretations, increases estimates of likelihood of future negative events, and risk aversion in decision making."[10]

The role anxiety plays is extremely important to understand about your opponent and about yourself. It appears that anxiety can cause a person to be overly risk averse and primarily concerned with identifying potential threats and minimizing potential negative outcomes.[11] This can work to your advantage if your opponent is anxious but could do you or your client a disservice if you are.

Finally, although the research is less developed than the research on anxiety, you should know that there is evidence that people who feel *disgust* may show the same interpretive biases as people experiencing anxiety.[12] If the facts of your negotiation include subject matter that can generate the emotion of disgust — like a sexual offender, a corporate toxic tort or a financial fraud — that emotion may result in overly pessimistic interpretation by the party fearing the outcome.

2. Judgment

Once a person has interpreted ambiguous information, the information (as interpreted) is used as the basis to predict outcome — or the likelihood of future events.[13] Once again, the research suggests that people who have anxiety are more likely to be pessimistic about the likelihood of a bad outcome and are therefore more risk avoidant than persons who are not anxious. People who are fearful of rejection tend to make more generous offers, as do people who feel guilt.[14] Research suggests that mindset can have a very clear effect on judgment. When negotiating (or advocating in general) it is important to understand that situational cues "can prime a way of making sense of the world that affects how people perceive evidence and receive arguments."[15]

3. Reasoning

Reasoning is supposed to be free of emotion. If A=B and B=C, then A=C. Simple and logical. But what about deductive reasoning involving emotional topics like murder, terrorism, pedophilia, etc.? As early as 1946, a study asked participants to determine the logical validity of a series of syllogisms. Some of the syllogisms were

---

[10] *Id.* at 585.

[11] *Id.*

[12] *Id.* at 570.

[13] *Id.* at 571.

[14] *See* Rob M.A. Nelissen & Marijke C. Leliveld, *Fear and Guilt in Proposers: Using Emotions to Explain Offers in Ultimatum Bargaining* 41 European Journal of Social Psychology 78 (2010).

[15] Barbara O'Brien & Daphna Oyserman, *It's Not Just What You Think, But Also How You Think About It: The Effect of Situationally Primed Mindsets on Legal Judgments and Decision Making*, 92 Marq. L. Rev. 149, 169 (2008-2009).

emotionally neutral, (e.g., All members of Phi Beta Kappa must be college students . . .) and some were emotionally charged (e.g., All Communists are believers in trade unions, therefore, all trade-unionists are Communists).[16] The study found that participants made substantially more errors in logic when the syllogisms were emotionally charged. Follow up studies have been consistent with these early findings.[17]

How does any of this apply to negotiation? What about the spouse negotiating a divorce triggered by adultery, the partners negotiating the company split, the employer negotiating with a former employee over what the employer sees as a theft of trade secrets? To what extent does emotion affect a brain that is trying to reason in a rational manner?[18] People who are affected by emotional considerations do not tend to think in a totally rational manner. What you think is logical may not seem logical to them. It is not just about how things *are*, but also about how they *feel*. In order to be most effective as a negotiator, understanding what is happening to you and the other participants can be critical.

C. WAYS IN WHICH NEUROSCIENCE MAY HELP US NEGOTIATE MORE EFFECTIVELY

There are numerous thoughtful articles being written that summarize the literature on neuroscience and the state of the knowledge on cause and effect when it comes to negotiating.[19] Here are some issues that are being explored and that will almost certainly be further explored through the use of fMRI and controlled experiments:

1. Fear and Timing of Bargaining

Fear induces the "fight or flight" response. When this emotion is induced, the executive functions of the brain (decision making, imagining alternatives) are temporarily impaired.[20] Therefore, if you are trying to get a client or opponent to brainstorm or to consider a possibly creative solution, you should avoid doing it when the person is in a state of fear.

---

[16] Blanchette & Richards, *supra* note 6, at 578 (citations omitted).

[17] *Id.* at 578-579.

[18] A classic children's poem by Eugene Field, *The Duel*, captures this concept. Available at http://en.wikisource.org/wiki/The_Duel_%28Field%29, last visited June 1, 2012.

[19] For an excellent summary of the research as it applies to *negotiation and mediation, see Richard Burke, Neuroscience and Settlement: An Examination of Scientific Innovations and Practical Applications* 25 OHIO ST. J. ON DISP. RESOL. 477 (2010).

[20] *See* Richard Burke, *Neuroscience and Negotiation: What the New Science of Mind May Offer the Practicing Attorney*, 17 DISP. RESOL. MAG. 4 (2011).

2. Loss Frames Reduce Creativity

What works best — an offer that the opponent will perceive as a loss or an offer that the opponent will perceive as a gain? Researchers using fMRI have studied the concept of loss aversion and the brain.[21] They found that when the brain received data that was perceived as a "gain" frame, it triggered the parts of the brain that react to pleasure — like dark chocolate and sex. But seeing things in the "loss" frame substantially *suppressed* the pleasure response, making it harder to imagine a positive outcome. This suggests that ultimatums to the opponent that would result in a perception of capitulation may be less effective than offers that give the opponent the sense of something positive.

3. Impact of Face to Face Negotiations

We discussed the importance of nonverbal communication in Chapter 7. Neuroscientists hypothesize that facial expressions are part of a universal language — regardless of culture or language spoken — and that humans have a neuron-based capacity to mirror the facial expressions of others and thereby to understand their intent. What impact might this have on negotiations? Consider the differing impact of written negotiations, telephonic negotiations and face to face negotiations. If you are trying to build a bridge and your client is sincere, consider having your client do the talking in a face to face meeting.[22]

D. CONCLUSION

We have barely scratched the surface but want you to be thinking. We encourage you to read the literature and to stay abreast. It is all part of being an intentional negotiator. Continue to reflect on these issues as we move forward into the next sections of this book.

---

[21] *Id.*

[22] *Id.* at 4.

EXERCISES

EXERCISE 9.1
SILENT NEGOTIATION EXERCISE

"ALL OR NOTHING" REVISITED

GENERAL DESCRIPTION OF EXERCISE: You will receive instructions in class.

PARTICIPANTS NEEDED: You will be divided into pairs.

ESTIMATED TIME REQUIRED:

35 minutes

LEVEL OF DIFFICULTY (1-5):

EXERCISE 9.1
REFLECTION

In Exercise 3.1, you decided how much money to give to your opponent or whether to accept the amount offered by your opponent. This time, you decided how much to *take* or whether to allow your opponent to take a portion of what you had. Did your considerations change at all in Exercise 9.1 when compared to Exercise 3.1? Logically, should your strategy have changed? If so, why? If not, why not? Did you feel any different emotions this time than you did when performing Exercise 3.1? If so, what was the difference?

Researchers have studied this issue and have drawn some interesting conclusions. It appears that high offers in the *giving* version of this exercise arise mostly from *fear* of being rejected. But in the *taking* version, higher offers arise mostly from a perception of *fairness*.[23] What emotions do you think are involved in the decision to accept the offer in the giving version? In the taking version? Studies suggest that people will sacrifice the money in order to punish a player who treats them unfairly.[24] When negotiating, how can you use your awareness of these emotional factors to improve your success?

---

[23] Nelissen & Leliveld, *supra* note 14, at 79.

[24] Sanfey, *supra* note 2, at 154.

EXERCISE 9.2
PRISONER'S DILEMMA

GENERAL DESCRIPTION OF EXERCISE: In-class non-verbal negotiation of whether to testify against each other.

SKILLS INVOLVED: Adaptability and self-observation.

PARTICIPANTS NEEDED: You will be divided into pairs in class.

ESTIMATED TIME REQUIRED:

75-90 minutes

LEVEL OF DIFFICULTY (1-5): 1

ROLES IN EXERCISE: You are acting as a co-suspect considering a plea bargain and testifying against your co-defendant.

THE EXERCISE

Assume that you and your partner have been arrested for a crime that you committed together. The prosecution wants at least one of you to confess to ensure the conviction of both. If only one confesses, he/she will be treated leniently, while the silent partner will be severely punished. If neither confesses, both will receive relatively short prison terms. If both confess, more substantial terms will be given to both. The problem is represented by the following diagram:

	PRISONER B	
	Does Not Confess	Does Confess
Does Not Confess	2 Years for A 2 Years for B	10 Years for A 6 Months for B
PRISONER A **Does Confess**	6 Months for A 10 Years For B	5 Years for A 5 Years for B

PARTICIPANT INSTRUCTIONS

Do five iterations of this exercise with your assigned partner. For each iteration, **_without any discussion or other communication between you_**, you each must write down "yes" or "no" with "yes" indicating that you will confess and with "no" indicating that you will not confess. After the first iteration, display your respective responses to each other and determine the sentence each would receive. Then go on to the second, third, fourth, and fifth iterations — ***without any discussion or other communication between you*** — displaying your answers simultaneously ***after each*** and calculating your respective jail terms. When you are done, you should determine the total number of years each of you would have to serve from the five iterations combined. You will be asked to report the results to your professor and will then receive additional instructions.

EXERCISE 9.2
PRISONER'S DILEMMA

REFLECTION

What choices did you and your partner make? Did they change with each iteration?[25] As you went forward, did you build trust? Distrust? To what extent did emotions play a factor in what choices you made? What were the emotions? Were they positive or negative or some of each? How would any of this effect negotiating between or among persons with an ongoing relationship? How, if at all, did your professor's subsequent instructions affect your behavior? Your partner's behavior?

This exercise has been studied using neuroimaging. Results have demonstrated that the positive feelings garnered by cooperation activate the striatum, which is an area of the brain that is active for basic rewards. It appears that it also activates for this more abstract reward of cooperation in social decision making.[26] Other brain imaging studies have shown that reward-related areas of the brain become active when punishing nonreciprocators.[27] When negotiating, how can you use your awareness of these emotional factors to improve your success?

---

[25] *See generally* ROBERT AXELROD, THE EVOLUTION OF COOPERATION (Basic Books 1984) (describing different approaches to Prisoner's Dilemma employed by economic game theorists).

[26] Sanfey, *supra* note 2, at 154.

[27] *Id.*

Part Two

MEDIATION

Chapter 10

INTRODUCTION TO MEDIATION

A. WHAT IS MEDIATION?

Mediation is a method of conflict resolution. It is a type of **negotiation** that involves the use of a neutral third party — called a "mediator." If successful, the parties still go through the 6 stages of negotiation, but the mediator facilitates the process. Instead of *direct* negotiation between the parties, the neutral mediator is in charge and facilitates the negotiation. Mediators employ their *negotiation skills* to assist the parties with their own discussions. What provides mediators with power is their detached status. They can ask questions and raise issues the parties might feel hesitant to address if their opponents raised them.

All mediation involves negotiation but not all negotiation includes the process of mediation. It may take place with or without litigation pending. Instead of negotiating directly with each other, the parties to the dispute work with — and often through — the mediator, who may or may not be a lawyer. There is usually only one mediator, but there can be more.[1] The mediator is trained to help the parties reach a **voluntary resolution of the dispute**. There is no adjudication as a result of mediation. If the parties do not reach a full agreement, the dispute remains active. But even when mediation does not totally resolve the dispute, it may help to narrow the issues. The parties may agree to some things but not to everything.

The concept of mediation has been around for years but has become increasingly common in the legal profession since the late 1970s — after the Pound Conference described in Chapter 1. Today, most state and federal courts and agencies have either voluntary or mandatory mediation programs. Many employers have mediation programs for employment disputes. Many disputes get privately mediated outside of the formal court process by mediators who work directly with the parties and/or counsel.

We encourage you to read this in conjunction with the **LexisNexis Webcourse** for this chapter where you will find video examples and other supplemental materials.

B. ARE THERE ANY BENEFITS TO MEDIATION VERSUS LITIGATION?

Effective mediation often has many benefits when compared to litigation:

---

[1] Students who wish to see a purely comic example of a co-mediated matter and who are not offended by adult content and language may wish to watch the opening scene of "The Wedding Crashers."

1. Monetary cost — Litigation is often extremely expensive, particularly the "scorched earth" variety. A timely settlement reached through mediation usually avoids substantial financial costs. Even when disputes are not resolved until the eve of trial, both trial and post-trial proceedings are avoided. The estimated future cost of the litigation is usually a factor that can be included when the parties calculate their BATNA when preparing for mediation.

2. Emotional Cost — Although some litigated matters are more emotional than others, all litigation involves emotional cost. The plaintiff has decided to *sue*. This usually means that the plaintiff feels wronged and often has feelings of anger. The defendant has been *sued*. This experience usually triggers an emotional response, which could be anger, denial, shame, etc. Engaging a lawyer is often an emotional matter. Whether plaintiff or defendant, the client often feels out of control in an unfamiliar forum. The litigation process includes meeting with lawyers, answering interrogatories, being deposed, testifying in court — all stressful events. By contrast, a settlement reached through timely mediation can usually avoid many of the psychological costs associated with trials. In addition, since the mediation process can allow the parties an opportunity to share their feelings in a controlled environment, it can be a cathartic process that allows the parties to actually *resolve* the matter and not just settle it.

3. Control — Meditation allows the parties to control their own destinies, instead of having adjudicated resolutions imposed upon them by judges, juries, or arbitrators. People usually feel more satisfied with terms they have had the opportunity to structure than with terms imposed upon them by others. Mediated settlements allow the parties to work through the negotiation stages discussed in Chapter 4, including the Cooperative Stage where value maximizing (making the pie larger) can occur. Judges, juries and arbitrators do not look for creative solutions, nor is that their function.

C. ARE THERE ANY DOWNSIDES TO MEDIATION VERSUS LITIGATION?

Not all lawyers and clients believe in the value of mediation. Some lawyers and their clients employ a "take no prisoners" attitude to litigation and see mediation as an expensive annoyance in the way of getting to trial. They believe that litigation is a test of strength and that mediation is a sign of weakness. These people tend to avoid mediation whenever possible and usually take a very tough stance when attending mandatory mediation. These lawyers and clients are usually known by reputation; they believe that their tough reputations will limit the number of lawsuits filed against them and will result in better settlements when they do occur.

Some attorneys may be hesitant to employ mediation, fearing that such sessions may be a waste of time and expense. They are afraid they may "show their cards" to the other side which may result in the imposition of disadvantageous terms. If the mediation is timely, such trepidations are nearly always incorrect but should be considered:

1. Waste of time and expense — As noted above, mediation is usually cost effective and time well spent. When entered into ***voluntarily*** by the parties, it is usually a serious opportunity to resolve the dispute or to at least narrow it. It is rarely a waste of time unless entered into on an ***involuntary*** basis. This is something that may be required by court order or by contract. In many jurisdictions, as discussed below, the courts have mandatory mediation programs. Some of those programs require mediation by a date certain, whether the parties are really ready for the mediation or not. Various contracts, such as employment contracts, may call for the mediation of disputes within "30 days," or some other fixed period of time. When mediations occur on this basis, they can sometimes be a waste of time and money, even though the rules often allow for sanctions for failing to "mediate in good faith." Even when mediation is mandatory, settlement remains voluntary. It is like the old saying that "You can lead a horse to water but you can't force him to drink." To avoid this outcome, advocates are sometimes able by agreement to delay the mandatory mediation to a time when the parties have done sufficient discovery to allow them to understand the strengths and weaknesses of their respective cases. Even when a postponement is not allowed, an involuntary mediation sometimes assists the parties in narrowing the issues and can sometimes lead to settlement.

2. Fear of showing their cards — Some advocates fear that mediation will expose their litigation strategy, thus leaving them at a disadvantage in the event that settlement is not reached. This is always something to consider, but is not usually an issue if the other side mediates in good faith. When advocates prepare their mediation outlines, they should consider what to look for from their opponents in the Preliminary Stage and Informational Stage to demonstrate an honest and mutual give and take. If the opponent is not forthcoming, the advocate can adjust the carefully planned concession pattern during the Distributive Stage.

3. Imposition of disadvantageous terms — Some advocates fear that the mediation will somehow force a settlement. This is not accurate. Even when mediation is mandatory, settlement is voluntary.

D. WHY MEDIATE WHEN YOU CAN NEGOTIATE DIRECTLY?

As discussed below, there are various mediator styles. But all skilled mediators are usually able to help the parties look at the dispute from a neutral perspective and realize that there is real risk in giving up control over the outcome. Because the parties generally work through the mediator rather than directly with each other, they are able to "test" theories and positions with the mediator and make concessions to the mediator that they would not usually risk making directly to the opposing side. The mediator helps the parties stay on track through the six stages of negotiation. A good mediator is usually able to help the parties maneuver through the emotional issues discussed in Chapter 9 and generally increases the chances of a satisfactory resolution.

E.   WHEN DOES MEDIATION OCCUR?

The mediation process may be initiated by court rule, contract, one or more of the parties involved, by referrals from secondary parties, or by appointment by an external agency. Mediation can occur at any time during the course of a dispute. Unless the timing of the mediation is required by court rule, administrative rule or contract, the parties are free to negotiate the timing.

1. ***When required by court or administrative rule*** — Some courts and administrative agencies believe that mediation can work best before the parties have spent large sums on discovery; those courts and agencies have written rules of procedure which try to short-circuit litigation by requiring mediation shortly after a case is filed. Other courts believe that settlements are more likely after the parties have done the discovery necessary to understand the strengths and weaknesses of the case; these courts require mediation after the close of discovery, when the parties have usually exchanged interrogatories, produced documents and taken depositions. Courts that require mediation usually require it by a certain deadline but leave the parties free to mediate sooner. Also, most courts allow the mediation to occur with a court-appointed mediator or privately, with a mediator selected by the parties. Even when the rule requires mediation by a time certain, most courts will entertain a motion to postpone the mediation for good cause.

2. ***When required by contract*** — Many contracts now have provisions requiring mediation prior to the initiation of suit. This can be true for contracts involving employer/employee, vendor/purchaser, licensor/licensee, etc. The theory behind these contractual provisions is that litigation increases the stakes and the costs for all parties and often makes it harder to resolve things once one of the parties has filed suit. Litigation also makes public that which can otherwise remain private and even confidential. No matter the subject, lawsuits can produce major emotions, which then need to be dealt with as part of the settlement process. Pre-suit mediation can avoid some emotional issues that up the ante.

3. ***When pursued by choice*** — Mediation may occur at any time during the course of a dispute but usually occurs after the parties have been unable to negotiate a resolution without the help of a mediator. The timing of mediation initiation can be critical and varies from case to case. ***Whenever control over timing is possible, advocates should seek to hold mediation at a time when it is most likely to result in appropriate resolution.*** Mediation is usually successful when the parties enter the mediation in good faith with the desire to resolve the dispute. Therefore, ***experienced lawyers and their clients usually want to mediate when the other parties to the dispute are ready.*** But the realities of the adversarial process can sometimes get in the way and cloud what would otherwise be clear communication. Inexperienced participants who would like to mediate may fail to show a desire to enter the mediation process, fearing that if they raise the possibility first, it would indicate weakness on their part. One or more sides may have employed negotiation tactics that discouraged their opponents. One or more may have

overstated or understated their actual goals to such an extent that nobody could back down without appearing weak. Communication channels may have been adversely affected because of intense pressure on the participants, or cultural differences may have caused misunderstandings. Rather than being pro-active and showing confidence, parties that are angry, frustrated or afraid to make the first move usually wait until mediation is required under the terms of the court rule or contract, sometimes missing an opportunity to resolve the dispute sooner, more cheaply and with less emotional and time investment. Most experienced advocates recognize these pitfalls and understand that successful mediation at the first appropriate opportunity is a desired goal. They try to keep communication channels open and avoid tactics that cause the parties to entrench. What matters is that advocates strategize and are intentional about what they are doing, rather than allowing events to control them. Here are the most common choices on when to initiate the mediation:

a. ***Early intervention (pre-suit)*** — Often, if mediation begins too soon, the parties are not ready for meaningful discussion and the bargaining process may break down. But there are cases where early mediation is the last best chance to avoid all out warfare. When the parties already have a good grasp of the facts, and litigation is going to be expensive and potentially damaging to both parties, early intervention is often a good strategy. For example, two businesses with an ongoing relationship arguing over contract rights or intellectual property rights may prefer a chance to mediate before the relationship is permanently damaged. Also, employers may see it as an opportunity to save employee relationships. Some sophisticated clients value mediation as a form of early intervention and have an aggressive policy of using it before commencing litigation as either a plaintiff or defendant. Another use of early intervention is in the situation of the sensitive case where confidentiality has real value. As in Exercise 4.1 in Chapter 4, a plaintiff making a claim against the defendant, such as sexual harassment or non-consensual touching, may not want the case to be public and also may have a great deal more negotiating leverage before it is.

b. ***Pre-discovery*** — When parties already know a fair amount about what happened, it is often appropriate to attempt mediation before a lot of expensive discovery has occurred and before positions become entrenched.

c. ***After initial discovery*** — Once a matter enters litigation, successful mediation is often unlikely until after the exchange of at least initial discovery. After the advocates have exchanged interrogatories and document production requests and have deposed the parties and perhaps key witnesses, they have a pretty good idea of what the case is going to look like at trial. They have evaluated the key players as witnesses and know most of the facts. But if the case continues to adjudication, there is still preparation cost involved and the uncertainty of outcome. This is the time when most cases are ready for resolution through mediation.

d. *After substantial discovery but before expert disclosure* — The parties usually know by this point what the case looks like. Depending upon the case, the production of expert reports followed by expert depositions will be a major expense. Assuming that the parties mutually agree that each party will produce an acceptable expert or experts, this is an opportunity to settle before incurring the additional expense.

e. *After the close of discovery* — This is when the parties know exactly what is available to try the case. Depositions have been taken, parties and witnesses have been evaluated, and defense counsel has submitted a pretrial report letter to the client and/or insurance carrier identifying the risks and giving a range of outcomes. Plaintiff's counsel has provided a full evaluation to the client and has worked on setting reasonable expectations. At this point, the parties can still save the cost of trial preparation and trial, and avoid the risk of a bad outcome.

f. *On the eve of trial* — Sometimes, mediation does occur on the eve of trial, after the parties have conducted full discovery and are nearly ready to try the case. Often, this is a second mediation session with the original mediator following an earlier incomplete attempt, or it may be a second mediation with a new mediator. Occasionally, it is the first attempt at mediation. Mediation at this phase of the litigation can be difficult, because the clients have usually paid the advocates to prepare for trial and are financially and emotionally invested in an outcome. By now, the parties may have locked themselves into unyielding positions they are unlikely to modify. As discussed in Chapter 9, emotions can make it much more difficult to look at possible creative resolutions rationally.

g. *During trial* — It is very unusual to begin a mediation during trial, but it occasionally happens. Sometimes, both parties do not like the way the trial is going and prefer to take back control over the outcome. It is more common to continue a mediation that commenced prior to trial. With the benefit of jury selection, opening statements, etc., parties may be willing to move from their last position in the mediation, notwithstanding the emotional hurdles discussed in Chapter 9.

F. SELECTING THE MEDIATOR

Once the parties have agreed to mediate (or have been ordered to), a mediator needs to be selected. Normally, the parties are free to choose a mediator. In some mediation programs, the parties are limited to choosing a mediator from an approved list. Rarely, a particular mediator is selected by the court or by contract. When choice is allowed, the parties negotiate over selection. Usually, they will exchange proposals of two or three mediators who would be acceptable to them and then agree to one who is named by both parties. But before the parties ever suggest the name of a mediator, they need to have done their due diligence to identify a mediator who has the style and experience that will best suit their client's needs, based upon the facts and personalities of the case. As with all aspects of bargaining interactions, skilled negotiators will control the selection of a mediator to the extent possible, making *intentional* choices based upon considered strategy, rather than being controlled by and reacting to the process. In approaching selection, it is important to get information about the mediator from others who have mediated with her. *Just like advocates, mediators develop reputations which should be carefully evaluated.*

To the extent possible, negotiators should always consider what style of mediator will best suit the needs of the client and maximize the opportunity for a favorable outcome. (Mediator styles are discussed in the next section.) All things being equal, skilled negotiators who merely wish to obtain bargaining assistance usually opt for a facilitative/elicitive neutral. Less proficient negotiators who need assistance with their bargaining interaction may prefer an evaluative/directive person. Individuals who will have to deal with each other in the future — such as business partners or spouses getting divorced with minor children — may prefer a transformative individual who will work to preserve the relationship even if the immediate controversy is not resolved through negotiation. But — as with all negotiation decisions — these generalizations give way to the specifics of the case. For example, in some cases, the problem with settlement may be that the *other* negotiator is difficult, insecure, inexperienced, etc. The experienced negotiator may decide to recommend a strong evaluative/directive mediator in order to make more progress with the other side. Sometimes the experienced negotiator may allow the other side to select the mediator, believing that such a mediator is more likely to influence the other side in a way that will lead to resolution. After all, since the mediation is not binding unless there is agreement, the stakes are lower than if one allowed the other side to select an arbitrator who would make a binding decision. As with timing, the point is to make an intentional, calculated decision.

G. MEDIATOR STYLES

Skilled mediators possess many common qualities no matter which style they employ. They are usually objective and fair-minded individuals. They possess good communication skills — they are good, empathetic listeners and assertive speakers. Most are adept readers of nonverbal signals. They possess good interpersonal skills that enable them to interact effectively with persons with diverse personalities. They also understand the negotiation process, and the ways in which they can enhance that process.

Both neutrals and advocates must appreciate the fact that mediator personalities influence mediator behavior. Although very few trained mediators approach every case in the same way, assertive and aggressive individuals tend to be more direct mediators who state opinions and give advice, while less assertive and more passive persons tend to facilitate and let the parties have more control over the process. Most mediators fall somewhere in between these styles and tend more toward one style or another depending upon the case and the personalities of the parties and lawyers involved.

There are three basic styles of mediation. Although few mediators stick exclusively to any one style, they do tend to develop their own blended style that will fall primarily into one of the three categories — Facilitative/Elicitive, Directive/Evaluative and

Transformative. Nonetheless, during mediation sessions, most mediators use facilitative, evaluative, and even transformative techniques at different times to move the parties toward agreement.

1. Facilitative/Elicitive Mediators

Facilitative/Elicitive mediators try to reopen blocked communication channels and generate direct inter-party discussions that will enable the parties to formulate their own agreements. These conciliators tend to be process-oriented. They hope to regenerate party-to-party discussions that will enable the parties to structure their own agreements. They view impasses as the result of communication breakdowns and/or unrealistic party expectations. They work to induce advocates to reconsider the reasonableness of their respective positions. They are elicitive in the way they use questions to generate positional reassessments and to get parties to consider innovative options. They prefer joint sessions during which they try to induce the parties to engage in more open face-to-face discussions. They resort to separate caucus sessions only when they conclude that face-to-face talks are not progressing well.

These mediators ask many questions that are designed to induce the parties to evaluate the reasonableness of their stated positions and to explore underlying party interests. They try to get participants to look behind their stated positions in an effort to appreciate the availability of alternatives that may prove to be mutually beneficial. Whenever possible, they get the parties talking and remain quiet while the parties interact.

2. Directive/Evaluative Mediators

Directive/Evaluative mediators tend to focus more on the substantive terms involved. They try to determine what terms would be acceptable to the parties and convince the parties to accept those terms. These neutrals are used to interacting with inexperienced negotiators who have difficulty reaching their own agreements. They often encounter advocates who do not know how to initiate meaningful negotiations or who are unable to explore the different issues in a manner likely to generate mutual accords. These neutrals tend to feel a need to control the bargaining interactions they encounter. Judicial mediators frequently employ this style, because they are used to telling litigants what to do and they sometimes lack the patience to allow the mediation process to continue for prolonged periods.

Transactions conducted by Directive/Evaluative mediators tend to resemble "parent"-"child" interactions. The "parent"-like neutrals attempt to ascertain the real needs and interests of the "child"-like advocates so they can let those persons know what they *should* accept. These mediators often prefer separate caucus sessions that will enable them to find out confidentially what the participants need to achieve. They then look for formulations that should be mutually acceptable and work to convince the parties that these are the terms they should accept.

Directive/Evaluative mediators do not hesitate to let the parties know how they feel about specific positions being taken. They suggest which terms are reasonable and which are unreasonable. These substantive-oriented neutrals act as "deal makers" who try to determine what terms would be best for the parties. Although some people think these mediators try to impose their own terms on the parties, this is often not accurate. Usually, they try to discover the terms the parties would be likely to accept, and then work to convince the participants that these are the terms that would be best for them.

3.   Transformative Mediators

An innovative group of mediators are described as Transformative. They work to demonstrate to participants that they possess power over their final outcomes and to generate mutual respect between the parties that will enhance their ability to solve their own problems.

Robert Baruch Bush and Joseph P. Folger, in *The Promise of Mediation*,[1] explored an innovative conciliation style which was primarily relationship-oriented. Unlike most traditional mediators whose primary objective concerns final agreements, transformative mediators do not worry about the resolution of the immediate disputes. They believe that mediators should work to ***empower*** weaker parties my demonstrating to them that they have non-settlement options they can accept if this alternative becomes necessary. By using this approach to empower parties, they hope to induce those individuals to explore the underlying issues and look for mutually beneficial agreements. They also wish to teach negotiators how to use their abilities to resolve future controversies.[2]

Transformative mediators also work to generate mutual respect between the parties. They do this through "***recognition***," which involves efforts designed to induce each party to respect the interests of the other party. They work to generate inter-party empathy resulting from their efforts to get both sides to appreciate the feelings and perspectives of each other. Instead of focusing primarily on the bargaining process, as do Facilitative/Elicitive mediators, or on substantive issues, as do Directive/Evaluative mediators, Transformative neutrals focus on the disputants themselves. They work to demonstrate to emotionally drained parties that they have options they can effectively pursue if the current discussions do not prove fruitful.

Some traditional mediators believe that they can be both facilitative and transformative mediators by focusing on both the present negotiations *and* the relationship between the parties. Bush and Folger maintain that this approach is not really possible, on the ground that mediators must be interested primarily in either the substantive discussions and the parties' efforts to achieve mutually acceptable terms *or* the ability of the parties to become empowered and resolve their own disputes.

---

[1] *See also* ROBERT BARUCH BUSH & JOSEPH P. FOLGER, THE PROMISE OF MEDIATION (Jossey-Bass 2005) (exploring responses to their 1994 book).

[2] This orientation is quite similar to Collaborative Law, which is described in Part Three.

4. Blended Styles

As noted above, most mediators are a blend of styles — particularly the first two. They vary their approach depending upon the situation, including the facts and the personalities. They may have a style where they are mostly Facilitative/Elicitive, but give opinions if asked. They may volunteer opinions on liability and value, but only after asking a lot of open ended questions to give the participants the feeling of being heard. Although Transformative mediators do not believe that this approach can be "blended" with the others, many mediators believe that it can.

H. BEFORE THE MEDIATION SESSION STARTS[3]

Once the parties have selected a mediator, she will begin to facilitate the process. This pre-session work is all part of the Preliminary Stage of the negotiation, since it is setting the stage and tone for what is to follow. There are several things to consider before the first session:

1. The mediation agreement — Before the actual mediation session begins, the mediator usually has the parties sign a *mediation agreement*. This is a *contract* intended to bind the parties. This document identifies the parties, the lawyers and the mediator. It usually states that the mediation is confidential to the fullest extent allowed by law. (As noted below, there are exceptions to confidentiality.) The document will often include an agreement that the parties will not call the mediator as a witness in the event of a later dispute. This is so the mediator can work candidly and unencumbered by undue fear of becoming a witness in the event that the mediation is not successful. The document usually includes an agreement to pay the mediator and recites the agreed upon compensation.

2. Confidentiality — Most mediators and participants consider the entire mediation process to be confidential. However, there are limits, discussed below, which you should understand from the beginning. Confidentiality in mediation and limitations on confidentiality can come from several sources.

a. *Legal evidentiary exclusions* — Generally, evidence regarding offers of settlement and compromise of disputed claims has been excluded in judicial proceedings because it is not considered probative as determinative of the value of a claim. Federal Rule of Evidence 408 and similar state rules set forth specific protections. However, the rules have many *exceptions*, including introduction of settlement discussions to show bias or prejudice of a witness, to impeach credibility or to prove a material matter other than liability. In addition, the rules only apply to negotiations in legal causes of action.

b. *Other court rules* — Another basis for confidentiality is court rules. For instance, rules of civil procedure may protect communications. If the mediation is held under the auspices of a court-connected program, there may be rules which specify confidentiality.

---

[3] Portions of this section were originally co-authored for an unpublished 2010 continuing legal education presentation by John Burwell Garvey, Melinda Gehris and Edward E. "Terry" Shumaker.

c. *Statutes* — If the mediation is held in a court-connected program, there may also be statutes that apply to provide for confidentiality of the proceeding. The jurisdiction where you are mediating may have adopted the Uniform Mediation Act (UMA) or have its own mediation act or statute which includes confidentiality for mediation[4]

d. *Contracts* — Mediation may also be confidential by contract. As noted above, a written contract in which the parties, counsel, and mediators agree to confidentiality may be the basis for not sharing information.

e. *Limitations on confidentiality* — Courts may refuse to enforce a confidentiality agreement if they are concerned about other issues. For instance, suppression of evidence needed in litigation is contrary to public policy and courts have used this reason to require testimony about issues discussed during mediation.[5]

3. Mediation summaries for the mediator — Lawyers for the parties usually submit mediation summaries to the mediator. These may be confidential, shared with the other parties, or partially confidential and partially shared. The mediator reads these summaries in advance and often calls the lawyers to have private conversations after reading them. These summaries are important for several reasons. First, they inform the mediator, who will be assisting in the negotiation. Second, to the extent shared, and unlike many pleadings in litigation, they are usually read by the opponent's client. Third, to the extent they are shared, they send important signals to the opponents about preparedness, strength of analysis and determination.

4. Pre-mediation conference — As noted above, many mediators want to speak privately with counsel after receiving the mediation statements and before the mediation actually begins. In most cases, this is a telephone discussion which gives the mediator a chance to better understand the case, to anticipate any matters of particular sensitivity, to discuss client-control issues and generally figure out how to be most helpful. In some cases, particularly when there are multiple defendants or plaintiffs, the mediator may request a pre-mediation meeting with all of the defendants or all of the plaintiffs. This is an opportunity to resolve many issues which could result in an impasse. For example, if there are two plaintiffs and there is limited insurance, the mediator may see whether the plaintiffs would agree to a percentage allocation of the total amount available. With multiple defendants, the mediator may attempt to resolve percentages of responsibility or at least reach initial agreement on how the offers will be made during the mediation. Pre-mediation conferences are sometimes very helpful in avoiding impasse or substantial and stressful delay at the mediation. For example, defendants who arrive at a mediation and argue among themselves for hours before the first offer is made can inadvertently create animosity on the part of

---

[4] The UMA can be viewed at http://www.uniformlaws.org/shared/docs/mediation/uma_final_03.pdf. As of 2012 it has been adopted in 10 states and the District of Columbia: http://www.uniformlaws.org/LegislativeFactSheet.aspx?title=Mediation%20Act, last visited 6-6-12.

[5] *See ABM Indus., Inc. v. Zurich Am. Ins. Co.*, 237 F.R.D. 225 (N.D. Cal. 2006) (court rejected argument that Fed. R. Evid. 408 would bar introduction of evidence that coverage counsel came to the mediation and refused coverage because the evidence is not excluded if it is offered for another purpose); ***Ladiser v. Huff***, 121 Wash. App. 1039 (Ct. App. 2004) (admitting privileged mediation statements to determine whether attorney's fees were appropriate sanction for bad faith participation).

the plaintiff which can make it much more difficult for the plaintiff's lawyer to properly manage the situation and control expectations.

I.   PREPARATION FOR MEDIATION SESSIONS

Both negotiating parties and designated neutrals should prepare for their interactions. Even if the parties have prepared for their own negotiations, they need to reassess their respective situations in light of the intervention of a neutral facilitator. They should review their current positions to see if they can continue to support those positions rationally. They must next decide how they plan to interact with the mediator. Based upon that person's style, what approach do they think will be most effective? Do they want to have the client speak in the open session, as discussed in Chapter 9? How much are they willing to disclose at joint sessions with the other side, and what are they willing to disclose in confidential separate caucus sessions with the mediator? They should try to go behind the stated positions of their side and of the other side to look for alternatives that might prove to be mutually beneficial. They should try to approach the mediated sessions with as open a mind as possible. As with any negotiation, they should prepare using an outline.

Many mediation rules require the actual clients to be present at the initial — and sometimes subsequent — mediation sessions. Even when the rules do not require it, many mediators insist upon having all decision makers in the room or at least connected by audio/visual means.[6] It thus becomes imperative for lawyers to prepare their clients for such sessions. The clients should be prepared for mediator comments they might find intimidating — especially where judicial officers are serving as the negotiation facilitators — since such persons tend to be rather directive/evaluative. They are used to telling parties what to do, and that predisposition carries over to their mediation encounters. The clients should be prepared to know when it is beneficial for them to speak and when they should allow their advocates to speak for them. If the mediator asks to meet with the clients alone — which occurs most often in business negotiations but can occur in other cases — the attorneys should carefully prepare the clients for such encounters.

The selected mediator must also prepare for the upcoming sessions. She should direct the nature and timing of the submissions and read them carefully — phrasing is often key. When she first contacts the parties individually — usually by telephone — she should ask each party to explain the nature of the dispute and their current position. She should ask about any personality issues, client control issues, etc. She needs to begin to appreciate the underlying interests and the possible alternatives that might be beneficially explored during face-to-face party discussions. The more the mediator knows prior to the initial formal session, the easier it tends to be for her to begin the discussions beneficially.

---

[6] When insurance is involved, many carriers will try to avoid personal attendance to save money and as a negotiation strategy. Whenever a decision maker is not physically present, it changes the negotiating dynamic. The carrier may try to employ the "limited client authority" or "nibble" techniques, described in Chapter 6.

J. THE ACTUAL MEDIATION[7]

Mediators generally conduct their sessions at neutral locations — the mediator's own office or another non-party site. What matters most is that it is a location suitable to all of the parties. Mediators prefer meeting arrangements that have sufficient room for all of the participants, with separate rooms for caucus sessions if they become necessary. Many mediators try to arrange the furniture in a non-confrontational configuration. Some use round tables to avoid having the parties sit directly across from each other in a confrontational setting. Even where square or rectangular tables are involved, mediators can deal with this issue by sitting on one side of the table and asking the parties to sit next to each other along the other side. This is a more cooperative configuration, and it encourages the parties to think mentally that they are on the same side.

The first formal mediation session is almost always a joint session, with all of the parties and counsel present, unless otherwise excused. The first portion of this session completes the Preliminary Stage; the parties and the mediator become acquainted and the mediator explains the neutral role of the mediator. Everyone is face to face, including parties that may not have seen each other since the dispute began. Parties are often nervous and are sizing each other up. An effective mediator sets the tone and takes charge of the process. Most neutrals explain the confidentiality of mediation sessions (and the limits discussed above) and describe the mediator's neutral facilitative function. They also indicate that if separate caucus sessions are conducted, the information shared with them by the parties during such sessions will not be disclosed to the other side without their consent. Most emphasize the fact they have absolutely no authority to tell the parties what to do; they are only there to assist the parties achieve their own agreement. Dispute mediators often talk about the fact that litigation is *backward looking*, with the parties using the court or arbitrator to determine which one was right. Mediation, on the other hand, tends to be *forward looking*, with the participants endeavoring to resolve their dispute and get on with their lives.

After the mediator's preliminary explanation of the mediation process, the participants then engage in an Information Exchange. Mediators usually ask the parties to summarize the issues to be addressed. This usually commences with oral presentations by counsel at a joint session. Opposing parties are asked not to interrupt, to provide each side with the opportunity to set forth their positions without direct conflict. Facilitative/Elicitive mediators tend to use questions to generate party discussions. They ask each party questions designed to induce them to appreciate their weaknesses and to rethink the appropriateness of their stated positions. Directive/Evaluative mediators tend to be more direct. They are more likely to indicate their own view of party positions. Transformative mediators ask parties questions designed to demonstrate that they possess viable nonsettlement options they can rely upon if the present discussions do not culminate in mutual accords. They also work to induce each side to

---

[7] For a complete description of a mediation from the mediator's perspective, see John Burwell Garvey, *"Mediator" is an Action Noun*, 46 New Hampshire Bar Journal 7 (2005), available on line at http://www.nhbar.org/publications/archives/display-journal-issue.asp?id=289.

have an appreciation for the other side's perspective, even if they do not agree with it, to develop a degree of mutual respect.

Depending upon the case, the presentation by each party may be quite elaborate — including exhibits and video — or it may be very brief. From each party's perspective, the presentation is for the benefit of the mediator but is also a chance to present a condensed case to the other party. Since lawyers, as a rule, do not get to speak directly to another party represented by counsel, this is a strategic opportunity to say things that the presenter knows will be heard by the opponent, without first being filtered through the opponent's lawyer. Effective negotiators will also have the client speak when the client will make a positive impression. As noted in Chapter 9, effective communication by the client can convey sincerity and can be powerful. An impressive client can often have a big impact on any of the opponent's decision makers who are at the mediation and have not met the client. As mediators, we have often seen this strategy cause real movement and reevaluation by the parties.

After the parties have completed the Information Exchange, the mediation moves into the Distributive Stage, as the parties begin making concessions. This may take place in joint session but often occurs in private caucus. In mediation, this stage can take a long time to get started, as both sides posture over who will move first. The experienced mediator will patiently work with the parties and make suggestions that can get the negotiations on track.[8] This is where negotiating using the mediator is quite different than direct negotiations. In essence, the parties negotiate *with* and *through* the mediator. They will try to convince the mediator of the strength and sincerity of their position so that the mediator will work to obtain the best outcome possible. At the same time, they will often tell the mediator things they would never share with the other side, hoping that the mediator can find a way to obtain a resolution with the knowledge but without disclosing it. It is somewhat like playing three dimensional tick tac toe, because the lawyer needs to keep track of the negotiation on several different levels — the client, the mediator, and the opponent.

The Distributive Stage is usually the longest part of the mediation. In our experience, there is usually a point during the Distributive Stage where the parties become discouraged and it begins to look like impasse is on the horizon. This is the time when skillful mediators reframe issues and get the parties to think about the benefits of controlling the outcome through agreement rather than risking an uncontrolled result. For example, in an automobile personal injury case where the defendant has insurance, a predominantly facilitative/elicitive mediator might ask the defense lawyer the following questions in the presence of the insurance adjuster:

    1. *"What did you think of the plaintiff?"*

    2. *"How do you think a jury will react to her?"*

    3. *"How do you feel about Attorney Smith? Will she do a good job for Ms. Plaintiff?"*

---

[8] *See id.*

4. *"How far along are you on discovery? If the case doesn't settle, what do you estimate as your costs through trial, including experts?"*

5. *"What do you see as your weakest points in this case?"*

6. *"If you tried this case five times, how many times would you win it?"*

In asking questions like the ones above, the mediator introduces the element of risk into the discussion through the answers of the defense. Most often, the defense lawyer will acknowledge that the plaintiff will make an average to above-average witness, and that the lawyer will do at least an adequate job. If the plaintiff made a favorable impression or if the lawyer is well regarded, that will usually be conceded. The defense will usually acknowledge some weakness in the case, which leads to a realization that the case could be won by the plaintiff. We have not yet met the lawyer who will say in front of a client and/or adjuster that she will win the case five times out of five, nor have we met the adjuster who will make that prediction to her supervisor! Even if the prediction is that the plaintiff would only win one out of five times, the mediator will ask the defense lawyer why she would lose on that one occasion. The answer will reveal the weakness that concerns the defense lawyer. If the prediction is that the plaintiff will probably win more often than that, then the danger of the case is further underscored. The goal is to get them thinking about risk — and through their own analysis rather than from an opinion stated by the mediator. (This process is later repeated with the plaintiff).

As the parties reevaluate and make further concessions, there is usually a breakthrough. Although the parties have not yet resolved the dispute, they get close enough so that they see that it is within their grasp. When this happens, parties usually enter the Closing Stage, where they try to reach a mutual accord. Experienced mediators will usually see a change in the body language, as we discussed in Chapter 7. The parties become psychologically committed to making a deal, and the mediator helps the parties to close the remaining gap. We remind you in your role as advocates, the Closing Stage is *not* a time for swift action: it is a time for ***patient perseverance***. This is a dangerous time for less skilled bargainers who will often make bigger concessions than required.

If the mediator does successfully maneuver the parties through the Closing Stage, and if the negotiation involves multiple issues, then the mediation can move into the Cooperative Stage, to see if the parties can expand the overall pie to be divided between them and simultaneously enhance their respective positions. Sometimes, this is really part of the Closing Stage, since the expanded pie or the non-economic considerations become the value added that actually closes the deal.

Finally, if a deal is reached, most mediators will insist that the parties reduce the agreement to writing before ending the mediation. If the necessary closing documents are too complicated to complete during the mediation, there should at *least* be a memorandum of agreement, signed by parties and counsel, outlining the terms in sufficient detail so that a contract has been made.[9] If the parties are not willing to sign

---

[9] With respect to the mediator's involvement in preparing the memorandum, see section [K][2][b] of this chapter, *infra.*

a memorandum of agreement, then there is a serious question as to whether there has really been a meeting of the minds. A signed memorandum can reduce the effectiveness of the "limited client authority" and "nibble" techniques, described in Chapter 6.

1.   Tactical Considerations for the Mediator

Most mediators undergo substantial formal training and also gain skill through experience. They come to mediation with their own unique personalities and develop their own sense of style and timing. They read literature on human behavior and stay abreast of the research described in Chapter 9. Like the parties, mediators need to be very intentional. They need to observe all of the things we have discussed with respect to negotiation. They listen for leaks, watch facial expressions and body language, and strategize on when and how to say things. A lot of the timing comes down to judgment and the facts and tone of the particular case. Sometimes, mediators explore things in joint session, sometimes in private caucus. Sometimes, the mediator asks pointed questions during the Informational Stage and sometimes chooses to wait until the Distributive Stage. Whatever the timing, there are certain categories of questions and events that tend to recur. Parties should anticipate these questions and events in the Preparation Stage when completing pre-mediation outlines.

Where legal disputes are involved, mediators try to ask both parties questions designed to emphasize party weaknesses. Claimants may be asked if there is a possibility they may not prevail at trial, to induce them to think of their *down-side risk.* Defendants, on the other hand, may be asked about the possibility the claimant might prevail and the possible outcomes if the claimant does to induce them to contemplate their *up-side risk.* The parties are also asked about potential transaction costs, recognizing that claimants must *subtract* those costs from anything they obtain, while defendants must *add* those costs to anything they must pay. This factor helps to move the parties toward one another.

When transactional interactions are involved, the mediators work to bring the parties closer together. Most ask questions designed to lower the demands being made by one side and to increase the offers being made by the other. Questions are used to explore the underlying needs and interests of the parties to look for ways the parties can expand the overall pie to be divided to maximize the joint returns achieved. By the time mediation is requested by transactional negotiators, the parties tend to be focused almost entirely on their areas of dispute. Skilled mediators try to change the focus from those distributive items to more cooperative items that the parties can exchange and simultaneously improve their respective positions. This technique gets the parties saying "yes" to each other. As they tentatively agree upon these different issues, they become psychologically committed to overall agreements. When they finally return to the more controverted items, they no longer seem as insurmountable as they did when the parties were at impasse. In addition, the parties have found many areas for joint gains, and they do not wish to have those tentative agreements lost at this point in the process.

Where emotional issues are involved, skilled neutrals can use joint sessions to allow cathartic venting in controlled environments, (or they may choose to let the party vent with the mediator in a private caucus). If done in a joint caucus, the upset parties are permitted to express their underlying feelings candidly, but without intemperate personal attacks that would only exacerbate the situation. After such disclosures, the other side may be encouraged to apologize in a manner designed to offset the emotional feelings that have been expressed. They may merely indicate how sorry they are that this situation has arisen or how sorry they are the other side feels the way they do. Such expressions can significantly diminish the negative emotions felt by the other side.

Disputing parties frequently characterize critical issues in one-sided terms designed to support their own interests. Neutral facilitators can often get them to reframe these issues in more neutral terms that will enable the parties to explore their different issues in a more detached fashion. Role reversals are occasionally employed to induce the parties to appreciate the positions being taken by each other. For example, a prospective business seller might be asked to evaluate the firm from a prospective purchaser's perspective, and the prospective buyer could be asked to assess the circumstances from the firm owner's perspective.

When joint sessions seem to be moving toward irreconcilable positions, it can be beneficial for mediators to ask the parties if they would be willing to allow separate caucus sessions designed to let the mediators explore the underlying issues more candidly with each party. As each separate session begins, the mediators should reiterate the confidential nature of these sessions. They should then ask each party what they should know that they do not already know. This question is designed to get the parties talking about matters they have been unwilling to discuss in the presence of the other side. Some party concerns may not be that significant, and the neutrals can try to get the parties to appreciate this fact. Other concerns may be quite real, and the mediators have to explore them carefully with the parties in ways that may enable them to look for ways to resolve them appropriately. Each side is asked where they might be willing to modify their current positions, as the mediator looks for ways to narrow the gaps between the different party positions.

Mediators constantly look for issues the parties value differently. This permits item exchanges that enhance the underlying needs of both sides. Where distributive issues are involved, mediators may use ***conditional offers*** — sometimes called bracketing — where each party is asked if it would agree to move closer to the other side if that side simultaneously moved toward it. Even where the quintessential distributive item — money — is involved, it can be converted into a less controversial matter by asking the parties to contemplate structured deals calling for payments made over many years or in-kind payments where goods or services are provided in lieu of cash.

During both litigation mediation and transactional mediation, it is important for neutral facilitators to make it appear that the parties are moving together. This appearance of fairness can be crucial if the parties hope to achieve acceptable agreements. It is also important for the parties to feel they were treated respectfully by both the mediator and the other side during conciliation sessions. Such an approach is likely to generate greater party satisfaction at the conclusion of the process, no matter how objectively beneficial the actual terms may be.

When negotiating parties approach or reach impasse, they are usually focusing on their areas of disagreement. They become locked into stated positions, with neither willing to budge for fear of appearing malleable. Neutral facilitators seek to move the parties away from their stated positions and to induce them to explore their underlying interests and alternative solutions. When the mediation is successful, dispute resolution occurs. When it is partially successful, the parties narrow their areas of disagreement, but the disputed issues remain.

2.   Tactical Considerations for the Bargainers

We have already generally discussed numerous strategic issues that must be considered by the parties. Keeping in mind that mediation is a form of negotiation, the parties should consider all that we discussed in Part One of this book. Here are some additional considerations:

a. *Arrive early* — Make sure that you and your client arrive a little early. You want to get settled, have any documents ready and be calm.

b. *Consider the best seating for what you plan to do* — If you get there first, you can usually pick seating to your client's best advantage. (That said, some mediators will ask you to sit in a particular location.) What do you plan to do during the plenary session? If you represent the plaintiff, this is your chance to speak directly to the defendant (if he/she is there) or face to face with the adjuster if there is one. The mediator will watch and listen, but the presentation is also for the other side. If you are the defense counsel, this is probably your only chance to speak directly to the plaintiff and to explain firmly and fairly why this case is not a sure thing for either side. In a personal injury case, it is your opportunity to express sincere sympathy to the extent possible and to consider having your client make a statement. Think about these opportunities when you are choosing seating.

c. *Be considerate of others* — In most cases, the actual parties will be unfamiliar with the mediation process. They will usually be nervous. If the mediation involves a litigated matter, emotions may be running high. In the typical insurance defense case, the defendant is not there. The plaintiff is usually the only one at the mediation who is not a professional. All lawyers and adjusters should be sensitive to that fact. Things are usually informal, but the non-professional participants should be treated with courtesy. Avoid conversations which make the plaintiff feel excluded. If something is discussed in a technical way, take time to explain in a non-condescending way. Remember that the plaintiff usually comes into the proceeding with some anger about what happened. In order to have a successful mediation, it is usually necessary to let that anger go. If plaintiffs are treated as equals who are central players to the proceeding, it usually has a very positive effect for all parties.

When defendants are present, the same rules apply to them. They have been sued. Even when it is "just business," it rarely ever is. The defendant is usually a combination of embarrassed, angry and scared. Treat a defendant as you would a plaintiff.

d. *Introduce yourself and your other participants* — Shake hands, look everyone in the eye, introduce the people with you. Making appropriate physical contact and eye contact is the beginning of an important cultural ritual and helps to create an environment where you are more likely to be well received.

e. *Turn off your cell phone, quit reading your e-mails and pay attention* — You want to project an attitude that this mediation is the only thing that is currently happening in your life. It is important and you are at the mediation to represent your client and only your client. This is not just a matter of client development. Remember that you are being evaluated by the other side as a potential adversary from the moment you arrive. Be formidable, not distracted.

f. *Have a plan for optimizing the use of the mediator* — Consider how you can effectively use the mediator as part of your negotiation plan. You can give the mediator messages to deliver to the other side. How will you phrase them? How will you time them? What will you tell the mediator in confidence and for what purpose? Here are some general recommendations:

i. *Do not tell the mediator your BATNA until you are approaching it* — If the mediator knows your BATNA early on, it will make it harder for her to do her job in negotiating with the other parties. She will not be able to surmise, conjecture, etc. when talking with your opponents. She can "guess" if she doesn't know. If she knows, she has to worry about making affirmative misrepresentations.

ii. *Make principled demands and offers* — Be able to explain why your first position is what it is. You should be able to explain how you arrived at it. You should give it to the mediator with an explanation to pass on to the other bargainers. Each time you change your position, you should tell the mediator why, and deliver a message through the mediator that the other side will hear as firm, fair and friendly. If you appear rational and prepared, you will appear all the more formidable.

iii. *Watch the mediator and listen carefully* — Mediators are often required to keep confidences. However, through body language or vague references, they can often communicate a lot. Usually, this is intentional. Sometimes, it can be inadvertent *leaks*. When you are in private caucus with the mediator, watch her and listen to her as you would an opponent – as we discussed in Chapter 7.

iv. *Consider whether and when to give the mediator "killer evidence"* — If you have information that you do not believe the other side is aware of, and which will improve your case, do you disclose it in your mediation summary, opening statement, early caucus, late in the day or not at all? Generally, if you disclose it too early, the other side absorbs it without any apparent change in position. In our experience as mediators, it is often helpful to use information like that later in the process — at the time when negotiations appear stalled. There are several ways you can handle disclosure to the mediator. You can tell the mediator early on and authorize her to disclose the information when she thinks the timing is right. You can tell the mediator early and tell her you will let her know when she is authorized to disclose. Or, you can disclose the information to the mediator when you think the timing is right. Your strategy can vary with the facts of the case, the parties involved and the mediator.

v. *Remember that you and your client are always "dancing"* — Mediation is a kind of dance which tends to go through the "steps" or stages described in Chapter 4. At the beginning of the dance (Preliminary Stage), things are somewhat formal. The mediator is respectful of your space and nobody is "touching." The pace is slow. Private caucuses (Informational Stage) tend to last a long time and mostly involve questions by the mediator and answers by you and your client. As the mediation progresses (Distributive Stage), the music tends to speed up and things usually get more relaxed. The mediator will often "cozy up" to you and your client. The private sessions become shorter. There is a tendency to let your hair down with the mediator — even when impasse appears on the horizon. By the time they get to this point, most bargainers do not want the music to stop. They enter the Closing Stage, and make the concessions they feel are necessary to finish the dance. We are not suggesting that this is inappropriate — the purpose of mediation is to resolve disputes. But as with all things involving advocacy, it is important that you remain intentional at all times. Understand what is happening and intentionally use the mediator as an extension of your negotiation strategy. Choose a skilled mediator but remain in charge of your case. This will enhance, not diminish, the mediator's capability.

K.   ETHICAL CONSIDERATIONS

Mediation has evolved greatly over the last several decades, since the Pound Conference mentioned in Chapter 1. For many years, there were no specific rules of conduct that applied to the process itself.[10] Parties would get together and work through a neutral third party. The neutral may or may not have had any facilitative experience. They may have been trained as a lawyer, a psychologist, a social worker or not at all. When it became obvious that mediation was becoming its own field of expertise, efforts were made to develop standards for mediators and conduct for participants. This has been only somewhat successful.

The Model Standards of Conduct for Mediators were prepared in 1994 by the American Arbitration Association, the American Bar Association's Section of Dispute Resolution, and the Society of Professionals in Dispute Resolution (SPIDR). As an example of the fluidity of mediation development, SPIDR later merged with the Academy of Family Mediators and the Conflict Resolution Education Network to form the Association for Conflict Resolution. In 2005, the original organizations and the new Association for Conflict Resolution revised the original standards.[11] Although these standards do not have the force of law, they can be adopted by a court, agency or other regulatory body.[12] In 2001, the National Conference of Commissioners on Uniform State Laws and the American Bar Association approved the Uniform Mediation Act (UMA), which includes rules of conduct and confidentiality. As with the Model Standards of Conduct, the UMA has no force of law unless adopted by a state or incorporated into the rules of a court, agency or other regulatory body. As of 2012, it had only been enacted as law in ten states and the District of Columbia, which leaves

---

[10] *See* EDWARD BRUNET, CHARLES B. CRAVER & ELLEN E. DEASON, ALTERNATIVE DISPUTE RESOLUTION 356-370 (LexisNexis 4th ed. 2012).

[11] The Model Standards of Conduct for Mediators, available at: http://www.americanbar.org/content/dam/aba/migrated/dispute/documents/model_standards_conduct_april2007.authcheckdam.pdf.

[12] For an interesting discussion on the pros and cons of adoption, see Michael L. Moffitt, *The Wrong Model, Again: Why the Devil is Not in the Details of the New Model Standards of Conduct for Mediators*, 31-33, and Joseph B. Stulberg, *The Model Standards of Conduct: A Reply to Professor Moffitt*, 34-35, DISPUTE RESOL. MAG., Spring 2006. Available at: http://www.americanbar.org/content/dam/aba/publishing/dispute_resolution_magazine/dispute_magazine_Spring06Unified.authcheckdam.pdf.

a lot of jurisdictions without any clear guidance.[13] Since mediators continue to come from various disciplines, there is nothing in most jurisdictions that provides either clear guidance *or* enforceable rules of conduct.

If you mediate in a jurisdiction without specific rules of conduct for mediation, you are always free to agree to rules as part of the mediation contract. You may also find that some courts and individual judges will apply rules for a case or as a general policy. When the mediator is not a lawyer and there are no applicable rules of conduct, you may wish to ask the mediator for the rules of engagement. When the mediator is a lawyer, is she subject to the same rules of professional conduct as the attorneys representing the parties? Interestingly, as discussed further in Section [2][b], below, it appears not. Unlike the other lawyers participating in the negotiation, the mediator is *not representing* a party.

1. Specific Considerations for the Advocates

a. *Candor to the Mediator* — In Chapter 5, we discussed the ethical boundaries and dilemmas of negotiation. Since mediation is a form of negotiation, the basic rules of ethics with respect to the lawyers who are representing parties apply. Lawyers representing parties are bound by the rules of professional conduct applicable in the jurisdiction, as described in Chapter 5. These rules usually involve some version of Model Rule 4.1 (Truthfulness in Statements to Others) and — when representations are made to a *judicial* mediator — Model Rule 3.3.[14] If the mediator is not a judicial mediator, then the Model Rules do not require any more candor to the mediator than to the opponent, but when a judicial facilitator is involved, not even misrepresentations of client settlement intentions or values are allowed due to the application of Model Rule 3.3(a).

b. *Duty to Inform Clients About ADR* — Should a lawyer advise a client of the ADR option before filing suit? An increasing number of jurisdictions require it.[15] Also, as noted in Chapter 1, an increasing number of courts require some form of ADR before reaching trial. Model Rule of Professional Conduct 1.4 requires the lawyer to "reasonably consult with the client about the means by which the client's objectives are to be accomplished."[16] Although Model Rule 1.4 does not state a specific duty to mention ADR, there is really no downside and it would be prudent to do so. Given the emotional and financial cost of litigation, we believe that describing the ADR process as a possible alternative should be part of obtaining "informed consent" prior to filing suit. Also, since lawyers usually make more money in litigation than in ADR, it helps

---

[13] *See supra* note 4.

[14] *See ABA Formal Opin. 06-439* (2006), available online at: http://www.illinoislegalmal.com/archives/06-439.pdf, site last visited 5-21-12.

[15] *See* Dwight Golan & Jay Folberg, Mediation: The Roles of Advocate and Neutral 414 (Wolters Kluwer 2011).

[16] Rule 1.4, ABA Model Rules of Professional Conduct, available online at: http://www.americanbar.org/groups/professional_responsibility/publications/model_rules_of_professional_conduct/rule_1_4_communi_cations.html.

to address any potential conflicts of interest with respect to the lawyer's economic advantage.

2.   Specific Considerations for the Mediator

a. *Training and Certification* — In most jurisdictions, there is no licensing or certification requirement in order to be a mediator. There is, in some court programs, a requirement that the person receives a certain amount of training and be certified for specific types of mediation — like family law and probate. Some court programs require general training for all mediators who wish to be on the "approved list." Most programs do not require that the mediator be an attorney.[17]

b. *Is the Mediator Practicing Law?* — There is an ongoing debate about whether mediating constitutes the *practice of law.* Since some mediators are not attorneys, and some attorney mediators mediate in jurisdictions where they are not licensed to practice, this would raise the issue of the *unauthorized* practice of law (UPL). Also, even when the mediator is mediating in a jurisdiction where she is licensed, this raises issues of legal malpractice and potential misconduct.

Some commentators have taken the position that mediation *is* the practice of law, while others have taken the opposite position.[18] In 2002, the ABA Section of Dispute Resolution issued a Resolution on Mediation and the Unauthorized Practice of Law which attempted to put this issue to rest.[19] The Resolution takes the following four positions: 1) mediation is *not* the practice of law and the parties are *not* represented by the mediator; 2) mediator discussions with the parties may involve legal issues, and this does *not* create an attorney-client relationship *nor* does it constitute legal advice; 3) mediators may assist in memorializing a settlement agreement *and* may even go beyond the terms specified by the parties, so long as all parties are represented by counsel *and* the mediator discloses that any proposal with respect to settlement terms is informational only — not the practice of law — and that the parties should consult with their own counsel; 4) mediators have an obligation to inform the parties in a mediation about the nature and limitations of the mediator's role, that the mediator is not there to provide legal representation, that a settlement may affect the parties' legal rights, and that each party has the right to legal counsel throughout the process and should seek counsel before signing a settlement agreement.

While the above described Resolution makes sense, the issue still remains somewhat murky. Comment 4 of the Resolution noted that the ABA Commission on Multijurisdictional Practice was considering proposals for modification of the Model Rules of Professional Conduct that would "eliminate, or at least reduce concerns about lawyer-mediators engaging in a multi-jurisdictional practice." More than a decade later, there is no such amendment.

---

[17] For a more in depth survey, see BRUNET, CRAVER & DEASON, *supra* note 9, at 367-375.

[18] *See* BRUNET, CRAVER & DEASON, *supra* note 9, at 362.

[19] Available online at: http://www.americanbar.org/content/dam/aba/migrated/2011_build/dispute_resolution/resolution2002.authcheckdam.pdf.

c. Subject Matter Expertise — Does the mediator need to have competence in the particular subject matter of the mediation? Again, some courts have specific training and certification programs for specific areas, like family law and probate. But what about where there is no specific requirement? Can a mediator with no employment experience mediate an employment case or a mediator with no environmental experience mediate an environmental case? In most jurisdictions, the answer is "yes." And even in those states that have adopted the UMA and/or the Model Standards of Conduct for Mediators (MSCM), the answer is still "yes." Section 9(f) of the UMA states that the Act "does not require that a mediator have a special qualification by background or profession." Standard IV(A)(1) of the MSCM states that "Any person may be selected as a mediator, provided that the *parties* are satisfied with the mediator's competence and qualifications." (Emphasis added.)

d. Conflicts of Interest — Lawyers always need to be mindful of conflicts of interest and how a relationship today can greatly impact one's ability to have a relationship tomorrow. If a mediator handles a five-hour mediation for Acme Corp., does that mean that both she and her firm will be conflicted out of taking a legal matter for or against Acme Corp. in the future? Lawyer-mediators need to be mindful of Model Rule of Professional Conduct 1.12(a), which states that "a lawyer shall not represent anyone in connection with a matter in which the lawyer participated personally and substantially as a . . . mediator or other third-party neutral, unless all parties to the proceeding give informed consent, confirmed in writing." And some states, in adopting this Model Rule, have not even allowed for consent.[20] Model Rule 1.12(c) states that "if a lawyer is disqualified by paragraph (a), no lawyer in a firm with which that lawyer is associated may knowingly undertake or continue representation in the matter unless: (1) the disqualified lawyer is timely screened from any participation in the matter and is apportioned no part of the fee therefrom; and (2) written notice is promptly given to the parties and any appropriate tribunal to enable them to ascertain compliance with the provisions of this rule." This rule does not create a total ban on future representation, but it does make it important for the lawyer-mediator to keep accurate conflict records and to anticipate the conflict consequences when accepting a mediation.

In addition to the *future* conflict issue, all mediators should be mindful of making full disclosure to the parties regarding any potential conflicts. Although the UMA and MSCM are not adopted in most jurisdictions, their rules of conduct are instructive. Section 9(a) of the UMA provides that, before accepting a mediation, an individual who is requested to serve as a mediator shall: (1) make an inquiry that is reasonable under the circumstances to determine whether there are any known facts that a reasonable individual would consider likely to affect the impartiality of the mediator, including a financial or personal interest in the outcome of the mediation and an existing or past relationship with a mediation party or foreseeable participant in the mediation; and (2) disclose any such known fact to the mediation parties as soon as is practical before accepting a mediation. The UMA does not call for mandatory recusal, but Standard III(e) of the MSCM does. "If a mediator's conflict of interest might

---

[20] *See* NH Rule of Professional Conduct 1.12, available online at: http://www.courts.state.nh.us/rules/pcon/pcon-1_12.htm.

reasonably be viewed as undermining the integrity of the mediation, a mediator shall withdraw from or decline to proceed with the mediation regardless of the expressed desire or agreement of the parties to the contrary."

EXERCISES

EXERCISE 10.1
PRACTICING MEDIATION SKILLS
"RODRIGUEZ v. DOUGLAS CHEMICAL COMPANY"

GENERAL DESCRIPTION OF EXERCISE: Mediation of a wrongful termination and defamation suit.

SKILLS INVOLVED: Representing parties at mediation; mediating a dispute between parties.

PARTICIPANTS NEEDED: Two attorneys and a mediator.

ESTIMATED TIME REQUIRED:

45 minutes for mediation and 30 minutes for discussion: 75 minutes.

LEVEL OF DIFFICULTY (1-5):

ROLES IN EXERCISE: You are acting as a lawyer for a party as identified in the exercise or as the mediator.

THE EXERCISE

Now it's time to get the feel of mediation! You will be divided into three groups. Your professor will assign one person to represent the plaintiff, one person to represent the defendant, and one person to be the mediator. Start by reading the General Information below. After that, read any confidential information and instructions provided by your professor.

GENERAL INFORMATION

The Douglas Chemical Company ("Douglas Chemical") produces various chemical products at its East Dakota facility. Several of its manufacturing processes involve the use of highly toxic substances regulated by the East Dakota Environmental Protection Act. The East Dakota Environmental Protection Agency requires chemical companies to detoxify hazardous substances before releasing them into rivers or ground waters. Substances that cannot be sufficiently detoxified must be removed by licensed toxic waste firms.

Alicia Rodriguez is a physical chemist. After she received her Ph.D. from the University of East Dakota fifteen years ago, she accepted a position with Douglas Chemical. Until last year, she worked in the Research and Development Department.

Last December 1, she was promoted to Director of the Environmental Protection Department. Her salary was increased to $75,000 per year.

When Dr. Rodriguez took over the Environmental Protection Department, she discovered that her predecessor had been falsifying Company records to permit the release of highly toxic substances into the Green River which flows past the Douglas Chemical plant. Dr. Rodriguez found that her predecessor had been filing false reports with the East Dakota Environmental Protection Agency. Those reports indicated that only detoxified substances were being released into the Green River.

Dr. Rodriguez immediately informed Ezra Douglas, the Company President, of her discovery. Mr. Douglas indicated that the East Dakota Environmental Protection regulations were overly strict. He said that the Company was not releasing an excessive amount of toxic substances into the Green River, and he suggested that no real harm was being caused by the Company's action. He told Dr. Rodriguez that she would have to be more of a "team player" if she wished to remain at Douglas Chemical. Dr. Rodriguez stated that she would not falsify Company records to permit the unlawful release of toxic substances. Mr. Douglas informed her that any disclosure of Company practices to the East Dakota Environmental Protection Agency would result in her termination.

Last December 15, Dr. Rodriguez met with Peter Connolly, Director of the East Dakota Environmental Protection Agency. She informed Dr. Connolly of the existing Douglas Chemical toxic substances release practice and provided him with copies of both the correct and the falsified Douglas Chemical records. On December 16, Dr. Connolly had water samples taken from areas of the Green River adjacent to the Douglas Chemical facility and discovered excessive levels of toxic substances. Samples taken from the Douglas Chemical release pipes were found to contain unusually high levels of toxic substances. On December 17, the East Dakota Environmental Protection Agency issued a citation against Douglas Chemical, and on December 20, it obtained a temporary restraining order prohibiting the further release of untreated toxic substances by Douglas Chemical.

On December 21, Mr. Douglas called Dr. Rodriguez into his office. He informed her that she was not working out in her new position. He said that he was unwilling to have a disloyal individual in his employ. Mr. Douglas then informed Dr. Rodriguez that she was being terminated.

On January 5, Mr. Douglas was contacted by Ed Barrett, a Vice President of the Jacobs Petroleum Company. Mr. Barrett told Mr. Douglas that Jacobs Petroleum was planning to ask Dr. Rodriguez to become its Director of Chemical Processing, a position that would have paid her $80,000 per year. Mr. Douglas told Mr. Barrett that Dr. Rodriguez had recently been discharged by Douglas Chemical because of her "poor attitude." He said that Dr. Rodriguez had been "a wholly uncooperative manager." On January 6, Mr. Barrett told Dr. Rodriguez that Jacobs Petroleum would be unable to offer her the Chemical Processing position, due to her "past difficulties" at Douglas Chemical.

Last February 1, Dr. Rodriguez filed a civil action in the East Dakota Circuit Court alleging: (1) that her termination based upon her unwillingness to falsify toxic chemical records contravened public policy and (2) that Mr. Douglas' statements to Mr. Barrett constituted defamation. She sought actual damages of $500,000 and punitive damages of $1,000,000.

No East Dakota statute or regulation expressly protects individuals who are terminated because of their unwillingness to participate in practices violating the State Environmental Protection Act. Although the East Dakota Supreme Court has followed the traditional "employment-at-will" doctrine, under which an employer may discharge an employee for "good cause, bad cause, or no cause at all," three of its seven Justices indicated in a recent decision that they might adopt a "public policy" exception if particularly egregious circumstances were involved. The East Dakota Civil Code specifically provides a "qualified immunity" against defamation liability for employers who provide reference information in response to requests for such information from other business entities.

Any monetary sum that Douglas Chemical agrees to pay to Dr. Rodriguez must be payable immediately. It may *not* be payable in future installments.

EXERCISE 10.1
PRACTICING MEDIATION SKILLS

REFLECTION

Whether you represented a party or acted as mediator, ask yourself what you learned from this exercise:

1. In what ways and to what degree did the mediator facilitate the interaction?

2. What did the mediator do to minimize party conflict and induce the parties to explore the underlying issues in a mutually beneficial manner?

3. What did the mediator do that you did not find helpful?

4. What could the mediator have done to be more effective in assisting in the negotiation process?

5. In what ways did this experience differ from directly negotiating with the parties?

Chapter 11

EXAMPLES OF TOPICS FOR MEDIATION

In Chapter 10, we discussed the general concept of mediation and how it works. In this chapter, we will give you examples of various areas of practice where mediation occurs and discuss matters unique to the various areas. There are many ways in which mediation is being used today. This chapter is not intended to be exhaustive, but illustrative. As you develop interests in law school and in practice, we encourage you to read further about mediation in your area of interest *and* to consider new applications. This is an emerging field of practice that will almost certainly expand during your career.

A. PERSONAL INJURY

When someone is physically injured and claims the injury was caused by the negligence of another, the usual remedy is litigation. The claims are typically based upon state common law or a particular state statute (dog bite, etc.) but can involve conflicts of law questions with respect to more than one state. These cases lend themselves well to mediation. Many courts now require that these cases be mediated before a trial is allowed. The fact patterns are usually fairly straightforward — a car accident, a slip and fall, a dog bite, etc. — but the issues at mediation can sometimes be quite complex. For example, there are often issues of whether there is insurance coverage, which insurance coverage is "primary," comparative negligence, contribution among joint tortfeasors, causation, pre-existing conditions, permanency, lost wages, loss of enjoyment of life, and loss of consortium.

In personal injury matters, the injured parties are most often strangers to litigation and usually feel like they are victims. The defendants often feel like the plaintiffs are just trying to milk the system. The insurance companies usually have control (under the terms of the insurance policy with the defendant) over whether there will be a settlement and for how much. Often, the defendant is not even present at the mediation. The dynamic can often be quite difficult for the mediator who must work to address the different needs of the stakeholders. The plaintiff is often emotional and needs a process that will allow him to "let go" of the case. The insurance company representative is usually dispassionate and deals with "the numbers" — within the limits of the insurance coverage. It is hard for a mediator to be creative, because the only thing being bargained for is money. There are few ways to make the pie bigger. Experienced mediators usually work privately with counsel for the parties in advance of the mediation to "set the table" for success. Whenever possible, the mediator usually encourages an apology from the defendant (or counsel) to take place at the opening session. After the apology, it is often helpful if the defense counsel is able to dispassionately explain to the plaintiff how the case will go if a trial occurs. This is an opportunity for the plaintiff to hear the other side directly from the defense lawyer — as will happen at trial. This usually gives the plaintiff something to reflect upon as the mediation goes forward. After the initial session, these mediations usually involve private caucuses, where the mediator explores the strengths and weaknesses with each party. The parties negotiate through the mediator as described in Chapter 10.[1]

B. EMPLOYMENT LAW

Employment disputes are well suited for mediation. There is a long history of mediation in the employment context. Some employment disputes can affect national security, and the United States government has historically been involved in the mediation of those disputes. These usually involve collective bargaining interactions between employers and representative labor organizations over the terms to be included in new bargaining agreements. For example, President Martin Van Buren facilitated a settlement of a strike by shipyard workers as early as 1838.[2] In 1947, Congress enacted the Labor-Management Relations Act of 1947 (Taft-Hartley Act), which created an independent government agency called the Federal Mediation and Conciliation Service. The agency's mission is to prevent or minimize the impact of labor-management disputes on the free flow of commerce by providing mediation, conciliation and voluntary arbitration.[3]

Most mediated employee disputes involve only one complaining employee. The employee is almost always the plaintiff. The employee has usually failed to get an "expected" promotion, been demoted or terminated. Sometimes, the employee has left the job because of the stressful conditions that she claims are unlawful. In these cases, the plaintiff claims that she was constructively discharged. The alleged illegal activity can be based upon a state and/or federal statute and/or common law and can be wide ranging, including but not limited to claims of sexual harassment, an unaccommodated disability, age, race, national origin, religion, or gender discrimination, whistleblower retaliation, and failure to provide for family and medical leave. Many of the statutory claims provide for attorneys fees and even enhanced damages.

Employment cases are almost always emotional. The plaintiff employee usually feels violated. The case may involve claims of wrongdoing by other employees — like sexual harassment or bullying. The other employee may be extremely defensive and even hostile. The employer's human resources professionals are sometimes quite defensive for "allowing" the illegal activity to continue.

Mediators in employment cases have many challenges, but they also have a lot to work with. Employment mediations are rarely zero sum negotiations. There are many things the parties can achieve at mediation that they cannot obtain at a jury trial. Most

---

[1] For a complete description of a mediation from the mediator's perspective, see John Burwell Garvey, *"Mediator" is an Action Noun*, 46 NEW HAMPSHIRE BAR JOURNAL 7 (2005), available on line at http://www.nhbar.org/publications/archives/display-journal-issue.asp?id=289.

[2] For a timeline of federal involvement, see Federal Mediation & Conciliation Service, A Timeline of Events in Modern American Labor Relations, available on line at http://www.fmcs.gov/internet/itemDetail.asp?categoryID=21&itemID=15810.

[3] *Id.*

employers and employees are interested in keeping the matter confidential. Employers are concerned with morale and the nonmonetary cost of ongoing litigation. Depositions of employees and managers are financially expensive and disruptive. If the case is one that allows for an award of legal fees to the plaintiff, the employer has to consider that it may be paying for all of the legal fees. Even if the employer only pays its own legal fees, the costs through trial can be steep. An employee claimant is often out of work at the time of the mediation. She would like to get on with her career — either with the former employer or in a new setting. She would like to have a clean employment record and a recommendation. The lawyer for the plaintiff usually has the case on a contingency fee and usually fronts the costs for depositions, expert fees, etc. Most lawyers representing the employee would rather settle at mediation if at all possible rather than risking the expense and uncertainty of proceeding to trial.

The experienced mediator recognizes that there are often many potential stakeholders and emotional barriers in an employment case. The plaintiff is usually angry and has gotten angrier as time has gone by. Her spouse and friends have supported her and have told her she was wronged. She has received positive attention and has not had to consider whether any of the problems at work were caused by her own behavior — such as tardiness, absenteeism, attitude, poor performance, etc. The spouse is not a party but usually feels like one, and the mediator needs to deal with this. From the spouse's typical point of view, the plaintiff worked hard and sacrificed family time and energy for this unappreciative despicable employer, only to pay the price for it along with the spouse.

On the employer's side, the supervisor is defensive, because she is being criticized for her actions and she is afraid that her job may be in peril if the case settles with a payment to the "wronged" employee. The human resources person is often defensive, because she believes that the claim, if paid, may reflect poorly on her and her department. Sometimes, the lawyer may be defensive, because she or her firm wrote the policy manual that is now being criticized or provided the personnel discrimination training, etc. When there is insurance, the insurance adjuster is wondering why she should pay anything on a case that the employer says is ridiculous, etc. To add even more tension, many employers keep insurance premiums lower by having a self-retained limit of exposure (similar to a deductible) where the employer pays the first $100,000 (or some other amount) of all costs, including legal fees, settlement payments, etc. This often creates tension between the employer (insured) and the insurance company. The insurance company wants the employer to resolve the matter within the limits of the self-retention amount. The employer would like to do that if it can be done at a level that provides any savings to the employer. But once that self-retention limit has been exhausted, the employer is usually more interested in "making the case go away," and no longer sees the payments as being employer money.

The experienced mediator is able to help the parties (and all stakeholders) to process the various emotions and concerns in a safe and controlled environment. Most employment mediators work with the lawyers in advance of the mediation to orchestrate the opening session. Who will be there? How will that affect the dynamics of the room? If the employer is planning to bring a person that makes the plaintiff very uncomfortable (think sexual harassment, etc.), should the parties be separated from the beginning or should they meet?

The plaintiff usually needs to feel heard. If she is going to let go of this case and move on, she needs to feel that she has told her story. Often, it is helpful if the plaintiff actually makes her own prepared statement during the opening session after her counsel has spoken. It is also usually helpful if the employer thanks the employee for her contributions and expresses regret that the relationship has come to this point. This statement needs to be carefully made to avoid injecting hope or unreasonable expectations into the mediation, but a sincere "thank you" focusing on the positive contributions of the employee can be very helpful. The opening session is also the time when the employer's lawyer can calmly explain why the case can be vigorously defended, even though the whole situation has obviously been very difficult for the plaintiff. Properly done, this usually injects a little reality therapy that the mediator can use as the mediation progresses.

After the opening session, most employment mediations involve private caucuses where the mediator can give both sides the opportunity to vent and save face. In our experience, employers usually state initially that they are not optimistic about the chances of settlement because of the weakness of the plaintiff's case. However, if they are given a chance to resolve the case without admitting liability or losing face (and often with the agreement that the employee will not apply to work for the company again), they will often pay more and provide more non-economic benefits (purging employment record, writing a recommendation, allowing the employee to remain on the payroll without pay long enough to vest for a company benefit, etc.) than it initially appeared they would do. As the mediation progresses and the offers get into the range where the employee has something to lose by going to trial, the plaintiff also gets more interested in settlement. The money is always important, but the non-monetary benefits of settlement are often the tipping point between settlement and trial, since the plaintiff comes to understand that controlling her own outcome gives her things she cannot obtain otherwise. Also, the mediator gently educates her that the possibility of a loss at trial would be a public matter that would be there for any future employer to consider. Even a win at trial would cause many prospective employers to pause.

C. FAMILY LAW

Family law is an area of practice where mediation is extremely common.[4] It usually involves the law of a single state but may involve conflicting laws of more than one state. Many courts that handle divorce matters or other family issues now have mandatory mediation programs. Because of the unique nature of this work, unlike most mediation, many courts require specific training and certification.

Obviously, the emotional level of many divorces is extreme. People who were once totally intimate are now permanently separating. They usually have personal property that they acquired together, including wedding gifts. Many of the personal items are charged with strong memories which are being torn apart by the divorce. The two spouses have usually exchanged personal and sometimes lavish gifts. Often, a spouse will have received something very personal from an in-law, like a painting, a special rug, or even a family heirloom. There are usually cars that each spouse thinks of as

---

[4] *See generally* ALISON TAYLOR, THE HANDBOOK OF FAMILY DISPUTE RESOLUTION (Jossey-Bass, 2002).

"theirs." There is often a home and other real estate to which both spouses have strong personal attachment. Some of the "attachment" to the personal and real property is based on perception of value, but a lot of it is based on strong emotion. Divorcing couples will sometimes spend thousands of dollars fighting over an item of personal property that could be duplicated for less than the cost of legal fees.

To make matters even more complex, the divorce is not usually just about property. Both parties have existing relationships with other people that are suddenly in flux. There are fathers-in-law, mothers-in-law, brothers and sisters-in-law. There are couples' friends and joint friends. And most significant, there are often children. There may be children of the marriage and children of prior marriages who have lived together during this marriage and have bonded as siblings.

The divorce may be occurring for a variety of reasons. It is rarely just a single reason, although the parties may think that is the case. There may be adultery, physical and/or mental abuse, prolonged periods of physical and/or emotional absence, addiction, incest, neglect, mental illness, physical infirmity, etc. It may be that the parties have grown apart for a variety of reasons, including poor communication skills. Unlike most litigation, the plaintiff is not always the party who feels most wronged. Sometimes the plaintiff is the moving party because they have a new relationship and want to be freed of the marriage. Sometimes, the plaintiff is the party who was physically absent through work for months at a time and came home to discover that their spouse was having "an affair." And sometimes, the plaintiff is the party who has been repeatedly abused, has filed the action with the help and encouragement of a support group, and is very frightened about going forward. There are very few "fill in the blanks" divorces, particularly the kind that come to mediation, and mediators need to be adept at identifying the legal and emotional issues, the stakeholders and creative, non-zero sum solutions to the extent possible. They must understand that divorce involving children means that the parties will have a continuing relationship — for better or worse. There may be economic, emotional and physical power imbalances. Any agreements may have far reaching consequences, and badly bargained agreements may be the subject of repeated litigation and orders to modify.

In most marital mediations where the parties are represented, lawyers submit mediation summaries that provide a lot of factual information about the marriage. The summaries include names of spouses and children, personal and real estate assets, liabilities, wages, salaries, pensions, etc. The submissions usually include proposals for asset distribution and, if there are minor children, a custody arrangement.

In any mediation, it is helpful to understand where the landmines are. In marital mediation, it is critical. The first thing marital mediators usually do after reading the summaries is talk privately to the lawyers by phone to get an "off the record" sense of personalities and major issues. If there are no lawyers (which is sometimes the case in court ordered mediation) then the mediator often chooses to meet the parties in person in the first instance to establish a relationship before asking background questions. In many marital mediations, the parties remain in session with the mediator throughout — there are no private caucuses. The mediator starts by discussing the process, and obtains agreement from the parties as to how the session will proceed. There is usually a comparison of the submissions and a discussion about any items on which there seems to be disagreement. An attempt will be made to reach agreement as to what the *facts* are — assets, liabilities, children, etc. Next, an attempt is usually made to agree on as many *dispositions* as possible by comparing the proposals. Sometimes, there is overlap as to what the parties seek. By starting with small agreements, the mediator can set a tone that may carry forward to the bigger issues.

The biggest issues in divorce usually center on children, child support and spousal alimony. Sometimes the fight over children is based upon each parent's legitimate interest in being involved with the children as much as possible. Sometimes, parents believe that whoever gets the children will retain the house and will receive child support and alimony. Sometimes, a parent will seek primary custody even though they do not really want it because they would feel ashamed not to seek it. This can be a very difficult issue for the mediator to negotiate. Experienced marital mediators understand that the emotions of the parties are complex and often conflicting. Mediators avoid shaming the parties or backing them into a corner. To the extent possible, they help the parties go positive. They help parents visualize what a stable situation would look like for the children. They draw out the positive connections that the parties still share and help them see that there could be positive times going forward if they commit to it. Whenever possible, mediators use external guidelines — like child support guidelines established by the jurisdiction — to discuss money matters. They work with counsel (when present) to expand the pie whenever possible. For example, they understand that alimony is tax deductible to the payor and taxable to the recipient but that child support is not. If the receiving spouse is in a substantially lower tax bracket than the paying spouse, then the payment of more alimony and less child support could be attractive. In order to succeed, marital mediators must be particularly attuned to both "heart and head." They must provide a safe forum to vent the heart issues — anger, betrayal, sadness, shame, empathy, love, etc. They must also help the parties to focus on the head issues — fair allocation of assets and liabilities, fair allocation of expenses going forward, appropriate arrangements for children, mechanisms to discuss issues in the future without resorting to litigation, etc. As mentioned above, there are no "cookie cutter" solutions, but there is some commonality in the issues that arise.

D. COMMERCIAL LAW

"Commercial Law" mediation is an extremely broad category which can include anything involving a dispute relating to a business relationship. It can involve parties from the same state, the same nation or nations from around the world. It can involve state, federal and international law as well as the law of other countries. This type of mediation is becoming increasingly common, and there are numerous organizations which provide these services. One organization, called the CPR Institute, is a nonprofit think tank whose mission is "to spearhead innovation and promote excellence in public and private dispute resolution and to serve as a primary multinational resource for avoidance, management and resolution of complex commercial disputes."[5] Such

---

[5] CPR Institute web page: http://www.cpradr.org/About/CPRsWork/FrequentlyAskedQuestions.aspx. CPR states that its membership includes General Counsel and senior lawyers of Fortune 1,000 corporations,

disputes are often between parties with long-term relationships which they want to continue, but are sometimes between (or among) parties who are dissolving a relationship or who are competitors. For example, the matter could be between a supplier and a manufacturer, a building contractor and a customer, or a bank and a borrower. It could involve a dispute between a small company and the seller of the company who made representations about the strength of client lists as part of the "good will" value. It could be between competing companies that supply an industry, where one company accuses the other with interference with a contractual relationship. The possibilities are really endless. The common thread is that the issues are commercial, which means that at least one of the parties is in business to make a profit.

Where parties have an ongoing relationship, the greatest appeal of mediation is the non-adversarial nature of it. Parties may be afraid of damaging or even destroying their relationship but need to resolve the dispute. Mediation can offer a quick and early attempt at dispute resolution before the matter is escalated. Even when there is no ongoing relationship to consider, commercial mediation is usually much less expensive than litigation and even arbitration. Many parties see it as a "no lose" first option before digging in for expensive, "no holds barred" litigation. Many corporate counsel now push outside counsel to mediate before authorizing litigation. Sometimes, corporate counsel will hire counsel who will not participate in the litigation to conduct the mediation, since there can be a perception that not all litigation counsel are focused on early resolution.

Although not required, commercial mediators usually have enough business background or business litigation experience to understand the issues in play. As with all mediations, they begin by trying to understand the factual issues and identifying the emotional concerns. They identify the stakeholders — both internally and externally. They work with the lawyers in the first instance. The parties tend to be fairly pragmatic in approaching the problems, but emotion is definitely involved. For example, in a supplier/manufacturer/seller case, assume that the supplier failed to provide by the time agreed upon the components needed to complete assembly of cell phones. As a result, the cell phone manufacturer failed to deliver the cell phones to the retail seller by the agreed upon date. The seller claims that the manufacturer's failure to deliver has caused the seller to lose market share because the competition has now launched a new phone with similar features. The mediator in this case would first look to the nature of the relationships among the disputants. If the relationships are ongoing, keeping them intact would be a major part of the mediator's approach. Further, the mediator would try to identify all of the individuals within the organizations who are feeling embarrassed, defensive, angry, etc. If any of those people are part of the decision-making process, the mediator would work with them to help them see the advantages of a cooperative resolution, rather than entrenching in expensive litigation that could make any perceived errors that much worse. Finally, the mediator would work with all of the parties on a pragmatic level to help them "crunch the numbers." A mediator would help the parties to see that a mediated resolution would eliminate the distraction, time commitments and financial cost of litigation. The parties

attorneys in the top law firms around the world, as well as leading judges, government officials, neutrals, and academics.

would be free to work together and incentivized to succeed. The mediator would look for creative ways to make the pie larger. For example, payment by the supplier for damages might include a discount for future parts supplied for a certain period of time. Likewise, the manufacturer might offer a discount to the retail seller in lieu of full payment for damages.

1. Intellectual Property Disputes

Intellectual property (IP) disputes are a kind of commercial dispute, but they are unique and usually involve specialized knowledge. The most common forms of intellectual property are patents, trademarks and copyrights. The disputes can involve state, federal and international law, as well as the law of other countries. With globalization, the IP field is expanding exponentially. Most disputes concern whether one party is infringing on the rights acquired by the other party with respect to the patent, trademark or copyright. By way of example, Alpha cell phone manufacturer claims that its competitor, Beta, infringed on several of its wireless and smartphone technologies. Beta counters that Alpha has violated some of its key patents related to operating system devices. Or a recording artist claims that a company is using her song for commercial purposes without her permission. Or Company A complains that Company B is using a trademark that is similar to Company A's and is likely to cause confusion. There are many examples. Mediators who handle these cases generally approach them using the techniques employed in other commercial mediations, but they usually have IP knowledge to help them navigate through the difficult substantive issues.

Many IP practitioners recommend mediation as being faster and less expensive than litigation. It is also recommended because, unlike trials before judges and juries, the parties can agree on a mediator who understands the field of law.[6] The World Intellectual Property Association (WIPO) now provides mediation workshops for mediators.[7] For an example of an international dispute involving a vodka trademark, go to Mock Mediation Video, Resolution Through Mediation: Solving a Complex International Business Problem, available at:

http://www.inta.org/Mediation/Pages/AboutADRandMediation.aspx.

This video is posted by the International Trademark Association in cooperation with CPR Institute.

2. Construction Disputes

Construction disputes can be large or small. They can involve a remodeling job for a homeowner, a multi-million dollar sewage treatment plant, or a multi-billion dollar highway project. The disputes are usually based upon contract interpretation. They can involve standard American Institute of Architects (AIA) contracts, government

---

[6] *See* Sara Tran, *Experienced Intellectual Property Mediators: Increasingly Attractive in Times of 'Patent' Unpredictability*, HARVARD NEGOTIATION LAW REVIEW, Vol. 13, 2008. Available at SSRN: http://ssrn.com/abstract=1763374.

[7] *See* http://www.wipo.int/amc/en/.

contracts, privately drafted contracts and handshakes. Generally, the mediator is someone who understands the principles of construction, including the contracts, change orders, delay damages, etc. Some construction mediations are held on an expedited timetable if the project is ongoing. Except for the particularized knowledge, the issues in construction mediation are similar to other commercial mediations — ongoing relationships, cost, stress, etc.

E. CONSUMER DISPUTES

When consumers buy a product and it breaks, what is their recourse? There may be a warranty. Some states have consumer protection statutes which provide for attorneys fees if the consumer prevails. There may be an applicable federal statute. The office of the state attorney general usually has a consumer protection bureau. But all of these remedies can be costly and time consuming. Many small claims courts, district courts and state bar associations now offer mediation diversion for consumer matters. The Federal Trade Commission encourages mediation (and arbitration) when possible.[8] These disputes are not usually complicated and are often handled by volunteer mediators. The basic principles of mediation, as described in Chapter 10, are used. This is a good way to get experience as a mediator.

F. CRIMINAL MATTERS

Victim Offender Mediation (VOM) is a growing area of the law. According to Mark Umbreit, the founding director of the University of Minnesota Center for Restorative Justice and Peacemaking, VOM is now used in over 1,300 communities in 17 countries around the world.[9] This is also called restorative justice, or reconciliation. Unlike typical mediation, it is not about two people trying to resolve a dispute through the services of a neutral party. Rather, the victim is clearly the aggrieved party and the offender is in the legal system. The mediation is considered part of the victim's healing process and part of the offender's correctional process. The mediation aims to obtain a restitution agreement that may include personal contact between the offender and the victim — like community service. There are various models of VOM so it is difficult to describe a "typical" program. If you are interested in mediation and criminal work, you should be aware of this emerging field. For further explanation and sample videos, go to the University of Minnesota Center for Restorative Justice and Peacemaking:

http://www.cehd.umn.edu/ssw/RJP/Video_Clips/default.asp.[10]

---

[8] *See* http://www.ftc.gov/bcp/edu/pubs/consumer/general/gen05.shtm.

[9] Comments of Mark Umbreit in *Overview of Victim Offender Mediation and Conferencing*, video available on line at: http://www.cehd.umn.edu/ssw/RJP/Video_Clips/default.asp.

[10] *See also* http://restorativejustice.org/.

EXERCISES

EXERCISE 11.1
PRACTICING THE MEDIATION PROCESS

"THE NOT SO PLEASANT LAKE MEDIATION"

GENERAL DESCRIPTION OF EXERCISE: Mediation of dispute over access to a beach and dock.

SKILLS INVOLVED: Mediation.

PARTICIPANTS NEEDED: You will be assigned one of five roles.

ESTIMATED TIME REQUIRED:

45 minutes for mediation and 30 minutes for discussion: 75 minutes

LEVEL OF DIFFICULTY (1-5):

ROLES IN EXERCISE: You are acting as a plaintiff, defendant, counsel for plaintiff, counsel for defendant, or the mediator.

THE EXERCISE

You will be divided into five groups — plaintiff, counsel for plaintiff, defendant, counsel for defendant, and mediator. Start by reading the general information below. After that, read any Confidential Information assigned to your role and follow the instructions that your professor provides.

General Information

Pleasant Lake is a 6,000 acre, natural, spring fed lake near Pleasantville. It has been the summer home for generations of families who have come there to enjoy fishing, canoeing, kayaking, hiking and marshmallows over the campfire. Although all bodies of water in excess of 100 acres are controlled by the state for purposes of state regulation, nearly all of the shoreline around Pleasant Lake is privately owned. There are two public boat ramps.

Pleasant Lake has a rich history. In the late 1800s, it was a favorite summer destination for city dwellers, who arrived in Pleasantville by train. From there they would transfer to horse drawn carriages, which took them on carriage roads to the boat dock. From there, they would board the Pleasant Laker, a paddleboat run by steam, which would make a big circle around the lake, dropping people off at various large docks. At the time, most of the docks were public. However, the steamer would also stop at various designated private docks when a red flag was raised on the dock's flag pole. The summer residents would offload at the various docks on the steamer's circuit, and young boys would then haul the trunks to the various summer camps — all within walking distance of the docks.

As of the mid-1800s, all of the land around the lake was owned by the state. Between 1850 and 1880, the state sold or granted the land in exchange for development agreements, including railroad development. The state also built a number of the docks where the steamship stopped. The eventual owners of these large tracts of land developed what amounted to summer villages around the lake. Most of the villages had a grand hotel and numerous small cottages, which were mostly rented to families. One such owner was Thomas Parkhurst.

Mr. Parkhurst was a railroad man. With the land he received in 1880, he built the small shoreline Village of Idlehurst. The original plans called for a grand hotel on the waterfront and 44 individual lots behind the hotel. The plans also showed an existing dock, but there are no records available to know whether it was built by Mr. Parkhurst or the state. The lots were all 1/4 acre in size, and were lined up on a grid. Mr. Hastings immediately built the hotel. The hotel was destroyed by fire in 1909 and was not rebuilt. After the fire, the waterfront land where the hotel had been remained vacant, except for the dock. Over time, Mr. Parkhurst built homes on 20 of the 44 lots. To help finance his development, he sold off the remaining 24 lots to various buyers. Over the years, all 44 lots were built upon.

When Mr. Parkhurst died in 1926, all of his remaining property went to his wife, Helen, who lived until 1949. She sold off some of the cottages during her lifetime, but kept a lot of them for her growing family. Her four children were each deeded two of the remaining cottages for themselves and their families. The whole area became a kind of summer compound for the Parkhurst clan. When Mrs. Parkhurst died, her four children inherited all of her remaining property in equal shares, including the vacant waterfront property. The waterfront property was always used as the beach area, and the dock was always used for sunbathing and mooring boats. The Parkhurst families always shared the expense of maintaining the beach and the dock. They never restricted other cottage owners from the area, and always felt that they were a generous clan. This happy situation continued through the next two generations, which brings us to a few years ago.

Over time, more of the Parkhurst cottages had been sold. The various great grandchildren now own a total of 10 cottages, and still own the waterfront area in common. Thirty-four cottages are owned by persons not related to the Parkhursts. During the past decade, the assessment for dock repair has been divided up on a per cottage basis among the ten Parkhurst cottages.

Last summer, in the early morning hours of July 5, 62-year-old Randy Parkhurst walked down to the dock to enjoy the sunrise. When he got there, he saw that the dock had been totally trashed. There were many empty beer cans, and a broken wine bottle. He even found a pipe and a little baggie of marijuana. There were cans floating on the water. He was upset, to say the least. He lately felt like the young kids around Idlehurst were ruining the neighborhood with their loud music, lewd clothes, loud parties and rude ways. Randy called a meeting of his family, since many of them were down for the 4th of July holiday. After a discussion, they decided that they needed to assert control over their property. It was agreed that they would build a fence and gate for their dock, and along the waterfront. Only the Parkhurst clan members would have keys.

Construction started as soon as permits were received. When some of the neighbors saw what was happening, they were upset. Idlehurst owners were used to using the beach and the dock. Many of them felt that they had a right to use it. When the Parkhursts refused to back down, an angry group of Idlehurst residents hired a lawyer and sued for access to the water. They claimed that they had a right to access under various theories:

1. Adverse possession

2. Implied easement

3. Rights based upon the original grants when Mr. Parkhurst laid out the plan showing the lots and the dock.

4. Right of public access to the dock, based upon its history as a public dock.

The case is scheduled to be tried in 5 months. The parties have agreed to attempt mediation. In addition to the mediator, the mediation will involve one Parkhurst (Jamie) authorized to speak on behalf of the family; the Parkhurst lawyer; one Idlehurst resident (Terry Tomaselli) authorized to speak on behalf of the residents, and; the residents' lawyer.

EXERCISE 11.1
PRACTICING THE MEDIATION PROCESS
"THE NOT SO PLEASANT LAKE MEDIATION"

REFLECTION

Whether you represented a party or acted as mediator, ask yourself what you learned from this exercise:

1. In what ways and to what degree did the mediator facilitate the interaction?

2. What did the mediator do to minimize party conflict and induce the parties to explore the underlying issues in a mutually beneficial manner?

3. What did the mediator do that you did not find helpful?

4. What could the mediator have done to be more effective in assisting in the negotiation process?

5. In what ways did this experience differ from directly negotiating with the parties?

6. In what ways was this mediation different from Exercise 10.1?

7. To what extent did it make a difference to have parties in addition to lawyers?

EXERCISE 11.2
PRACTICING THE MEDIATION PROCESS
MULTI-PARTY MEDIATION

"THE MULTIPLE CAR ACCIDENT CASE"

GENERAL DESCRIPTION OF EXERCISE: Mediation of multiple vehicle accident claims.

SKILLS INVOLVED: Mediation.

PARTICIPANTS NEEDED: You will be assigned one of nine roles.

ESTIMATED TIME REQUIRED:

120 minutes for mediation and 30 minutes for discussion: 180 minutes

LEVEL OF DIFFICULTY (1-5):

ROLES IN EXERCISE: You are acting as a plaintiff, defendant, counsel for plaintiff, counsel for defendant, or the mediator.

THE EXERCISE

GENERAL INFORMATION
AVAILABLE TO ALL STUDENTS

You will be divided into groups of 9 — plaintiff Terry Gustaf, counsel for Plaintiff Gustaf, Plaintiff/Defendant Charlie Goshen, counsel for Plaintiff Goshen, counsel for Defendant Goshen, Defendant Dale Gustaf, counsel for Defendant Dale Gustaf, counsel for Defendant Fran Noonan (Fran Noonan will not appear in person), and the Mediator. Start by reading the general information below, including the mediation statements. After that, read the Confidential Information assigned to your role and follow the instructions that are provided.

General Information

Two years ago last February 13, defendant Fran Noonan was traveling by car to New York from New Hampshire non-stop into the night and fell asleep at the wheel. Noonan woke up when the vehicle began to leave the highway and was able to regain control of the car.

Two years ago last February 15, while returning to New Hampshire non-stop from New York, Noonan again fell asleep at the wheel sometime after 11 p.m. When Noonan fell asleep this time, the car was headed northbound on Interstate 93, a four-lane divided highway with two lanes in either direction. The vehicle struck the left guardrail, went across the road, struck the right guard rail, and then came to a stop while perpendicular to oncoming traffic and completely blocking the left travel (passing) lane. At the time of the crash, the weather was clear and the road was dry. Noonan woke up and left the vehicle where it came to rest without activating any lights. The location of the abandoned Noonan vehicle was shortly beyond a hill-top with respect to oncoming traffic. As a result, vehicles traveling over the hill in the passing lane had a limited opportunity to avoid the Noonan vehicle.

Dale Gustaf was driving a vehicle north on Interstate 93 and came upon the scene. Gustaf successfully avoided the Noonan vehicle, and then promptly pulled over on the right side of the road to investigate the accident. Gustaf parked in the breakdown lane off Interstate 93 near the exit to the Windham Weigh Station on Rt. 93. Gustaf used a cell phone to call 911 and got out of the car to render assistance. Gustaf had a passenger in the vehicle — Gutaf's 16 year-old child — Terry Gustaf. After Gustaf pulled over, several vehicles came upon the scene and navigated the situation without having an accident. While Dale Gustaf was still out of the vehicle, a car driven by Charlie Goshen was traveling North on Interstate 93. Goshen swerved to avoid the Noonan vehicle. Goshen lost control of the vehicle and it went into a roll, coming to a halt on top of the Gustaf vehicle. As a result of the Goshen vehicle landing on top of the Gustaf vehicle, Terry Gustaf was seriously injured, suffering a grade 3 concussion on a 3 scale. Terry was unconscious for a period of time, and had double vision and lethargy as well as decreased sensation to touch on the left side of the face.

Charlie Goshen was also injured. Goshen sustained a head injury and has no memory of the accident. In addition, Goshen had a large lump on the head, 4 fractured teeth, a sprained ankle, rib fractures and general bruising. Goshen claims ongoing symptoms from a traumatic brain injury.

Prior to the accident, Noonan had a lengthy history of erratic sleep and for years was regularly taking medication that included the side effect of drowsiness. Goshen was prescribed the medication by Dr. John Nether, a New York psychopharmacologist, who was managing Noonan's pharmacology.

Noonan provided blood samples at the hospital at 2:10 a.m. and 3:15 a.m. after the accident at the request of the police to check for drugs and alcohol. The tests were negative for drugs and alcohol.

In this matter, there are two plaintiffs and their cases have been consolidated for the purposes of discovery. The court has not yet ruled on whether the cases would be consolidated for trial, but it is likely. Terry Gustaf has brought a claim against Charlie Goshen and Fran Noonan. Goshen has brought a claim against Fran Noonan and Dale Gustaf. Each of the defendants has a lawyer hired by their insurance company under the terms of the insurance policy. Noonan has a policy with a single limit of $250,000. Gustaf has a policy with limits of $100,000 per person/$300,000 per accident. Goshen has a policy of $25,000 per person/$50,000 per accident. Each plaintiff has a lawyer retained for the purpose of pursuing the personal injury claim. Therefore, Goshen has an insurance defense lawyer to defend *and* a separate lawyer to pursue the personal injury claim. There are 4 parties and 5 lawyers.

The cases are in suit. New Hampshire is a comparative fault state. That is, the plaintiff can recover as long as his/her fault is not more than the combined fault of all other parties — including "parties" unnamed in the action. The recovery of a comparatively negligent plaintiff will be reduced by his/her percentage of fault. For example, if the jury finds for the plaintiff in the amount of $100,000, but also finds that the plaintiff's fault is 50%, the verdict will be reduced to $50,000. If the plaintiff is found to be 51% at fault, he/she will recover nothing. As another example, if the jury finds for the plaintiff in the amount of $100,000 and finds that the plaintiff is 25% at fault, the defendant is 50% at fault and a person unnamed in the action is 25% at fault, the plaintiff will recover $50,000.

MEDIATION STATEMENT OF PLAINTIFF TERRY GUSTAF

HILLSBOROUGH COUNTY   **SUPERIOR COURT**
NORTHERN DISTRICT

Sandy Gustaf, MNF of Terry Gustaf
v.
Charlie Goshen and Fran Noonan
216-2011-0000

MEDIATION SUMMARY OF PLAINTIFF TERRY GUSTAF

NOW COMES Terry Gustaf and submits the following Mediation Summary:

STATEMENT OF FACTS CONCERNING ACCIDENT

Terry Gustaf was a passenger in a vehicle being driven by parent Dale Gustaf, that was involved in a motor vehicle collision two years ago on February 15, at approximately 11:40 p.m. in Windham, New Hampshire, on Interstate 93. While traveling in the left hand lane Dale Gustaf noticed another vehicle bouncing from guardrail to guardrail and settling in the left hand lane. Dale Gustaf cut over to the right hand lane and pulled into the breakdown lane about 100 yards away from the disabled vehicle. The disabled vehicle was later determined to be operated by Fran Noonan who was traveling back from Long Island, New York to Southern New Hampshire University.

It was also later determined that Noonan had ingested certain pharmaceutical substances that had impaired Noonan's ability to drive a motor vehicle, which was further complicated by the fact that Noonan had commenced the motor vehicle trip back to New Hampshire on an insufficient amount of sleep. The New Hampshire State Trooper investigating this accident, Trooper Chris Rose, recorded in the Police Report that Noonan had fallen asleep while driving.

Dale Gustaf recalled in deposition that the Noonan vehicle was blocking the left hand lane of Interstate 93 and its lights were off. Dale Gustaf believed that the Gustaf vehicle was the first vehicle to pull over into the breakdown lane on the right hand side of Interstate 93 in order to possibly render assistance to Noonan. Dale Gustaf recalls that maybe one or two vehicles pulled up ahead of the Noonan vehicle after it was parked. Dale Gustaf exited the vehicle and dialed 911 on a cell phone, leaving Terry Gustaf in the vehicle parked on the right hand side of the road with its lights on and hazard lights activated. Dale Gustaf then walked towards the disabled Noonan vehicle on the right hand side of Interstate 93 and was able to speak to Noonan (who was out of the vehicle and on the side of the road) to ascertain whether Noonan was OK. Shortly thereafter, Charlie Goshen was also traveling northbound on Interstate 93 and came upon the scene. Because Goshen was driving at such a high rate of speed, Goshen was unable to safely navigate around the Noonan vehicle. Goshen apparently executed an emergency swerve around the Noonan vehicle causing the Goshen vehicle to roll over and collide with the Gustaf vehicle parked on the right hand side of the road. Dale Gustaf recalls that there were at least two or three other vehicles that had passed by the scene prior to Goshen arriving and crashing into the Gustaf vehicle and those vehicles had been able to safely avoid a collision with the Noonan vehicle or other vehicles like Gustaf's which were parked on the side of the road. The Gustaf vehicle was totaled and Terry Gustaf was severely injured.

Terry Gustaf asserts this case is governed by Marshall v. Nugent, 222 F. 2nd 604 (1st Cir., 1955). As cited in the Marshall case, Noonan negligently operated a vehicle in such a manner as to place the vehicle in a disabled position on Interstate 93 such that Noonan could reasonably be held liable for all subsequent collisions caused by the fact that the Noonan vehicle was blocking traffic and was not visible due to the fact that Noonan failed to activate hazard lights and had inexplicably turned off the running lights. Goshen is concurrently liable because all other drivers who came upon the disabled Noonan vehicle were able to avoid a collision with other vehicles. From this fact we can infer Goshen was traveling at too high a rate of speed given the nighttime and winter conditions on the section of Interstate 93 in question.

STATEMENT OF INJURIES TO TERRY GUSTAF

After seeing the Goshen vehicle crash into the Gustaf vehicle, Dale Gustaf raced back to find the Goshen vehicle resting on the rear left corner of the Gustaf vehicle. Terry Gustaf was unconscious in the front passenger seat. Emergency responders took Terry to the Parkland Medical Center, and it was Dale Gustaf's recollection that Terry remained unconscious until sometime after arrival at the emergency room.

At the Parkland Medical Center, in addition to receiving emergency treatment, Terry was seen by Dr. Jeffrey Rand. It was Dr. Rand's assessment that Terry Gustaf had suffered a significant concussion, grade 3 to grade 4, depending upon the rating system, but certainly the worst grade in either system. Terry was suffering from double-vision and lethargy as well as decreased sensation to light touch on the left side of the face. An MRI done on February 16 was interpreted by Dr. Rand as indicating a contusion of the corpus callosum on the right of the midline. Terry also complained of neck and back pain. X-rays were negative and further treatment was postponed because of the head injury.

Terry was discharged from the Parkland Medical Center on the 18th of February and later admitted to Northeast Rehabilitation for one day of rehabilitation treatment. Nearly a year later, on February 5, Terry was seen by a neurologist named Dr. Ronald Sprague. On physical exam Dr. Sprague detected slight abnormalities in Terry's right eyelid with the right pupil set slightly larger than the left and some limitation of the movement of the eyes. It was Dr. Sprague's assessment that Terry was recovering from traumatic brain injury and diplopia or double-vision.

Terry Gustaf began receiving chiropractic care for the neck and back injuries at Straight Chiropractic and those treatments continued from March 18 through August 26 on the year of the accident. Terry was seen for continuous speech and language therapy at the Southern New Hampshire Medical Center for more than a year. Terry was also seen by Joseph Romer, M.D. at the Massachusetts Eye and Ear Infirmary for a neuro opthomological evaluation. The first assessment by Dr. Romer two months post-accident found that Terry had traumatic brain injury; at his follow-up assessment a year later, Dr. Romer stated that it was his impression Terry had traumatic brain injury with residual right hypotropia with diplopia. This is the same assessment that Dr. Romer gave after a further follow up two years post-accident, that Terry still had traumatic brain injury with residual double-vision on the extremes of vision.

At the time of the accident Terry Gustaf was a junior at Banter High School. Terry was out of school for nearly five weeks. During that time Terry received speech and language therapy assistance from New Hampshire Medical Center. It was recommended that Terry receive a 504 accommodation plan and that plan was approved by the high school to provide Terry untimed and extended times for tests, a reduction of work load per course limitation, limitation on oral presentations, limiting team work to one partner, limiting homework to two hour blocks with teachers monitoring and encouraging walks, water, breaks, snacks to minimize fatigue.

Terry Gustaf received a comprehensive neurological assessment by Margaret Dana, PhD, and in her report eighteen months post-accident she concluded that although Terry had a history of having a learning disorder prior to the motor vehicle accident on February 15, it was her assessment that the continued problem with rapidly alternating attention was likely secondary to the traumatic brain injury from the motor vehicle accident. Dr. Dana did recommend continuing academic accommodations for Terry at UNH.

It is Terry's assessment that it takes a longer period of time to complete mental tasks since the accident and that it is harder to concentrate. Terry manages these problems as best as possible. As a result of the accident, with the exception of track and field, Terry did not return to any pre-accident sports at high school, which included lacrosse and basketball, because of the fear of having another concussion causing a more severe brain injury. Terry does continue to experience headaches when working on mental tasks for a long period of time. Terry feels it takes longer to do academic tasks because things have to be repeated more often. Terry continues to have double-vision when looking out of the corner of the eye and sometimes sees double when sitting at a desk and looking up at a screen. Generally, Terry Gustaf has been able to overcome or compensate for any difficulties and has worked hard to achieve a 3.5 grade point average at UNH.

Total medical expenses for Terry Gustaf are $49,809.42.

DEMAND

Terry Gustaf suffered a brain injury and other serious injuries that caused substantial pain and suffering and impacted on Terry's future quality of life. Demand is made against Noonan and Goshen in the total amount of $600,000.00. There has been no offer. This demand is made without prejudice and for the purpose of settlement discussions only.

Respectfully submitted,
By Terry Gustaf's attorneys,

Terry Gustaf

Date: _____

_____
(Attorney for Gustaf) NHBA #3333
9855 Apple Street
Manchester, NH 03104
(603) 668-0000

CERTIFICATE OF SERVICE

I hereby certify that on this date I emailed a copy of the above Mediation Summary for Plaintiff Terry Gustaf to all counsel of record and to the neutral mediator.

_____
Counsel for Terry Gustaf

MEDIATION STATEMENT OF DEFENDANT NOONAN IN GUSTAF CASE

STATE OF NEW HAMPSHIRE

Hillsborough, ss.   Superior Court
Northern District

Terry Gustaf
v.
Charlie Goshen and Fran Noonan
Docket #: 216-2011-CV-000

DEFENDANT, FRAN NOONAN'S MEDIATION SUMMARY

NOW COMES the Defendant, Fran Noonan, and respectfully submits the following MEDIATION SUMMARY pursuant to N.H. Superior Court Rule 170, without prejudice, and objects to its use for any other purpose.

STATEMENT OF THE FACTS:

This case is pending before the Hillsborough County Superior Court. The deposition of Charlie Goshen has been taken. Parties have exchanged and responded to interrogatories.

This suit arises from an accident which occurred two years ago February 15, in Windham, New Hampshire. Defendant, Fran Noonan, fell asleep while driving north on Interstate 93 at approximately 11:37 p.m. and was involved in a one vehicle accident in which the Noonan vehicle came to rest in the left hand lane.

Upon seeing Noonan's disabled vehicle, co-defendant Dale Gustaf, who had been travelling in the same direction as Noonan, pulled over into the right hand breakdown lane of I-93 N to see if Noonan needed assistance. Gustaf activated emergency flashers, stepped out of the Gustaf vehicle and was attempting to contact emergency personnel while the passenger, Plaintiff Terry Gustaf, remained in the vehicle. After several vehicles had driven by the Noonan vehicle, Goshen approached, swerved abruptly to the right to avoid the vehicle, lost control and proceeded to roll approximately 2-3 times, landing on the roof and rear compartment of Gustaf's vehicle. Goshen was able to exit the vehicle without assistance and was ambulating at the scene.

DAMAGES:

Injuries and Treatment:

Terry Gustaf claims to have the following injuries as a result of the motor vehicle accident: upper back, neck and head injuries with loss of consciousness, vision problems and short term memory loss as well as cognitive dysfunction.

Gustaf was brought by ambulance to Parkland Medical Center early morning on February 16, and was treated for a concussion and diplopia (double vision.) Gustaf was discharged on February 18 with orders of no lifting, no running and no driving. Gustaf was referred to outpatient neuro-rehabilitation.

Gustaf was seen at Northeast Rehab Health Network on February 19, where prognosis was reported as excellent. Gustaf was told to wear an eye patch on alternating eyes to assist with the diplopia.

At Gustaf's March 5 neurology appoint with Dr. Sprague, less than a month after the accident, he noted the patient was improving and that the diplopia occurred with up and down gaze, but not lateral gaze. Gustaf was eager to go to school and participate in activities. No difficulty with balance or coordination was noted. Dr. Sprague stated that other than the diplopia, which was improving, Gustaf was virtually asymptomatic. Gustaf was released to resume activity, return to school for half days. Gustaf was restricted from playing lacrosse and contact sports but was otherwise free to participate in athletics.

In the meantime, Gustaf attended 6 therapy sessions. The March 18 therapy notes indicate the patient was making rapid gains and was not having double vision, even at night. Gustaf continued with a busy social life going to the mall without difficulty and planning for track, running cross-country. By March 26, about six weeks after the accident, Gustaf reported no difficulty while presenting a speech at school. Gustaf had almost complete resolution of symptoms and only noticed diplopia with extreme upward or downward gaze. No further physical therapy was recommended and Gustaf was discharged.

In March, about 5 weeks post-accident, Gustaf had an evaluation for speech language rehabilitation. At this testing Gustaf indicated concern about a slower reading rate, which was not a new problem. When young, Gustaf needed speech therapy and reading help as early as kindergarten. It was recommended the patient have a 504 School Accommodation Plan in place to modify the work load, accommodate learning needs with testing and projects as well as be given additional time to accomplish tasks and take home tests. This plan was put in place at school in May following the accident. An SAT prep course was also recommended to assist in learning test-taking skills and strategies (no course was taken). Gustaf was referred to a neuro-optometrist for reassessment of visual tracking vs. reading rate differences. Speech and language therapy was also recommended, though Gustaf did not follow through on this treatment and recommendation until August.

At an April 9 neuro-ophthalmological consult less than 2 months post-accident, Gustaf reported that the diplopia had resolved 2 weeks prior and had not returned. Gustaf's parents reported that functioning was almost back to baseline. The exam was normal with the exception of a small left hypertropia in upgaze to the right but given that the patient was asymptomatic it was felt there was no need to address this small misalignment.

In August following the accident, Gustaf returned for speech and language therapy after not having been seen since the March evaluation. Gustaf attributes the gap in treatment to a decision to take the summer off and also due to family illnesses. At this point in time, Gustaf's mother wanted Terry re-assessed partially due to the fact that Terry did not want an IEP plan in place at school. Gustaf was retested and the scores had improved since spring testing. In the spring Gustaf had tested "baseline normal" but now had an 11 point gain and was scoring "average normal." Though Gustaf continued to test within normal limits and managed to do well at school, speech and language therapy continued and focused on SAT preparation and college essay writing.

Throughout the school year Gustaf managed to hold on to a busy school schedule and social life while maintaining a 3.13 GPA in school. It is important to note that at the pre-accident baseline Gustaf was an A-B student. Now, upon return to school, not only did Gustaf have a heavy course load, but also participated in the following activities and events during the school year:

*   math and robotics team;
*   community service at a local elementary school;
*   part-time at the Info Center;
*   track and field;
*   a very active social life, going out with friends on Friday nights;
*   a rock concert in November;
*   SATs in October and November;
*   ACTs in December;
*   part-time work in the high school library;
*   30 weekly speech and language therapy sessions to assist with organization and executive functioning;
*   applied to colleges

By October, it was reported that Gustaf's reading skills were closer to pre-morbid levels and by January the following year Gustaf's mother felt Terry was 90% back on track. Throughout the speech and language therapy sessions Gustaf's overloaded school and social calendar were continually addressed as the late nights and long hours were causing fatigue. Gustaf was continually urged by medical providers and parents to make better use of time for school work.

Upon discharge from speech and language therapy, Gustaf was urged to develop goals for a 504 plan at college and to register with the Study Support Center at college, neither of which was followed through on.

A neuro-ophthalmological exam 15 months post-accident showed Gustaf to be doing well with no diplopia or change in vision. Neither Terry nor the parents noted any cognitive impairment. Terry's exam was normal except for the right hypotropia in upgaze with a slight limitation of elevation of the right eye in abduction. The exam was stable and no further neuroradiographic workup was recommended. Given that Terry was asymptomatic, there was no need to address the continued small misalignment.

At a psychology/neuropsychology evaluation 15 months post-accident, it was again documented that the diplopia resulting from the motor vehicle accident had resolved. During this evaluation Terry's prior developmental history was reviewed. It was noted that early in Gustaf's developmental stages there had been some issues with language delay and Terry had received early intervention. Terry had Title 1 Programming for reading and language arts in kindergarten through 3rd grade. In addition, Terry was monitored because of concerns about varying levels of attention. At this evaluation, Gustaf reported to Dr. David that Gustaf currently had a significant problem with spelling and was always a slow reader. Despite this, Terry had always maintained A and B grades with a lot of hard work. Also noted was a family history of ADHD and learning issues.

Dr. David concluded that Gustaf's developmental history suggested learning difficulties early on in elementary school which continued to manifest. He suspected that what Terry was experiencing was residual from a learning disorder. The continued difficulty with rapid word retrieval was consistent with a history of reading difficulties from earlier in childhood. While math and problem solving skills were in the high average to above average range, reading and writing skills had always been a problem area for Terry. Because of this, Dr David said it was unknown whether the results of the neuro-psych testing stemmed from a learning disorder, or from the motor vehicle accident. He suggested Terry have appropriate college level accommodations including a reduced course load while in college.

Gustaf graduated high school on time with a 3.3 GPA, grades ranging from A+ to B- and had served 42 community service hours. Terry began classes at UNH the next fall and had a 3.83 GPA during the first semester. Terry did not use the resources available at college, such as the Study Support Center recommended by the therapist and Dr. Davis, though Terry did reportedly file paperwork allowing additional time for tests. As of the fall semester of sophomore year, Gustaf was maintaining a 3.66 GPA.

Medical Specials:

The plaintiff is claiming medical specials of approximately $51,126.75. There is no claim for lost wages.

Conclusion:

Terry Gustaf claims to be suffering from lingering problems of diplopia (double vision) but medicals since 5 weeks post-accident have indicated that the double vision has resolved. Gustaf has a history of a reading disability and has always had to work hard at school. Since the accident, Terry has continued to do well in school and is an A-B college student with a 3.6 GPA. Terry has opted not to use the Study Support Center resources which are readily available. Gustaf has made an excellent recovery and is no longer treating.

> Respectfully submitted,
> Fran Noonan
> By Fran Noonan's Attorneys,

Date: _____

> By: _____/s/_____
> Attorney
> NH Bar No. 9999

1838 Apple Street
Manchester, NH 03104
(603) 668-0000

CERTIFICATE OF SERVICE

I hereby certify that a copy of the within Mediation Summary has this day been sent to all counsel of record and the neutral mediator.

/s/

Attorney for Noonan, Esq.

MEDIATION STATEMENT OF DEFENDANT GOSHEN IN GUSTAF CASE

THE STATE OF NEW HAMPSHIRE

HILLSBOROUGH, ss   SUPERIOR COURT
Northern District

Docket #11-CV-000

Terry Gustaf
v.
Charlie Goshen and Fran Noonan

CHARLIE GOSHEN'S MEDIATION SUMMARY

NOW COMES Charlie Goshen, and hereby submits the following Mediation Summary:

1. This personal injury action arises from a motor vehicle collision that occurred late at night two years ago on February 15 on Interstate 93 north in Windham, New Hampshire. Gustaf was following a vehicle being operated by Fran Noonan. Gustaf witnessed Noonan carom off of two guardrails, coming to rest in the left travel lane — blocking the entire left lane of travel. Gustaf pulled the Gustaf car over into the breakdown lane to assist Noonan, who had fallen asleep at the wheel. Terry Gustaf was in the front passenger seat of the Gustaf vehicle. At the same time, Terry Goshen, who was operating a vehicle on Interstate 93 northbound, came upon Noonan's vehicle in the dark, without lights on, and apparently swerved to avoid hitting Noonan. Goshen then lost control and crashed into Gustaf's vehicle, which was parked in the breakdown lane.

2. Fault for this accident rests primarily with Noonan, who fell asleep at the wheel and crashed just past a curve in the highway. Although Charlie Goshen has no memory of this accident because of head trauma, the evidence shows that as Goshen came around a bend in the road Goshen was confronted with an emergency situation and reacted instinctively by swerving to the right to avoid striking the Noonan vehicle. Unfortunately, Goshen lost control and the vehicle rolled, coming to rest on top of the Gustaf vehicle, which was parked in the breakdown lane in an unsafe position. Gustaf, by parking in the breakdown lane so close to the Noonan vehicle, caused any approaching vehicle to thread the needle to pass through the crash site.

3. At trial, Goshen will be entitled to sudden emergency and/or instinctive action instructions that will instruct the jury that Goshen cannot be found at fault for actions in trying to avoid the collision with the Noonan vehicle.

4. Although no one knows exactly how fast Goshen's vehicle was traveling at the time of this accident, Charles LaPonte, a motor vehicle accident reconstructionist, has performed an investigation and rendered an opinion that Goshen would have had to be

traveling less than 40 mph in the high speed lane of travel to have sufficient perception and reaction time to avoid this collision.

5. Since 40 mph is the minimum speed allowed at that section of Interstate 93, no reasonable juror could find Mr. Goshen at fault for this accident.

6. Terry Gustaf was injured in the accident and sustained a mild traumatic brain injury with loss of consciousness. Gustaf initially presented with some cognitive deficits that resolved within a couple of days. Gustaf had some residual problems with double vision, which reportedly resolved about 5 weeks post-accident, and balance issues, for which Gustaf sought physical therapy. Gustaf also treated with physical therapy and chiropractic for a period of time to address some neck stiffness and back pain following the accident.

7. Terry Gustaf was released to return to school for half days in early March following the accident. Once Terry returned, there was reportedly some difficulty with organization and management of the course load because of the traumatic brain injury. Terry was evaluated by a speech language pathologist who recommended instituting a Section 504 accommodation plan at school that would allow extra time and modify assignments, etc. Terry did not seek regular speech/language pathology therapy until August following the accident. Testing indicated that Terry had problems with reading rate and vocabulary based on age. However, Terry did have a pre-existing reading disorder since childhood. The speech/language therapy sessions consisted of vocabulary building, organizational skills, SAT preparation and practice writing essays for college applications. It was strongly recommended that Terry get established with the center for learning disabilities at UNH to ensure success in college.

8. Terry underwent a neuropsychological evaluation about 15 months post-accident. The evaluator assessed Terry as having a "residual language based learning disorder affecting reading and writing expression," some of which may have been exacerbated by the head injury. However, the report noted that it would be difficult to ascertain what features of the neuropsychological evaluation were residual from the learning disorder, and what might represent changes in cognitive functioning from pre-accident abilities. The evaluator did think that the issue of rapidly alternating attention was more likely to be a result of the head injury.

9. Terry is claiming approximately $39,586.92 in medical bills. Gustaf is not making a claim for lost wages.

10. Terry Gustaf fully recovered from the effects of this accident and is excelling at the University of New Hampshire with a 3.5 grade point average.

> Respectfully submitted,
> Charlie Goshen
> By Charlie Goshen's attorneys,

Dated: _____

By: _____ /s/ _____

Attorney NH Bar #7777
175 River Street
Manchester, NH 03101
(603) 612-0012

CERTIFICATE OF SERVICE

I hereby certify that on this day, a copy of the within was forwarded electronically to all counsel of record and to the neutral mediator.

_____/s/_____
Attorney for Goshen

MEDIATION STATEMENT OF PLAINTIFF CHARLIE GOSHEN

STATE OF NEW HAMPSHIRE

HILLSBOROUGH, ss.   SUPERIOR COURT
                                               216-2010-CV-00000

CHARLIE GOSHEN
v.
DALE GUSTAF AND FRAN NOONAN

PLAINTIFF, CHARLIE GOSHEN'S MEDIATION SUMMARY

NOW COMES the Plaintiff, Charlie Goshen, and submits the following mediation summary pursuant to Superior Court Rule 170:

FACTS AND LIABILITY

Charlie Goshen was 43 years old at the time of the accident. Charlie is single and resides in Allenstown, New Hampshire.

Charlie earned a BA from St. Anslem's College in Manchester. Since graduation, Charlie has worked at Bowling Lanes in Allenstown. At the time of the accident, Charlie was the League and Marketing Supervisor, which involved mostly desk work, outside sales, and mechanical work. Charlie was earning $1,344.00 per week.

MEDICAL HISTORY

Charlie Goshen was in very good health at the time of the accident. There was no history of smoking, alcohol or recreational drug use. Charlie had no surgical history.

Prior to the accident, Charlie enjoyed golf, and performed the usual household duties and yard work. There were no orthopedic restrictions. In short, Charlie was in overall good health.

FACTS OF THE CRASH

The crash occurred two years ago on February 15, while Charlie was traveling north on Route 93 in Windham, NH. Charlie had just finished work at 11:00 p.m. and was headed home. Defendant Fran Noonan ("Noonan") moments earlier had been traveling north on Route 93 and fell asleep, crashed off two guard rails and ended up in the left travel lane at 11:37 p.m. Noonan's vehicle had no lights on and it was completely dark at the crash scene. Charlie, traveling within the speed limit of 65 mph, approached by turning to the right on a curve and going over a hill so that the view of Noonan was impaired. In a last-second attempt to avoid crashing into Noonan's vehicle, Charlie swerved to the right and lost control of the motor vehicle which rolled over and collided with the automobile operated by Defendant Dale Gustaf ("Gustaf") which was parked in the right breakdown lane.

The evidence will show that Noonan had taken an unorthodox and unauthorized psychotropic cocktail of Tesretrol (800 mg), Klonopin (.5 mg), and Zoloft (100 mg) prior to the accident.

The New Hampshire investigating officer, Trooper Chris Rose, placed fault squarely upon Noonan. His report stated in part:

> "Vehicle 1 fell asleep while driving in the left hand lane and left the roadway, striking the guard rail along the left side of the roadway. Vehicle 1 then moved across both marked lanes of travel and struck the guard rail along the right side of the roadway. Vehicle 1 came to rest in the left lane of Interstate 93 northbound, blocking the entire lane of travel . . . As a result of this crash, a subsequent crash occurred wherein a vehicle attempted to avoid Vehicle 1, which was blocking the left lane of travel, lost control and rolled over onto a second vehicle which was parked in the breakdown lane . . . Based on the investigation of the crash scene, the driver of Vehicle 1 was found to be at fault for causing the crash, and the subsequent crash . . . The driver of Vehicle 1, who had admitted to falling asleep and leaving the roadway, was found to be in violation of RSA 265:22."

Trooper Rose estimated Goshen approached Noonan's vehicle in the left hand lane at 11:39 p.m. Noonan's vehicle had no lights on and it was dark. Goshen also approached by turning to the right on a curve and going over a hill so view was impaired. In fact, Windham Police Officer Brian Smyth, when responding to the accident and already aware of the location of the Noonan vehicle, reported that he barely missed Noonan's vehicle because it was impossible to see it due to the curve, hill and darkness.

In addition to the obvious negligence of Noonan, Dale Gustaf bears responsibility. As Charlie explained during deposition, the location of the Gustaf vehicle made it necessary to attempt a sharp swerve around the Noonan vehicle. As motor vehicle accident reconstructionist Robert G. Laton will testify, the combination of the location of the Noonan vehicle and the Gustaf vehicle made it nearly impossible for Charlie Goshen to avoid this crash while going the authorized speed limit of 65 m.p.h., and the fault thereof rests solely on Defendants Noonan and Gustaf.

DAMAGES

As a result of the collision, Officer Rose reported (with regard to Goshen):

> "the driver of Vehicle 2 sustained a head injury. The driver was unable to remember anything about the crash, had a bloody nose, and was complaining of pain to the ribs, left ankle, and neck."

At the hospital, Charlie underwent a plethora of x-rays and scans. Charlie spent approximately six hours at the hospital because of injuries, diagnostic studies and treatment. Charlie was in significant pain and was prescribed Vicodin and Zofran. Charlie was diagnosed with head injury, multiple rib fractures (left 4th and 5th). Injuries also consisted of a large lump on the head, 4 smashed/fractured teeth, and a severely sprained ankle that required crutches for 2 weeks. In addition, Charlie's neck was very stiff and hurt for many months after the accident.

Throughout the months of June, July, August and September following the accident, Charlie underwent a total of eleven (11) post and core, root canal and crown procedures for broken and fractured teeth. During that four month period, Charlie could not eat solid food and suffered significant pain and discomfort.

Three months after the accident, Charlie's primary care physician, Dr. Khalil Khan, reported in part: "The patient was taken to the ER at Parkland, was diagnosed with 2 fractured ribs and multiple bruises from head to toe. Patient was on pain meds and it took 7-8 weeks before the pain subsided. Patient was regaining normal activities slowly. Patient continues to have pain with bending over anteriorly and when carrying objects with arms extended, . . . persistent rib pain vs neuropathic pain vs de-conditioned, will start high dose NSAIDS for 2 weeks and then stop, if still persist may consider referral to ortho for further eval and management."

Charlie returned to see Dr. Khan as instructed. There was no improvement. The physician reported: "The patient was placed on high dose NSAIDS for 2 weeks and stopped. Patient continues to have pain in the sternum with bending forward and with attempts to lift anything with arms extended straight in front . . . rib pain . . . persistent pain . . . will refer to ortho and follow recommendations."

Gradually Charlie's condition improved, but there has not been a complete recovery. Eighteen months post-accident, Charlie visited an orthopedic specialist who reported: "Today patient reports mild dull aching pain predominately over the left sternal border, which is noted when patient bends over. Patient also has pain when lifting something heavy with arms outstretched in front. Patient has had some difficulty sleeping and, therefore, has been sleeping in a recliner. At worst the pain is 3/10 on the pain scale . . . Assessment: rib sprain/strain, possible costochondritis on the left side . . . consideration may be given to trigger point injection to the tender areas."

Costochronditis is an inflammation of the cartilage that connects a rib to the breast bone (sternum). It causes short pain in the costesternal joint and/or dull and gnawing pain, usually on the left side. The only treatment is to ease the pain while waiting for costochronditis to improve on its own.

SPECIAL DAMAGES

As a result of the injuries sustained by Charlie Goshen, a total of $26,505.55 were incurred. The detailed breakdown has been provided to all counsel.

LOST WAGES

At the time of the accident, Charlie Goshen was salaried at the rate of $1,344.00 per week. According to Charlie's employer, Bowling Lanes, Charlie was absent from work from February 16, to March 1, and worked half days from March 2 to March 16. **Total lost wages are $4,002.00.**

EVALUATION

As to the question of damages, in addition to the special damages stated above, we have taken into consideration Charlie Goshen's traumatic emergency room and hospitalization experience lasting over 6 hours on February 16, plus extreme pain, not only with the head to toe bruises, soft tissue injuries, but fractured ribs, and extensive dental repair work. We have also considered the residual pain that Charlie still has although admittedly on a more occasional basis than before.

DEMAND: $250,000 without prejudice
OFFER: None as of this date.

Dated:_____

Respectfully submitted,
CHARLIE GOSHEN
By Charlie Goshen's attorneys

_____/s/_____
(Attorney for Goshen) NHBA #2222
9800 Peach Street
Manchester, NH 03104
(603) 666-0000

CERTIFICATE OF SERVICE

I, (Attorney for Charlie Goshen), hereby certify that on this date I emailed a copy of the above Mediation Summary for Plaintiff Charlie Goshen, to all counsel of record and to the neutral mediator.

_____/s/_____
Counsel for Charlie Goshen

MEDIATION STATEMENT OF DEFENDANT FRAN NOONAN IN GOSHEN CASE

STATE OF NEW HAMPSHIRE

Hillsborough, ss.   Superior Court
Northern District

Charlie Goshen
v.
Fran Noonan and Dale Gustaf
Docket No: 216-2011-CV-0000

DEFENDANT, FRAN NOONAN'S MEDIATION SUMMARY

NOW COMES the Defendant, Fran Noonan, and respectfully submits the following MEDIATION SUMMARY pursuant to N.H. Superior Court Rule 170, without prejudice, and objects to its use for any other purpose.

STATEMENT OF THE FACTS:

This case is pending before the Hillsborough County Superior Court. The deposition of Charlie Goshen has been taken. Parties have exchanged and responded to interrogatories.

This suit arises from an accident which occurred two years ago February 15, in Windham, New Hampshire. Defendant, Fran Noonan, fell asleep while driving north on Interstate 93 at approximately 11:37 p.m. and was involved in a one vehicle accident in which the Noonan vehicle came to rest in the left hand lane.

Upon seeing Noonan's disabled vehicle, co-defendant Dale Gustaf, who had been travelling in the same direction as Noonan, pulled over into the right hand breakdown lane of I-93 N to see if Noonan needed assistance. Gustaf activated emergency flashers, stepped out of the Gustaf vehicle and was attempting to contact emergency personnel while the passenger, Plaintiff Terry Gustaf, remained in the vehicle. After several vehicles had driven by the Noonan vehicle, Goshen approached, swerved abruptly to the right to avoid the vehicle, lost control and proceeded to roll approximately 2-3 times, landing on the roof and rear compartment of Gustaf's vehicle. Goshen was able to exit the vehicle without assistance and was ambulating at the scene.

DAMAGES:

Injuries and Treatment:

At the scene of the accident, Goshen initially refused treatment but was convinced by Derry Fire and EMS to be checked out at the emergency room. Goshen was transported to Parkland Medical Center and was diagnosed with 2 fractured ribs and a head injury. Goshen was released the same day.

More than a year later, Goshen met with primary care provider Dr. Shamin for persistent rib pain. Goshen was treated with NSAIDs. Dr. Shamin referred Goshen to an ortho for further evaluation.

It was not until eighteen months post-accident that Goshen consulted with Dr. Batlivala for mild pain on the left side of the sternum when bending over or lifting with outstretched arms. X-rays did not reveal any issues and no treatment other than basic stretching and strengthening were recommended. No other doctor's visits have taken place since this appointment.

In the few years prior to the accident, Goshen had been seeing a dentist regularly, correcting teeth that needed posts and crowns or other repairs. Just two months prior to this accident, Goshen's dentist made a treatment plan of the teeth that needed repair or treatment which included 15 out of Goshen's 21 teeth. Included on this chart were upper front teeth 2-1, 1-1, 1-2 (also known as 7, 8, 9) all needing root canals, post/core and crowns. When Dr. Ferramo called Goshen's house coincidently a few days after the accident to report on the cost estimate for a tooth needing repair, Goshen informed him that Goshen had injured teeth in an accident and would need these teeth looked at prior to the crown repair Dr. Ferramo was calling about.

Only days after the call, Dr. Ferramo wrote up an insurance estimate that included work on the four upper front teeth, 1-2, 1-1, 2-1 and 2-2 (also known as teeth 7, 8, 9 and 10). His treatment plan for these teeth was identical to the pre-accident treatment plan, with the exception of tooth #10. Tooth #10 had previous root canal, post/core and crown treatment and was not on the earlier list.

Goshen made no complaints to any of the EMS attendants at the scene of the accident regarding an injury to teeth, nor is there any injury of that type recorded in the emergency room records. Goshen's teeth 7, 8 and 9 were scheduled for root canal, post/core and crown treatment prior to the accident taking place. Further, there is no indication that Goshen's tooth #10 was injured in the accident requiring it to have a replacement crown. Therefore, the defendant Noonan disputes the dental bills Plaintiff Goshen has claimed in this incident.

Past Medical History:

Goshen's history is significant for extensive ongoing dental treatment.

Medical Specials:

The plaintiff is claiming medical specials of approximately $26,505.55. This total includes $7,050 in dental treatment.

Goshen's lost wage claim totals $4,002.00.

Conclusion:

There is no question that Goshen did in fact sustain 2 fractured ribs on the night of the accident. However, that a total of 2 doctors' visits in the years since the accident took place proves that Goshen has been well enough to continue day to day activities without any lingering problems. The last of the 2 visits occurred just 2 months prior to filing suit in this matter. What does draw a red flag is the fact that Goshen is claiming the $7,050 incurred in dental fees to be related to this incident, with no medical records following the accident to prove Goshen had sustained any dental injuries. Further, this dental work was already scheduled to take place prior to the accident even occurring.

Many vehicles came upon the Noonan crash and were able to slow down and drive between the Noonan and Gustaf vehicles safely. Goshen's speed and/or inattentiveness contributed to the inability to keep the vehicle in control, which ultimately caused the injury. Goshen created an emergency situation by failing to slow down and by failing to be on the lookout for an accident when it was easy to observe several cars parked in the breakdown lane including Gustaf's which had its emergency flashers activated. Goshen was the only driver whose car flipped over on the night in question. A jury will undoubtedly conclude that Goshen was inattentive and speeding. It is difficult to come to any other conclusion.

Respectfully submitted,
Fran Noonan
By Fran Noonan's Attorneys,

Dated: _____

By: _____/s/_____
Attorney
NH Bar No. 9999
1838 Plum Street
Manchester, NH 03104
(603) 634-0003

CERTIFICATE OF SERVICE

I hereby certify that a copy of the within Mediation Summary has this day been sent electronically to all counsel of record and the neutral mediator.

_____/s/_____
Attorney for Noonan, Esq.

MEDIATION STATEMENT OF DEFENDANT DALE GUSTAF IN GOSHEN CASE

THE STATE OF NEW HAMPSHIRE

HILLSBOROUGH, ss   SUPERIOR COURT
Northern District

Charlie G. Goshen
v.
Fran Noonan
and
Dale Gustaf
216-2010-CV-00000

MEDIATION SUMMARY OF DEFENDANT
DALE GUSTAF

NOW COMES defendant Dale Gustaf and submits the following statement in anticipation of the mediation in these matters:

Facts: Two years ago, on February 15, at approximately 11:30 PM defendant Gustaf was driving a vehicle northbound on Interstate 93 in Londonderry, NH, with Terry Gustaf riding in the front passenger seat. Defendant observed a car traveling in front (later determined to have been driven by defendant Fran Noonan) bouncing from one guard rail to the other, eventually coming to rest perpendicular to traffic flow in the left of the two northbound travel lanes. The defendant slowed down and passed the stopped Noonan vehicle and parked in the right breakdown lane about 100 yards beyond the Noonan car, leaving the motor running, headlights on, and activating the flashers to warn approaching traffic of the danger. Terry Gustaf stayed in the car. Defendant then called 911on a cell phone to report the accident and walked down the breakdown lane toward the Noonan car to see if Noonan needed assistance. Meanwhile, somewhere between two and seven northbound vehicles came upon and through the scene without losing control, and one or two of them of them pulled over and parked beyond Gustaf's car in order to be of assistance. One of them was operated by witness Karen Cantor, who (as she related to the investigating trooper) pulled into the breakdown lane herself and stopped to render aid, just as Dale Gustaf had. As Cantor and defendant Gustaf walked toward the Noonan car to determine if Noonan needed help, both Cantor and Gustaf (who was still on the cell phone with the 911 operator) saw the vehicle operated by defendant Goshen approach the scene from the south, lose control as it passed by them and flip onto the roof of the Gustaf car parked in the breakdown lane, causing physical injury to passenger Terry Gustaf. Charlie Goshen also sustained physical injury in the impact with the Gustaf car.

Liability: Dale Gustaf has been sued by Charlie Goshen on the theory that Gustaf's actions on the night in question did not meet the standard of ordinary care and were the proximate cause of injuries sustained by Goshen. Terry Gustaf has not brought suit against Dale Gustaf.

The injuries in this case were the proximate result of the loss of vehicular control by Fran Noonan and/or Charlie Goshen, for which Dale Gustaf bears no legal liability. The actions of motorists encountering the Noonan accident scene, even as it appeared after Gustaf had parked in the breakdown lane and was walking with others back to the Noonan car, prove that the scene could have been, and was, encountered safely and without loss of vehicular control by oncoming traffic. Several cars came upon, and through, the Noonan accident scene without incident, and even stopped to offer aid, as did Gustaf. These other people have not been joined as defendants. Only Goshen lost control, and Goshen has no recollection of the accident.

Dale Gustaf's actions on the night in question were reasonable and responsible under all the circumstances and did nothing to cause Goshen's loss of control. The only thing Dale Gustaf could have done differently that might conceivably have prevented the injuries to Gustaf's child, Terry Gustaf, was to have ignored the plight of distressed fellow motorist Noonan and to have kept on driving. The law does not require a motorist to turn an indifferent eye toward the predicament of others on the highway. While there may be no clearly defined statutory or common law duty of a motorist to stop and render aid to a fellow motorist in need of it (but see, e.g., *Soule v. Stuyvesent Insurance Co*, 116 N.H. 595 (1976)) nevertheless Gustaf's actions in so doing cannot be said to reflect a lack of ordinary care. Gustaf acted with prudence and circumspection in light of all the circumstances and none of Gustaf's actions were proximately causal of any injury.

Respectfully submitted,
DALE GUSTAF
By Dale Gustaf's attorneys,

Date: _____

By_____
(Attorney for Dale Gustaf)
74 Proctor Street
Newmarket, N.H. 03857
(603) 293-0000
NH Bar #6666

State of New Hampshire
Rockingham, s.s.

I hereby certify that I have this day electronically forwarded a copy of the foregoing to all opposing counsel of record and the neutral mediator.

_____
(Attorney for Gustaf)

EXERCISE 11.2
PRACTICING THE MEDIATION PROCESS
MULTI-PARTY MEDIATION
"THE MULTIPLE CAR ACCIDENT CASE"

REFLECTION

Whether you were a party, represented a party, or acted as mediator, ask yourself what you learned from this exercise:

1. In what ways and to what degree did the mediator facilitate the interaction?

2. What did the mediator do to minimize party conflict and induce the parties to explore the underlying issues in a mutually beneficial manner?

3. What did the mediator do that you did not find helpful?

4. What could the mediator have done to be more effective in assisting in the negotiation process?

5. In what ways did this experience differ from directly negotiating with the parties?

6. In what ways was this mediation different from Exercises 10.1 and 11.1?

7. To what extent did it make a difference to have parties in addition to lawyers *and* two lawyers with different interests representing the same client?

Part Three

COLLABORATIVE LAW

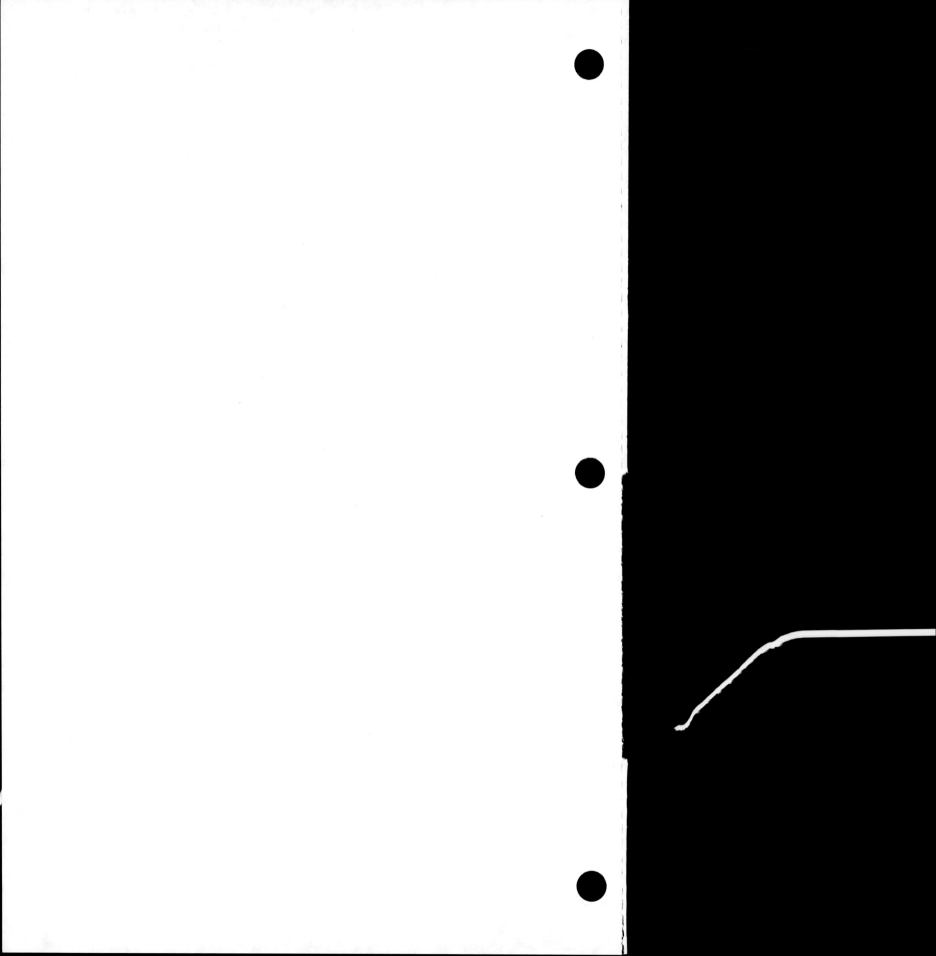

Chapter 12

INTRODUCTION TO COLLABORATIVE LAW

We encourage you to read this in conjunction with the **LexisNexis Webcourse** for this chapter where you will find video examples and other supplemental materials.

A. WHAT IS COLLABORATIVE LAW?

Collaborative law is a unique form of resolving disputes. Clients are represented by lawyers. There is usually no mediator or other third party. The parties and lawyers commit that they will collaborate in resolving the conflict using ***cooperative strategies***. The lawyers and parties agree that, if the case is not resolved through collaboration, the lawyers involved in the collaboration (and the lawyers' firms) will NOT represent the clients in litigation or other adversarial proceedings.[1]

B. HISTORY OF COLLABORATIVE LAW

The concept of collaborative law was developed by Stuart G. Webb, a Minnesota attorney who gave up his trial practice in 1990 to devote himself exclusively to a "family law settlement practice."[2] (Emphasis in original.) This later became known as a Cooperative Law Practice, or "CLP." Although the use of this approach is still most commonly seen in matters involving family law, it is also available for all types of civil matters.[3] Two decades later, Attorney Webb's idea has spread to almost all states in the U.S., most of the Canadian provinces, and over 20 countries around the world.[4] There is now an International Academy of Collaborative Professionals which is very active.[5]

---

[1] *See generally* Pauline H. Tessler, Collaborative Law: Achieving Effective Resolution in Divorce Without Litigation (A.B.A. Sect. of Family Law 2d ed. 2008); Forest S. Mosten, *Collaborative Law Practice: An Unbundled Approach to Informed Client Decision Making*, 2008 J. Disp. Res. 163 (2008); Richard W. Shields, *On Becoming a Collaborative Law Professional: From Paradigm Shifting to Transformative Learning Through Critical Reflection and Dialogue* 2008 J. Disp. Res. 427 (2008).

[2] Letter from Stuart G. Webb to The Honorable A.M. "Sandy" Keith, Justice, Minnesota Supreme Court, February 14, 1990. Copy of letter on file with author.

[3] Massachusetts Collaborative Law Council website http://www.massclc.org/civil-practice.php, last viewed 4/25/12.

[4] *Id.* http://www.massclc.org/about-collaborative.php, last viewed 4/25/12.

[5] https://www.collaborativepractice.com/_t.asp?M=3&T=About, last viewed 5/9/12.

At this point in its development, "collaborative law is governed by a patchwork of state laws, state Supreme Court rules, local rules, and ethic opinions."[6] In an attempt to provide uniformity and in recognition of the fact that collaborative law has become a significant method of dispute resolution, the Uniform Law Commission (ULC) has drafted a Uniform Collaborative Law Rules/Act (UCLR/A).[7] The history of this proposed act is a good case study in how change occurs in the legal profession – often with substantial resistance from the traditional bar. The UCLR/A has the support of the Section of Dispute Resolution of the American Bar Association but has thus far failed to gain the full support of the ABA House of Delegates.[8] Even without the ABA's blessing, the Act has been introduced in a number of state legislatures and has already been adopted in several states.[9]

C. THE LIKELY FUTURE OF COLLABORATIVE LAW DURING YOUR CAREER

It is likely that the Uniform Collaborative Law Rules/Act will continue to spread even without the ABA's full endorsement. Whether or not it does, collaborative practice is here to stay. Lawyers who practice family law will need to know how to do it or turn clients away who want to use the approach. More and more, other areas of practice will probably turn to the collaborative process. As Collaborative Practice California[10] notes, collaborative practice is an approach to apply "to disputes involving employment law, probate law, construction law, real property law, and other civil law areas where the participants are likely to have continuing relationships after the current conflict has been resolved."[11] The Civil Resolution Section of the Massachusetts Collaborative Law Council states:

> Civil disputes are particularly well-suited to resolution through the Collaborative Law process. While almost all court cases settle, civil disagreements (such as business disputes, workplace and employment disputes, landlord-tenant matters, and probate contests), need not begin in the court system, as they do not require a court-mandated resolution. The Civil Resolution Section is committed to the intentional pursuit of settlement of business disputes as the positive, beneficial outcome of legal representation through Collaborative Law.[12]

---

[6] http://www.uniformlaws.org/Shared/Docs/UCLA/UCLR-A%20Short%20Summary.pdf, last viewed 5/9/12.

[7] National Conference of Commissioners on Uniform State Laws. http://www.uniformlaws.org/Act.aspx?title=Collaborative Law Act.

[8] http://www.abajournal.com/news/article/the_aba_house_of_delegates_rejected_resolution_110b/, last viewed 5/9/12.

[9] http://apps.americanbar.org/dch/committee.cfm?com=DR035000, last viewed 5/9/12.

[10] This is a statewide organization of collaborative practice groups. http://www.cpcal.com/AboutCPCal-new.aspx#AboutCP, last viewed 5/9/12.

[11] http://www.cpcal.com/Content.aspx?T=AboutCP, last viewed 5/9/12.

[12] http://www.massclc.org/civil-practice.php, last viewed 5/9/12.

Although the use of collaborative law in areas other than family law is still in the early stages, it is important to remember how far mediation has come since Warren Burger's comments at the Pound Conference in 1976. Law school students (and most lawyers) had never heard of mediation, much less had any exposure to it. Today, mediation is a common part of practice, and it has become institutionalized by most courts. It is likely that some forms of collaborative law will evolve in the same manner.[13] In-house counsel who manage litigation for large companies and who contract with outside litigation counsel could be key to this development.[14]

D. HOW DOES THE COLLABORATIVE LAW PROCESS WORK?

Negotiation in collaborative law is interest based, rather than positional. In other words, through a series of steps designed to build trust and transparency, the parties and their lawyers attempt to ascertain all of the true interests and needs of the parties and find solutions that meet as many needs as possible, rather than taking more extreme positions from which they intend to negotiate. This is a radical departure from the traditional concepts of negotiation that we discussed in Chapter 3.

The idea of pursuing the collaborative approach may first be raised by either client or counsel. Particularly in family law, lawyers now advertise that they provide collaborative services. Referral services and counselors are often aware of the option and mention it to individuals seeking a divorce. In the business context, where there is an ongoing relationship that the parties to the dispute want to maintain, in-house counsel may ask outside counsel to make the process available. If outside counsel would generally be litigation counsel, the matter may get referred to a different firm that does not handle the company's litigation, since collaborative counsel agrees to withdraw in the event an agreement is not reached.

In *Collaborative Law*, Pauline Tesler compares the collaborative process ". . . to a well-constructed three-act play."[15] The acts are as follows:

1. Act One

A client meets with her lawyer and explains the dispute. The lawyer gives the client lots of information about the options available, including collaborative law. If the client wishes to pursue collaborative law, the lawyer confirms this in writing in an engagement letter to the client. (This is no different than other matters.) If the other party is not yet represented by counsel, the lawyer then writes to the other party and encourages that party to consider collaborative law and to obtain a lawyer that will be willing to assist in a collaborative law effort. If the other party is already represented, the lawyer writes to the other party's lawyer and asks whether collaborative law would be possible. If both sides wish to pursue collaborative law, the lawyers work together to set an agenda for a first four-way meeting with the clients and lawyers.

---

[13] For a general discussion, see PAULINE H. TESLER, COLLABORATIVE LAW 191-220 (ABA 2008).

[14] *Id.* at 198.

[15] *Id.* at 53.

The lawyers exchange sufficient information on behalf of their clients so that they can establish trust, agree to process rules and set the groundwork for a successful first meeting. Act One ends at the conclusion of the first meeting, where the parties and lawyers sign the collaborative agreement which sets forth the operating rules as to how the parties will proceed to resolve the dispute. What makes the process unique is that the contract provides for the mandatory withdrawal of the lawyers if settlement is not achieved. The parties usually sign this agreement at the conclusion of the first meeting, in a kind of ceremony.

2.   Act Two

Now that the parties have given informed consent to act collaboratively, the lawyers begin to work with their clients in earnest to gather and share information, clarify aspirations and needs, establish priorities, brainstorm possible solutions and finally seek agreement. During this phase, depending upon the type of case, the parties may agree to engage neutral experts (rather than adversarial experts paid separately to testify on behalf of a particular party) in order to gather information necessary to the decision-making process. For example, in a divorce case, the parties may need input from a business or real estate appraiser, forensic accountant, estate appraiser, child psychologist, vocational consultant, stock option appraiser, retirement benefits appraiser, etc. It is important that things proceed along an agreed upon path, rather than attempting to short cut the[16] process. The orderly approach is important to ensure that the parties reach an optimal result.[17]

During Act Two, there are usually a series of carefully planned meetings with lawyers and clients present. The participants work on the various issues that are in need of resolution. When there are a number of issues to resolve, the meetings may focus on one or two of the issues rather than attempting to resolve everything globally. Although traditional adversarial litigation-mode negotiators often make settlement of any item conditional upon a global settlement, this is not the spirit of collaborative law. Collaborative lawyers attempt to reach a series of interim agreements and tentative understandings.[18] The parties may choose to have interim agreements be tentative and subject to the final comprehensive agreement, but collaborative negotiators would not use this as an "all or nothing" positional tactic. Rather, the goal would be resolution. If the collaborative negotiation is successful, Act Two ends with an agreement in principle.

3.   Act Three

This is the stage where all of the loose ends are tied up.[19] Since collaborative law is usually used in matters involving ongoing relationships, this stage is more than just drafting and signing the written settlement agreement. After the terms of settlement

---

[16] *Id.* at 67-68.

[17] *Id.* at 64.

[18] *Id.* at 68.

[19] *Id.* at 68.

have been properly documented in writing by the lawyers, there is usually a final meeting of the parties and counsel. The meeting is both substantive and ceremonial. The lawyers may take turns reading and explaining the terms of the written agreement to both parties. They help the clients review the progress they made during the collaborative process and identify the positive actions of both parties that allowed agreement to be possible. They acknowledge that future disputes may well arise and express confidence in the parties and their capacity to resolve future disputes together or again using the collaborative process, as set forth in the agreement. Often, there is a kind of signing ceremony, which provides a kind of closure — particularly in marital cases.[20] Whether or not the matter is marital, Act Three provides parties with an ongoing relationship a memory of a shared experience that arose out of discord was but resolved with mutual care and concern. This positive memory can serve as a template for future disputes and reduces the likelihood that future disputes will be contentious.

E.   ETHICAL CONSIDERATIONS AND COOPERATIVE LAW

When collaborative law was first introduced, the question arose as to whether it was ethical to create a four-way agreement (among two clients and two lawyers) that provided for the mandatory withdrawal of counsel in the event that agreement was not reached. There was also concern expressed about whether such an agreement was consistent with the lawyer's duty of zealousness to the client. Prior to 2007, a number of states reviewed this question and issued ethics opinions. With the exception of Colorado, all states concluded that the four-way agreement is not inherently inconsistent with the Model Rules of Professional Conduct. Colorado declared that the four-way agreement created a non-waivable conflict of interest under Rule 1.7(a)(2).[21] In 2007, the ABA Committee on Ethics issued a formal opinion which declared "that collaborative law practice and the provisions of the four-way agreement represent a permissible limited scope representation under Model Rule 1.2, with the concomitant duties of competence, diligence, and communication."[22] The ABA opinion specifically rejected the Colorado opinion.[23]

In rejecting the Collaborative Law model on ethical grounds, the Colorado Committee went on to note the availability of **Cooperative Law** agreements which incorporate the general good faith, cooperative, openness, and interest-based aspects of Collaborative Law agreements, but which *do not require participating attorneys to withdraw if litigation becomes necessary.*[24] These more limited Cooperative Law arrangements are permissible in all jurisdictions.

---

[20] *Id.* at 70.

[21] Colorado Bar Ass'n Eth. Op. 115 (Feb. 24, 2007), *Ethical Considerations in the Collaborative and Cooperative Law Contexts*, available at http://www.cobar.org/group/display.cfm?GenID=10159&EntityID=ceth.

[22] ABA Formal Ethics Opinion 07-447.

[23] *Id.*

[24] *See* Scott R. Peppet, *The Ethics of Collaborative Law*, 2008 J. Disp. Res. 131 (2008).

F.   ADVANTAGES AND DISADVANTAGES OF COLLABORATIVE LAW[25]

Most lawyers are not trained in the process of collaborative law. Because it is collaborative and not adversarial, some lawyers dismiss it as a "soft" process that would limit the client's options and results. Some trained adversaries believe only in "winners" and "losers." If there is no "winner," then everyone loses. But trained collaborative lawyers believe that the process is often the best way to truly resolve disputes by focusing on the interests of all of the parties and making choices that maximize benefits while minimizing the costs.[26] These lawyers believe that the financial and emotional cost of litigation rarely makes winners of anyone but cynical lawyers. Collaborative law practitioners do their best to spread the word, hoping that people and companies with disputes will see the potential benefits in collaborative dispute resolution.

1.   Advantages

a.   Atmosphere of cooperation, which benefits ongoing relationships. In divorce cases, it can make a huge difference — particularly in situations with children. In business cases, it can foster an ongoing relationship, which can be strengthened rather than destroyed.

b.   Brainstorming is encouraged during the negotiation problem-solving process, which can promote better interest-based outcomes.

c.   There is a strong incentive for both parties to settle the matter, which keeps them focused on resolution as a goal.

2.   Disadvantages

a.   Particularly in divorce cases, some parties are just too angry to work in a collaborative environment.

b.   If the lawyers are not properly trained, they may be unable to make the mental shift in approach necessary for a successful collaboration, thus dooming the process to failure. A failed collaborative negotiation can create additional emotional cost to the parties and can limit their ability to work constructively in any type of ongoing relationship.

c.   Some parties — particularly divorce clients — do not have the resources to pay for a failed collaborative divorce *and* for litigation counsel. If collaborative negotiation fails, it can make the divorce that much more stressful financially and emotionally.

---

[25] *See* David Hoffman & Pauline Tesler, *Collaborative Law And The Use Of Settlement Counsel*, Chapter 41 *in* THE ALTERNATIVE DISPUTE RESOLUTION PRACTICE GUIDE (B. Roth, ed. West Publishing 2002), available at: http://bostonlawcollaborative.com/blc/people/attorneys/david-hoffman/publications-list.html?branch=main&language=default.

[26] In this regard, collaborative practitioners often use the interest based approach described in ROGER FISHER & WILLIAM URY, GETTING TO YES (Houghton Mifflin 1981).

G. POSSIBLE TRAPS FOR UNWARY COLLABORATIVE AND COOPERATIVE LAW MODEL LAWYERS

The Collaborative Law and Cooperative Law movements have almost certainly excluded competitive/adversarial style negotiators from their groups. This can be a beneficial thing, since persons who are overtly competitive and adversarial tend to be ineffective negotiators, as was found by Professors Gerald Williams and Andrea Schneider in their studies of attorney bargaining behaviors, previously discussed in Chapter 8.[27] Collaborative Law and Cooperative Law members clearly wish to include only cooperative/problem-solvers in their groups. If they could accomplish this objective, their interactions would be pleasant and their agreements would be mutually beneficial.

What if some individuals the Collaborative Law and Cooperative Law members think are cooperative/problem-solvers are actually competitive/problem-solvers? On the surface, both types of negotiators behave similarly. They are courteous and professional, and they seek to generate efficient agreements. They appear to be open with their critical information; they begin with reasonable opening offers; and they seek "fair" results. Nonetheless, proficient competitive/problem-solvers disingenuously reflect the styles of cooperative/problem-solvers for the purpose of claiming more of the joint surplus for their own clients. Their first objective is to obtain beneficial terms for their own side, before they work to maximize the joint returns achieved. If they are able to delude cooperative/problem-solving opponents into believing that they are also cooperative/problem-solvers, they can exploit the naïve openness of such persons. Such competitive/problem-solvers are actually the most deceptive negotiators. They induce opponents into thinking that they are being completely open and direct, when their openness is actually limited and they are employing subtly deceptive behavior to advance their own interests.[28]

How can Collaborative Law and Cooperative Law practitioners avoid exploitation by opportunistic and manipulative competitive/problem-solvers? They can disclose their important information slowly. If they are convinced their openness is being reciprocated, they can continue to be open and cooperative. On the other hand, if they suspect that their openness is not being fully reciprocated, they must either behave more strategically themselves by being less open to avoid being taken advantage of or they may wish to call the other side on the behavior and withdraw from or terminate the process if the manipulation continues. If they fail to use such caution and continue to be naively open and cooperative, their clients will obtain less beneficial terms than are achieved by their deceptive adversaries.

---

[27] *See* GERALD R. WILLIAMS, LEGAL NEGOTIATION AND SETTLEMENT 18-20 (1983); Andrea Kupfer Schneider, *Shattering Negotiation Myths: Empirical Evidence on the Effectiveness of Negotiation Style*, 7 HARV. NEG. L. REV. 143, 146-148 (2002).

[28] *See* Keith G. Allred, *Distinguishing Best and Strategic Practices: A Framework for Managing the Dilemma Between Creating and Claiming Value*, 16 NEGOT. J. 387, 394-395 (2000) (finding that the most successful negotiators are persons whose opponents believe they were completely open and cooperative but who admitted to being somewhat closed and manipulative).

EXERCISES

EXERCISE 12.1
PRACTICING THE COLLABORATIVE LAW PROCESS

"GOIN' THROUGH THE BIG D" REVISITED

GENERAL DESCRIPTION OF EXERCISE: Preparation for collaborative resolution of property division, custody arrangement, child support, and alimony in a divorce.

SKILLS INVOLVED: Collaboration preparation.

PARTICIPANTS NEEDED: One person

ESTIMATED TIME REQUIRED:

60 minutes: 20 minutes for preparation, 40 minutes for discussion

LEVEL OF DIFFICULTY (1-5):

EXERCISE

Return to Exercise 6.2. Review your Negotiation Preparation Form. In what ways would your strategies have changed if your client had agreed to a collaborative process? Redo the preparatory outline, using your same confidential information, so that it anticipates a collaborative meeting.

EXERCISE 12.1
PRACTICING THE COLLABORATIVE LAW PROCESS

"GOIN' THROUGH THE BIG D" REVISITED

REFLECTION

1. Did you find yourself thinking at all differently in preparing for a collaborative meeting, as opposed to an adversarial negotiation? If yes, in what ways? If no, why not?

2. Do you think the actual resolution of this case — the allocation of money, property, parental rights and responsibilities — would have been any different if you had first approached it collaboratively instead of through traditional negotiation? If yes, in what ways? If no, why not?

3. Do you think the emotional issues going forward between the parents and among the parents and children would have been any different if you had first approached it collaboratively instead of through traditional negotiation? If yes, in what ways? If no, why not?

4. As you compare the methods of approaching the resolution of this dispute, can you think of other types of disputes and compare how they might be resolved through collaboration as opposed to traditional negotiation? What about the other previous traditional negotiation and mediation exercises? Think about the various *alternatives* for resolving the same disputes.

Part Four

ARBITRATION

Chapter 13

INTRODUCTION TO ARBITRATION

A. WHAT IS ARBITRATION?

In the previous sections of this book, we discussed alternative ways of resolving disputes without *adjudication*. Whether through direct negotiation, mediation, collaboration or cooperation, any resolution we discussed was *voluntary*. If the parties could not agree to settle the dispute, then it continued. This differs from ***arbitration***, which results in *adjudication*. In arbitration, the parties present evidence and argument to a third party, who makes a *decision* as to what is going to happen. Arbitration is an ancient form of dispute resolution. Stories involving forms of arbitration appear in Greek and Egyptian mythology, and there are numerous Biblical references.[1] There are stories of Poseidon and Helios fighting over ownership of Corinth, with the dispute being decided by the giant, Briareus. There is the famous story of King Solomon ruling on paternity as between the two fighting mothers.

Arbitration has evolved over the years and now appears throughout the world in numerous variations. In this section, we will begin by discussing the overall characteristics of binding arbitration.[2] Even though there are different forms and there are numerous exceptions, certain characteristics are usually present.

B. BASIC CHARACTERISTICS OF ARBITRATION[3]

1. Trial Substitute

Arbitration is a kind of trial. It is usually less formal than a trial in court, but it is adjudicatory. There may be a sole arbitrator or a panel of three or more. Parties present evidence to the arbitrator(s). The arbitrator(s) act(s) as judge and jury to render a decision.

---

[1] For an interesting history of arbitration, see GARY B. BORN, INTERNATIONAL COMMERCIAL ARBITRATION, VOL.1, 7-63 (Wolters Kluwer 2009).

[2] Arbitration can also be non-binding, which is much less common. If it is non-binding, it is more in the nature of an advisory opinion which can become final if neither party appeals it.

[3] *See* EDWARD BRUNET, CHARLES B. CRAVER & ELLEN E. DEASON, ALTERNATIVE DISPUTE RESOLUTION 431-451 (4th ed. LexisNexis 2012).

2. Expeditious

Arbitration is generally intended to streamline the litigation process in order to resolve disputes expeditiously with less expense. Whenever arbitrators have discretion over the process — such as whether to grant discovery requests — questions of speed and expense are usually considered.

3. Arbitrators Usually have Subject Matter Expertise

Trial lawyers in complex cases often complain that they cannot really get a jury of their clients' peers. For example, claims involving medical malpractice, construction, labor, and intellectual property usually involve matters of particular expertise. Many times, the parties would rather have the matter decided by someone who understands the field. With arbitration, the parties have a chance to agree on an arbitrator or arbitrators with expertise or to use an arbitration organization that will provide arbitrators with such expertise.

4. What Happens in Arbitration Usually Stays in Arbitration

For the most part, arbitrations are private proceedings. The hearings are usually closed sessions. By contract, the parties can agree that arbitrations are confidential to the fullest extent allowed by law. (As with mediations, discussed in Chapter 10, there are exceptions.) Even when arbitrations are not confidential, they are almost always private. This means that interested onlookers, including the press, are not allowed to observe. This can be very important to some parties. For example, a doctor or hospital might agree to arbitration instead of facing the possible negative publicity of an open trial. The plaintiff might agree to this, because the rules of evidence would be relaxed and the case would be less expensive, as explained below. A product manufacturer of an allegedly defective product might agree to a private trial for the same reason. Others who often want privacy include banks, securities brokers, clergy, lawyers and any parties where publicity could be perceived as negative regardless of the outcome.

In addition to the closed session nature of arbitration hearings, the decisions are usually quite cryptic. Unless the parties request otherwise, the arbitrators usually make a bare bones award. If the dispute is monetary and the plaintiff prevails, the award will usually read something like, "Plaintiff is awarded the gross amount of $_____ for all claims." If the dispute involves matters other than money, the award is usually as cryptic as possible while fulfilling the charge of deciding the matter.

5. Arbitration Procedure is Usually Informal

Arbitration is usually much more informal and flexible than judicial proceedings. Parties can agree to their own rules or can follow the rules of existing organizations that have rules in place. For example, the American Arbitration Association (AAA) — a large not-for-profit organization which administers arbitrations (and mediations) —

has its own sets of rules for various types of arbitration.[4] In most arbitration, there is no required form of pleading. Document discovery is usually voluntary between the parties or substantially limited. Depositions may or may not be allowed.[5] The rules of evidence are generally not applied except as to those of legal privilege. Affidavits can usually be submitted in lieu of live witness testimony. There are usually witnesses, but in much smaller numbers than typical court trials. Also, the examination is usually quicker and to the point, since there is no jury present and all participants understand the process.

6.   Arbitrations are Usually Shorter than Court Trials

Arbitrations usually take less time to try than court trials. Without a jury, there are no time-consuming "side-bar" discussions between the judge and the lawyers. With the rules of evidence relaxed, many things are simply submitted to the arbitrator(s), without laying elaborate foundations. The C.V.'s of experts are usually submitted in advance of their testimony, rather than having lengthy testimony about their credentials. Also, their reports are usually submitted and are then elaborated upon. (If the rules of evidence applied, the reports would normally be inadmissible hearsay and the expert would need to lay the foundation and then testify as to each conclusion.)

7.   Arbitrators are not Strictly Bound by Law

Generally speaking, arbitrators are *not* bound by principles of substantive law.[6] As Justice Blackmun stated in *Shearson/American Express, Inc. v. McMahon*, 482 U.S. 220, 259 (1987) (Blackmun, J., concurring in part and dissenting in part), "[A]rbitrators are not bound by precedent."[7] Although most arbitrators are lawyers, many are not. Some arbitrators are experts in the field but have no legal training. They may rule based upon their perception of what is fair as determined by common practice in the industry without regard to what the actual law might be. Certainly, lawyer arbitrators are generally concerned with applicable law, but most arbitrators attempt to reach a *fair* result as they perceive it — harking back to the days of King Solomon.

Can the parties require the arbitrators to follow the law? Interestingly, the law on this issue is unsettled. Historically, as noted above, arbitrators are not bound to follow

---

[4] AAA Rules for various forms of arbitration and mediation available at: http://www.adr.org/aaa/faces/rules/searchrules?_afrLoop=496180704947523&_afrWindowMode=0&_afrWindowId=6a6nbsyn0_216#%40%3F_afrWindowId%3D6a6nbsyn0_216%26_afrLoop%3D496180704947523%26_afrWindowMode%3D0%26_adf.ctrl-state%3D6a6nbsyn0_244.

[5] *See* AAA Commercial Arbitration Rule L-4, which contemplates the use of depositions in large, complex, commercial cases "for good cause shown," available at: http://www.adr.org/aaa/faces/rules/searchrules/rulesdetail?doc=ADRSTG_004130&_afrLoop=497660917735781&_afrWindowMode=0&_afrWindowId=6a6nbsyn0_241#%40%3F_afrWindowId%3D6a6nbsyn0_241%26_afrLoop%3D497660917735781%26doc%3DADRSTG_004130%26_afrWindowMode%3D0%26_adf.ctrl-state%3D6a6nbsyn0_293.

[6] *See* EDWARD BRUNET, CHARLES B. CRAVER & ELLEN E. DEASON, ALTERNATIVE DISPUTE RESOLUTION 432-433 (4th ed. LexisNexis 2012).

[7] Cited in *id.*, at 432.

the law. When the Uniform Arbitration Act (UAA) was reviewed and revised in 2000 (RUAA), the Drafting Committee considered whether to add a provision to Section 23, entitled "Vacating Award." The provision would have allowed parties to "opt in" to judicial review of arbitration awards for errors of law or fact or any other grounds not prohibited by applicable law. In Comment 2 to Section 23, the Committee stated that "no issue produced more discussion and debate . . ."[8] The Committee Comment carefully explains the pros and cons of allowing an "opt in" provision and explains that the Committee decided against it, saying, "This decision not to include in the RUAA a statutory sanction of expanded judicial review of the 'opt-in' device effectively leaves the issue of the legal propriety of this means for securing review of awards to the developing case law under the FAA and state arbitration statutes. Consequently, parties remain free to agree to contractual provisions for judicial review of challenged awards, on whatever grounds and based on whatever standards they deem appropriate until the courts finally determine the propriety of such clauses." The Federal Arbitration Act (FAA) and the RUAA will be discussed further, below.

8. Arbitrations are Considered Final

With few exceptions, binding arbitration awards are final. The grounds for appeal are extremely limited and generally involve fraud, corruption, bias, etc. There can also be an appeal for an "evident miscalculation" or an "evident material mistake", but these exceptions are extremely limited in scope. The grounds are set forth in Sections 12 and 13 of the UAA, Sections 23 ar . 24 of the RUAA and Sections 10 and 11 of the Federal Arbitration Act (FAA).[9] T .e whole concept is to get a decision and to move on. If there were extensive gr .nds for appeal, it would eliminate the expeditious nature of the process.

C. THE LAW O' ARBITRATION

As noted abov with certain possible "opt out" exceptions, arbitrators are not strictly bound ʰ follow the law *that applies to the subject matter of the dispute*. But there *is* a b .y of law that applies *to the arbitration process* as a whole. Either the FAA or sᵗ .e law (usually patterned after the RUAA) control.

1 Federal Arbitration Act (FAA) — 9 U.S.C. §§ 1-16

Historically, courts did not favor arbitration contracts because they limited the courts' jurisdiction over legal disputes. In 1925, "in response to widespread judicial hostility to arbitration agreements," Congress enacted the United States Arbitration Act, also known as the Federal Arbitration Act (FAA).[10] The FAA provides for the enforceability of arbitration agreements in maritime matters and contracts involving commerce. Section 2 reads as follows:

---

[8] RUAA Comment 2 to Section 23, available at: http://www.uniformlaws.org/shared/docs/arbitration/arbitration_final_00.pdf.

[9] Federal Arbitration Act (FAA) 9 U.S.C. § 10, available at: http://www.law.cornell.edu/uscode/text/9/10.

[10] AT&T Mobility LLC v. Concepcion, 131 S. Ct. 1740, 1745 (2011).

> A written provision in any maritime transaction or a contract evidencing a transaction involving commerce to settle by arbitration a controversy thereafter arising out of such contract or transaction, or the refusal to perform the whole or any part thereof, or an agreement in writing to submit to arbitration an existing controversy arising out of such a contract, transaction, or refusal, shall be valid, irrevocable, and enforceable, save upon such grounds as exist at law or in equity for the revocation of any contract.

Since it was enacted, the Supreme Court has "described this provision as reflecting both a 'liberal federal policy favoring arbitration' . . . and the 'fundamental principle that arbitration is a matter of contract.' "[11] A great deal of law has developed with respect to the enforceability of arbitration agreements. The Supreme Court has given an expansive interpretation to the language of the statute, "extending the Act's reach to the limits of Congress' Commerce Clause power . . ."[12] Under this interpretation, the vast majority of contracts to arbitrate are subject to this statute and may be enforced under its provisions in either state or federal court. And under the doctrine of preemption, state laws that restrict arbitration or that place limitations on what the parties may agree to in the arbitration agreement have been consistently "displaced by the FAA".[13] This leaves state statutes to only those matters involving purely local transactions which are not subject to the broad powers of the Commerce Clause or matters involving insurance transactions. (In separate legislation, Congress created the McCarran Ferguson Act, 15 U.S.C. §§ 1011-1015, which gives states the right to regulate insurance, including whether arbitration clauses are permissible in insurance contracts.)[14]

2.   Uniform Arbitration Act (UAA)

The UAA was approved by the National Conference of Commissioners on Uniform State Laws (NCCUSL) in 1955, with minor amendments approved in 1956. This is the version of the Act that was adopted in at least some form in 49 states.[15] It is still the dominant form of the Act in use, since the RUAA has only been adopted in 14 states and the District of Columbia.[16] According to the Commissioners' Prefatory Note, "Th[e] Act covers voluntary written agreements to arbitrate. Its purpose is to validate arbitration agreements, make the arbitration process effective, provide necessary safeguards, and provide an efficient procedure when judicial assistance is necessary." As noted above, the UAA (where adopted) is applicable when the FAA is not.

---

[11] *Id.*

[12] Allied-Bruce Terminix Companies, Inc. v. Dobson, 115 S. Ct. 834, 836 (1995).

[13] *See AT&T Mobility* at 1747.

[14] McCarran Ferguson Act, 15 U.S.C. § 1011 available at: http://www.law.cornell.edu/uscode/text/15/1011.

[15] *See* Uniform Law Commission legislative status report: http://www.uniformlaws.org/Act.aspx?title=Arbitration%20Act%20%282000%29.

[16] *Id.*

3. Revised Uniform Arbitration Act (RUAA)

In 2000, the NCCUSL approved a revised and more expanded Act. In the Commissioners' Prefatory Note, they explained the need for the revisions as follows:

> The UAA did not address many issues which arise in modern arbitration cases. The statute provided no guidance as to (1) who decides the arbitrability of a dispute and by what criteria; (2) whether a court or arbitrators may issue provisional remedies; (3) how a party can initiate an arbitration proceeding; (4) whether arbitration proceedings may be consolidated; (5) whether arbitrators are required to disclose facts reasonably likely to affect impartiality; (6) what extent arbitrators or an arbitration organization are immune from civil actions; (7) whether arbitrators or representatives of arbitration organizations may be required to testify in another proceeding; (8) whether arbitrators have the discretion to order discovery, issue protective orders, decide motions for summary dispositions, hold prehearing conferences and otherwise manage the arbitration process; (9) when a court may enforce a preaward ruling by an arbitrator; (10) what remedies an arbitrator may award, especially in regard to attorney's fees, punitive damages or other exemplary relief; (11) when a court can award attorney's fees and costs to arbitrators and arbitration organizations; (12) when a court can award attorney's fees and costs to a prevailing party in an appeal of an arbitrator's award; (13) which sections of the UAA would not be waivable, an important matter to insure fundamental fairness to the parties will be preserved, particularly in those instances where one party may have significantly less bargaining power than another; and (14) the use of electronic information and other modern means of technology in the arbitration process. The Revised Uniform Arbitration Act (RUAA) examines all of these issues and provides state legislatures with a more up-to-date statute to resolve disputes through arbitration.

The revisions definitely made the Act more complex. Whether for this reason or others, as of 2012, the RUAA had only been adopted in 14 states and the District of Columbia.[17]

D. WHAT ARE THE MOST COMMON SOURCES OF ARBITRATION?

The statutes discussed above do not create arbitration — they provide a way to enforce it. There are several ways in which the right to (or requirement of) arbitration is created.

1. Pre-Dispute Arbitration Agreement

The right to arbitration is usually created by contract in the first instance, before the dispute leading to arbitration ever arises. There are two basic ways this happens:

---

[17] *Id.*

a. *Negotiated by contract before a dispute arises* — Parties with a business relationship often agree to arbitrate disputes as they arise. The parties negotiate language that forms part of their contract. They may agree to language that comes from a third source — like the arbitration clause for commercial arbitration used by the AAA. They may modify "standard" language or use their own. The important distinction is that the parties negotiate the agreement to arbitrate and it provides a binding process for resolving disputes before a dispute arises. This is called a "pre-dispute arbitration agreement."

b. *Boilerplate arbitration agreements* — With some contracts, there really is no opportunity to negotiate the terms. This can be true with many things, including most employment contracts, consumer service contracts (think mobile phone contracts), sales contracts, securities contracts, etc. The employee or the consumer takes the job or the service or does without. The contract has a nonnegotiable arbitration clause, written by lawyers for the company providing the job, the service, or the product.

2. Arbitration by Statute or Court Rule

Some states require the arbitration of certain disputes in the first instance. This can include certain categories of cases filed in court. When this happens, it is almost always non-binding (see footnote 2, above), because most statutory binding arbitration (in the absence of a contract) would be subject to constitutional challenge.

3. Arbitration by Treaty

Countries may include arbitration in treaties. The North American Free Trade Agreement (NAFTA) is a good example. Chapter 11 of NAFTA was the first international trade agreement provision to give foreign investors a direct cause of action for investment disputes against the host government in a binding international tribunal, commonly known as "investor-state arbitration."[18] Countries also enter treaties and conventions which allow for the enforcement of arbitration agreements. The United Nations Convention on the Recognition and Enforcement of Foreign Arbitral Awards of 1958, generally referred to as the "New York Convention," is the basis for the entire international arbitration system as it exists today.[19]

4. Arbitration Agreed to after a Dispute Arises

When disputes arise, parties are free to negotiate an agreement to arbitrate. This "post-dispute arbitration agreement" is similar to a "pre-dispute arbitration agreement" except that it is negotiated after the tension of the dispute already exists. Rather than negotiating for an arbitration process when neither side knows what the facts of the dispute will be, there is already a dispute in play. Parties usually have a

---

[18] For the actual NAFTA language and a good overview, see NAFTA Secretariat, available online at: http://www.nafta-sec-alena.org/en/view.aspx?x=275.

[19] For an interesting tutorial on international arbitration, see Proskauer Rose L.L.P. on International Litigation and Arbitration: Managing, Resolving, and Avoiding Cross-Border Business or Regulatory Disputes, available online at: http://www.proskauerguide.com/toc.

view as to who has the stronger position, and the dispute itself may affect the terms agreed upon.

E. THE TYPICAL ARBITRATION PROCESS

1. Commencing the Arbitration Process

If the parties have a pre-dispute arbitration agreement, the contract will provide the manner in which a party commences the arbitration. Usually, it is a written notice of or demand for arbitration sent to the other party. If the contract calls for the parties to have the matter handled by an administrative agency, like AAA, then the demand is sent to the agency, with a copy to the other party, as prescribed under the administrator's rules. The contract may call for a notice of arbitration, followed by a waiting period (to give the parties a chance to address the issue without arbitration), then followed by a formal submission. There are numerous variations, and the language of the contract controls.

If the arbitration is by statute or court rule, it usually is triggered by the filing of litigation. The court rule or statute requires or provides the opportunity for non-binding arbitration (or agreed to binding arbitration) at some time designated by the court or agreed to by the parties.

Like pre-dispute arbitration, arbitration by treaty or convention is commenced based upon the provisions of the document. Some provisions are quite formal and others are much less so. As one example, Chapter 11, Articles 1119 and 1120 of NAFTA requires that the disputing party submit written notice followed by a waiting period, followed by submission.[20]

Arbitration agreed to after the dispute arises does not require a formal method of commencement. The fact that the parties agree to arbitrate a dispute already in existence is the actual commencement of the process. Because the dispute has already arisen, the negotiation for the terms of the arbitration can be difficult. The parties need to agree to numerous things, including the subject matter of the arbitration, the method (binding or non-binding), the number of arbitrators, the authority of the arbitrators, the names of the artibitrator(s) or the method of appointment, the type of decision (unanimous, majority, super majority), the form of decision (general decision, detailed findings, etc.), whether the arbitration will be administered, and the allocation of arbitration costs.

2. Preparing for the Arbitration

Although lawyers in complex business disputes are now asking for increasingly burdensome discovery in arbitration, arbitration is generally supposed to be quicker and simpler than trial by judge or jury. As a result, most parties attempt to keep the discovery streamlined and efficient. If there are interrogatories, they are usually kept

---

[20] NAFTA, Chapter 11, Articles 1119-1120, available at: http://www.nafta-sec-alena.org/en/view.aspx?conID=590&mtpiID=142#A1119.

to a minimum. Depositions are the exception but are sometimes done by agreement. The parties often create a written stipulation of fact as to all they can agree upon so that the issues in dispute can be narrowed. Documents may be exchanged informally — with protective orders where appropriate. The goal in the typical arbitration is to efficiently gather the facts and strip the case of the superfluous.

Efficiency, however, should not be confused with lack of preparation. Experienced arbitration advocates prepare for arbitration with the same intensity as when they prepare for trial. They use the less formal rules to streamline their preparation but they still strive to learn all they can about the facts of the case. Because the rules of evidence are not strictly applied, lawyers may interview potential witnesses and take affidavits in lieu of testimony. (As a tactical matter, they may choose to have the live testimony of a particularly important witness, but the testimony of many witnesses can be appropriately submitted through affidavits.) Advocates often prepare detailed submissions that carefully explain their arguments and support them with attached exhibits — something that could never be done with a typical jury. They use the informality to their advantage to create a powerful submission that will be submitted to the arbitrator(s) before the hearing begins — a carefully constructed road map that not only tells the arbitrator(s) what to expect, but that also provides supporting evidence.

3. Pre-Hearing Conference

In cases of any complexity, arbitrators usually schedule a pre-arbitration session. This may be in person or by conference call. This session is run by the arbitrator(s) and deals with any matters that need resolution before the arbitration actually occurs. This is the time to focus on any discovery requests, scheduling, evidentiary issues, etc. It is like a combination of a preliminary and final pretrial conference in court.

4. Arbitration Hearing

Although parties may agree to have the case determined based upon written submissions, there is usually a hearing. Depending upon the nature of the case, the hearing may last a day, a few days, or may be spread out over weeks and even months. The schedules of the arbitrators and lawyers can often make a lengthy, continuous session difficult. This is quite different than most trials, since the arbitrators in long cases are often required to retain information with gaps in time when they have had to listen to other unrelated matters or handle their own private practice. When that occurs, the well presented written submission with supporting exhibits is all the more important.

During the hearing, the arbitrators sit as judge and jury. If there is more than one arbitrator, one is usually designated as the lead arbitrator for the purpose of handling objections, discovery requests, etc. Most arbitrators confer with the other arbitrators before making all but the most routine rulings.

Depending upon the case, it is common to have the arbitrators take a "view" of the scene as the first event in the actual information process. This may be important in a construction case, a motor vehicle case, or any other matter where the scene is important. This is similar to taking a "view" with a jury. What the arbitrators see is evidence that can be considered in their deliberations.

Even though the parties have usually submitted written statements in advance of the hearing, most advocates also make an opening statement to the arbitrators. When working with experienced arbitrators, most advocates do not repeat the content of their written submissions, but focus on particular matters that they expect will occur during the mediation in order to further clarify and highlight their arguments. As with court trials, the party making the claim usually goes first. The other party or parties may make an opening right after the claimant or wait until the claimant's case is presented.

Because the rules of evidence are relaxed, the advocates have different strategy considerations than in trial. Do they submit documents first, or through a witness? Do they submit an affidavit, or call the witness live? How much visual information do they use? Do they have a big chart or separate notebooks for each arbitrator? Like a court trial, the advocate needs to know the rules of the proceeding so that intentional choices can be made.

After the claimant's case is submitted, the other parties present evidence. When the evidence is finished, most advocates make closing statements to sum up the case. In complicated cases, this is often done by way of detailed written summaries. In more straightforward matters, it is usually done orally. Either way, most experienced advocates understand that the arbitrators are not lay jurors and the presentation is designed to appeal to the experience and wisdom of the arbitrator.

5. The Award

The decision of the arbitrator(s) is called an "award." It is sometimes made orally but is usually made in writing, signed by all of the arbitrators.[21] As noted above, it is often very brief and simply states an amount. Sometimes, usually when the parties request it, the award is detailed and includes findings of fact and rulings.

6. The Appeal

As noted earlier, there are usually very limited grounds for an appeal.[22] If the matter involves maritime or is subject to the Commerce Clause, then the FAA is the enforcing statute. If not, then state law applies, which in 49 states is some version of the UAA or RUAA.

F. BENEFITS AND LIMITATIONS OF ARBITRATION

We have now discussed the basic characteristics of arbitration and have described the general process. Is it the right solution for all matters? What are the benefits? Any downsides? Should you ever consider mediation first?

---

[21] *See* UAA § 8, available at: http://www.law.upenn.edu/bll/archives/ulc/fnact99/1920_69/uaa55.pdf.

[22] *See* Section [B][7], *supra.*

The characteristics of arbitration are neither positive nor negative — it all depends upon what the parties are looking for. Arbitration offers privacy, which is often desired. But sometimes, a party wants the matter to be public. Parties to an arbitration have much more control over the process than in court. That can be good when the parties have equal resources and power, but what about when the contract to arbitrate is in a consumer agreement or an employment contract that was not negotiated? Is arbitration best for the weaker complainant? Parties often get to select an arbitrator with expertise or an arbitrator from an approved panel. That is usually a good thing for businesses involved in a technical case. Is it good for a purchaser of securities who is required to arbitrate a securities case in front of an arbitrator from a list approved by the securities industry?

Arbitrations are usually expeditious and lack formal discovery. That is usually a great cost savings to both sides. Is it a good thing for a complainant who thinks there was misconduct and who is looking for a "smoking gun" document? The rules of evidence do not strictly apply. That makes it easier and usually cheaper to try a case. But what about the admission of evidence that would be inadmissible in a court on the basis of lack of reliability — like hearsay? Arbitration orders are usually quite brief. Is that a good thing for the development of case law in the field? Does it help others know what to expect next time? And what about appeals? Arbitrations tend to be final, which is great if you win. What if you do not? What if you think the arbitrators made egregious mistakes?

As with all dispute resolution procedures, arbitration is not always the best forum. Even when it is, it does not guarantee a satisfactory result. As noted earlier, parties to an arbitration give up control over the resolution of the dispute. Because of this, many parties attempt mediation before they arbitrate. Some pre-dispute arbitration agreements call for mediation as a condition precedent to filing a notice of arbitration. As long as the parties negotiate the terms of dispute resolution before a dispute arises, they have great flexibility in how they can approach it. Experienced practitioners consider all of the options when drafting agreements *before* the disputes arise whenever possible.

G. ETHICAL CONSIDERATIONS

As with mediation, the ethical rules regarding arbitration are less than clear, and are drawn from several sources. There are various "models" that are not enforceable unless they have been adopted in the applicable jurisdiction. It is important that practitioners look at the rules as they apply to the local jurisdiction. We will highlight the basic issues that arise for both advocates and arbitrators.

1. Specific Considerations for the Advocates

When lawyers represent clients in arbitration, are they bound by the rules of professional conduct that apply to litigation? We believe that the answer should be "yes," although the law is not so clear. Given recent amendments to the Model Rules of Professional Conduct which specifically mention arbitration and include arbitrators in the definition of "tribunal," we think that persons practicing in jurisdictions that have adopted the Model Rules should assume that the rules apply generally to conduct in connection with arbitration proceedings.

a. *Candor to the arbitrator* — In Chapter 5, we discussed the ethical boundaries and dilemmas of negotiation. Since arbitration may include negotiation, the basic rules of ethics with respect to the lawyers who are representing parties apply. Lawyers representing parties are bound by the rules of professional conduct applicable in the jurisdiction, as described in Chapter 5. These rules usually involve some version of Model Rule 4.1 (Truthfulness in Statements to Others).

Arbitrators in binding arbitration proceedings fall under the definition of a "tribunal" in Model Rule 1.0(m). As such, advocates owe a more expansive duty of candor to the tribunal, as set forth in Model Rule 3.3(a).[23] Even though Comment 2 to Rule 4.1 permits misrepresentations with respect to client settlement intentions and values based upon the view that such issues are not "material," Rule 3.3(a) does not contain the word "material," nor does it except such puffing and embellishment. As a result, the ABA has indicated that attorneys may not misrepresent such matters when communicating with tribunals.[24]

b. *Duty to Inform Clients About ADR* — Should a lawyer advise a client of the ADR option before filing suit? As we noted in Chapter 10, an increasing number of jurisdictions require it.[25] Also, as noted in Chapter 1, an increasing number of courts require some form of ADR before reaching trial. Model Rule of Professional Conduct 1.4 requires the lawyer to "reasonably consult with the client about the means by which the client's objectives are to be accomplished."[26] Although Model Rule 1.4 does not state a specific duty to mention ADR, there is really no downside and it would be prudent to do so. Given the emotional and financial cost of litigation, we believe that describing the ADR process as a possible alternative should be part of obtaining "informed consent" prior to filing suit. Also, since lawyers usually make more money in litigation than in ADR, it helps to address any potential conflicts of interest with respect to the lawyer's economic advantage.

c. *Unauthorized Practice of Law* — Arbitrations often occur in locations where the lawyer is not licensed to practice. Does this constitute the unauthorized practice of law? Once again, the law is not clear and depends upon the rules of the particular jurisdiction. Model Rule 5.5, as recently revised, seems to give lawyers the opportunity to practice temporarily in other jurisdictions, but the rule is somewhat confusing – even after reading the 21 comments that follow the rule![27] Practitioners

---

[23] *See ABA Formal Opin.* 06-439 (2006), available online at: http://www.illinoislegalmal.com/archives/06-439.pdf, site last visited 5-21-12.

[24] *ABA Formal Opin.* 06-439.

[25] *See* Dwight Golan and Jay Folberg, Mediation: The Roles of Advocate and Neutral 414 (Wolters Kluwer 2011).

[26] ABA Model Rules of Professional Conduct, available online at:

http://www.americanbar.org/groups/professional_responsibility/publications/model_rules_of_professional_conduct/rule_1_4_communications.html.

[27] Comments to ABA Model Rule of Professional Conduct 5.5, available online at: http://www.americanbar.org/groups/professional_responsibility/publications/model_rules_of_professional_

must carefully check with the applicable jurisdiction.

2.   Specific Considerations for the Arbitrator

As with lawyer advocates, the ethical rules pertaining to arbitrators can vary depending upon the jurisdiction and the rules agreed upon by the parties. There are guidelines and rules promulgated by various organizations which may be controlling — depending upon the rules of the arbitration. For example, the ABA and AAA have approved The Code of Ethics for Arbitrators in Commercial Disputes.[28] This code is applicable to all AAA commercial arbitrations, and other organizations sometimes adopt it by reference. For instance, the Financial Industry Regulatory Authority (FINRA), a self-regulatory organization that regulates securities firms doing business in the United States, has adopted the Code of Ethics for Arbitrators in Commercial Disputes.[29] There are other codes of conduct which can be applicable, depending upon whether they have been adopted in the jurisdiction. (We previously discussed the UAA and the RUAA which both have sections dealing with arbitrator fairness and neutrality. This is discussed further, below.)

a. ***Training and Certification*** — In most jurisdictions, there is no licensing or certification requirement in order to be an arbitrator. There is, in some court programs, a requirement that the person receives a certain amount of training and be "listed" on the court's approved list for specific types of arbitration. Most administrative agencies, like AAA, JAMS ADR, etc., require that prospective arbitrators apply to the administrative agency in order to be vetted prior to being placed on the approved list. Most programs do not require that the arbitrator be an attorney.

b. ***Duty to Be Impartial*** — Except in limited circumstances, discussed below, arbitrators are expected to be impartial. UAA § 12 and RUAA § 12 both place obligations on an arbitrator selected as a neutral. One of the very limited grounds for appeal, set forth in UAA § 12(2), includes that "There was evident partiality by an arbitrator appointed as a neutral or corruption in any of the arbitrators or misconduct prejudicing the rights of any party." RUAA § 12 requires full disclosure by the arbitrator of "any known facts that a reasonable person would consider likely to affect the impartiality of the arbitrator in the arbitration proceeding . . ." Failure of a neutral to disclose such facts can be grounds for vacating the award.

c. ***Duty of Party-Appointed Non-Neutral Arbitrators*** — Sometimes, the parties agree or the rules provide that each party selects one arbitrator, who in turn jointly select the third arbitrator. The arbitrators appointed by the parties are generally considered to be non-neutral, and are more like inside advocates who are appointed to make sure that each side has a full hearing during the deliberations with the neutral

---

conduct/rule_5_5_unauthorized_practice_of_law_multijurisdictional_practice_of_law/comment_on_rule_5_5
_unauthorized_practice_of_law_multijurisdictional_practice_of_law.html.

[28] Available online at:

http://www.americanbar.org/content/dam/aba/migrated/dispute/commercial_disputes.authcheckdam.pdf.

[29] *See*

http://www.finra.org/ArbitrationAndMediation/Arbitrators/Responsibilites/CodeofEthics/index.htm.

arbitrator. In effect, each non-neutral is ready to vote in favor of the side who selected her, and the deciding vote will be cast by the neutral. This type of arbitration is disfavored internationally.[30] The Code of Ethics for Arbitrators in Commercial Disputes allows for it in domestic arbitrations in the United States but states in its "Note on Neutrality" that "it is preferable for all arbitrators — including any party-appointed arbitrators — to be neutral, that is, independent and impartial, and to comply with the same ethical standards."[31] Even when the arbitrators are non-neutrals, they are required under Canon X to act in good faith and with integrity and fairness, but this is a very vague standard to apply on appeal. When advocates enter into a process where they each select an arbitrator who selects a neutral, they should make sure they know what the rules are with respect to the arbitrator they selected. An advocate would do a true disservice to her client if she instructed her selected advocate to be neutral when the other one was not.

---

[30] *See* Carrie J. Menkel-Meadow, Lela Porter Love, Andrea Kupfer Schneider & Jean R. Sternlight, Dispute Resolution: Beyond The Adversarial Model 508 (2d ed. Aspen 2011).

[31] *Supra* note 28.

EXERCISES

EXERCISE 13.1
PRACTICING THE ARBITRATION PROCESS
MULTI-PARTY ARBITRATION

"THE MULTIPLE CAR ACCIDENT CASE"

GENERAL DESCRIPTION OF EXERCISE: Arbitration of multiple vehicle accident claims.

SKILLS INVOLVED: Arbitration.

PARTICIPANTS NEEDED: You will be assigned one of nine roles.

ESTIMATED TIME REQUIRED:

120 minutes for arbitration and 30 minutes for discussion: 150 minutes

LEVEL OF DIFFICULTY (1-5):

ROLES IN EXERCISE: You are acting as a plaintiff, defendant, counsel for plaintiff, counsel for defendant, or an arbitrator.

THE EXERCISE

GENERAL INFORMATION
AVAILABLE TO ALL STUDENTS

Turn back the clock. In Exercise 11.2, you mediated a multiple car accident case. You either arrived at a settlement or failed to do so. What would have happened if the parties had agreed to arbitrate instead of mediate? Let's find out! You will again be divided into groups. Unless your professor advises otherwise, the roles will include Plaintiff Terry Gustaf, counsel for Plaintiff Gustaf, Plaintiff/Defendant Charlie Goshen, counsel for Plaintiff Goshen, counsel for Defendant Goshen, Defendant Dale Gustaf, counsel for Defendant Dale Gustaf, counsel for Defendant Fran Noonan and the Arbitrator(s). Start by reading the general information below, including the arbitration statements. After that, read the Confidential Information assigned to your role and follow the instructions that are provided. For the purposes of this arbitration, the parties will stipulate that all of the *facts* stated in the arbitration submissions would be the subject of an affidavit by a person with personal knowledge of the particular facts stated. In other words, the arbitrator(s) may consider, but need not accept, any factual representations made in the submissions. Your professor will tell you what arbitration rules to apply.

General Information

Two years ago last February 13, defendant Fran Noonan was traveling by car to New York from New Hampshire non-stop into the night and fell asleep at the wheel. Noonan woke up when the vehicle began to leave the highway and was able to regain control of the car.

Two years ago last February 15, while returning to New Hampshire non-stop from New York, Noonan again fell asleep at the wheel sometime after 11 p.m. When Noonan fell asleep this time, the car was headed northbound on Interstate 93, a four-lane divided highway with two lanes in either direction. The vehicle struck the left guardrail, went across the road, struck the right guard rail, and then came to a stop while perpendicular to oncoming traffic and completely blocking the left travel (passing) lane. At the time of the crash the weather was clear and the road was dry. Noonan woke up and left the vehicle where it came to rest without activating any lights. The location of the abandoned Noonan vehicle was shortly beyond a hill-top with respect to oncoming traffic. As a result, vehicles traveling over the hill in the passing lane had a limited opportunity to avoid the Noonan vehicle.

Dale Gustaf was driving a vehicle north on Interstate 93 and came upon the scene. Gustaf successfully avoided the Noonan vehicle, and then promptly pulled over on the right side of the road to investigate the accident. Gustaf parked in the breakdown lane off Interstate 93 near the exit to the Windham Weigh Station on Rt. 93. Gustaf used a cell phone to call 911 and got out of the car to render assistance. Gustaf had a passenger in the vehicle – Gustaf's 16 year-old child — Terry Gustaf. After Gustaf pulled over, several vehicles came upon the scene and navigated the situation without having an accident. While Dale Gustaf was still out of the vehicle, a car driven by Charlie Goshen was traveling North on Interstate 93. Goshen swerved to avoid the Noonan vehicle. Goshen lost control of the vehicle and it went into a roll, coming to a halt on top of the Gustaf vehicle. As a result of the Goshen vehicle landing on top of the Gustaf vehicle, Terry Gustaf was seriously injured, suffering a grade 3 concussion on a 3 scale. Terry was unconscious for a period of time, and had double vision and lethargy as well as decreased sensation to touch on the left side of the face.

Charlie Goshen was also injured. Goshen sustained a head injury and has no memory of the accident. In addition, Goshen had a large lump on the head, 4 fractured teeth, a sprained ankle, rib fractures and general bruising. Goshen claims ongoing symptoms from a traumatic brain injury.

Prior to the accident, Noonan had a lengthy history of erratic sleep and for years was regularly taking medication that included the side effect of drowsiness. Goshen was prescribed the medication by Dr. John Nether, a New York psychopharmacologist, who was managing Noonan's pharmacology.

Noonan provided blood samples at the hospital at 2:10 a.m. and 3:15 a.m. after the accident at the request of the police to check for drugs and alcohol. The tests were negative for drugs and alcohol.

In this matter, there are two plaintiffs and their cases have been consolidated by agreement for the purposes of arbitration. Terry Gustaf has brought a claim against Charlie Goshen and Fran Noonan. Goshen has brought a claim against Fran Noonan and Dale Gustaf. Each of the defendants has a lawyer hired by their insurance company under the terms of the insurance policy. Noonan has a policy with a single limit of $250,000. Gustaf has a policy with limits of $100,000 per person/$300,000 per accident. Goshen has a policy of $25,000 per person/$50,000 per accident. Each plaintiff has a lawyer retained for the purpose of pursuing the personal injury claim. Therefore, Goshen has an insurance defense lawyer to defend *and* a separate lawyer to pursue the personal injury claim. There are 4 parties and 5 lawyers. The insurance companies have agreed to arbitrate both cases in exchange for an agreement that there can be no award in excess of the insurance coverage in force for each company. In the event that Noonan's total coverage is exceeded, the plaintiffs will recover based upon the percentage that their award bears to the total combined award. For example, if Plaintiff Gustaf and Plaintiff Goshen are each awarded $150,000 as against Noonan, they will each receive $125,000 from the Noonan policy, which is 50% of the total coverage. The plaintiffs have agreed to this because arbitration is less expensive and much quicker than a formal trial. The arbitrator(s) will be told of the coverage agreement, and any award in excess of the coverage will be reduced to the total coverage.

New Hampshire is a comparative fault state. That is, the plaintiff can recover as long as his/her fault is not more than the combined fault of all other parties – including "parties" unnamed in the action. The recovery of a comparatively negligent plaintiff will be reduced by his/her percentage of fault. For example, if the jury finds for the plaintiff in the amount of $100,000, but also finds that the plaintiff's fault is 50%, the verdict will be reduced to $50,000. If the plaintiff is found to be 51% at fault, he/she will recover nothing. As another example, if the jury finds for the plaintiff in the amount of $100,000 and finds that the plaintiff is 25% at fault, the defendant is 50% at fault and a person unnamed in the action is 25% at fault, the plaintiff will recover $50,000.

ARBITRATION SUBMISSION OF PLAINTIFF TERRY GUSTAF

HILLSBOROUGH COUNTY   SUPERIOR COURT
NORTHERN DISTRICT

Sandy Gustaf, MNF of Terry Gustaf
v.
Charlie Goshen and Fran Noonan
216-2011-0000

ARBITRATION SUBMISSION OF PLAINTIFF TERRY GUSTAF

NOW COMES Terry Gustaf and submits the following:

STATEMENT OF FACTS CONCERNING ACCIDENT

Terry Gustaf was a passenger in a vehicle being driven by parent Dale Gustaf, that was involved in a motor vehicle collision two years ago on February 15, at approximately 11:40 p.m. in Windham, New Hampshire, on Interstate 93. While traveling in the left hand lane, Dale Gustaf noticed another vehicle bouncing from guardrail to guardrail and settling in the left hand lane. Dale Gustaf cut over to the right hand lane and pulled into the breakdown lane about 100 yards away from the disabled vehicle. The disabled vehicle was later determined to be operated by Fran Noonan who was traveling back from Long Island, New York to Southern New Hampshire University.

It was also later determined that Noonan had ingested certain pharmaceutical substances that had impaired Noonan's ability to drive a motor vehicle, which was further complicated by the fact that Noonan had commenced the motor vehicle trip back to New Hampshire on an insufficient amount of sleep. The New Hampshire State Trooper investigating this accident, Trooper Chris Rose, recorded in the Police Report that Noonan had fallen asleep while driving.

Dale Gustaf recalled in deposition that the Noonan vehicle was blocking the left hand lane of Interstate 93 and its lights were off. Dale Gustaf believed that the Gustaf vehicle was the first vehicle to pull over into the breakdown lane on the right hand side of Interstate 93 in order to possibly render assistance to Noonan. Dale Gustaf recalls that maybe one or two vehicles pulled up ahead of the Noonan vehicle after it was parked. Dale Gustaf exited the vehicle and dialed 911 on a cell phone, leaving Terry Gustaf in the vehicle parked on the right hand side of the road with its lights on and hazard lights activated. Dale Gustaf then walked towards the disabled Noonan vehicle on the right hand side of Interstate 93 and was able to speak to Noonan (who was out of the vehicle and on the side of the road) to ascertain whether Noonan was OK. Shortly thereafter, Charlie Goshen was also traveling northbound on Interstate 93 and came upon the scene. Because Goshen was driving at such a high rate of speed, Goshen was unable to safely navigate around the Noonan vehicle. Goshen apparently executed an emergency swerve around the Noonan vehicle causing the Goshen vehicle to roll over and collide with the Gustaf vehicle parked on the right hand side of the road. Dale Gustaf recalls that there were at least two or three other vehicles that had passed by the scene prior to Goshen arriving and crashing into the Gustaf vehicle and those vehicles had been able to safely avoid a collision with the Noonan vehicle or other vehicles like Gustaf's which were parked on the side of the road. The Gustaf vehicle was totaled and Terry Gustaf was severely injured.

Terry Gustaf asserts this case is governed by Marshall v. Nugent, 222 F. 2nd 604 (1st Cir., 1955). As cited in the Marshall case, Noonan negligently operated a vehicle in such a manner as to place the vehicle in a disabled position on Interstate 93 such that Noonan could reasonably be held liable for all subsequent collisions caused by the fact that the Noonan vehicle was blocking traffic and was not visible due to the fact that Noonan failed to activate hazard lights and had inexplicably turned off the running lights. Goshen is concurrently liable because all other drivers who came upon the disabled Noonan vehicle were able to avoid a collision with other vehicles. From this fact the arbitrator(s) can infer Goshen was traveling at too high a rate of speed given the nighttime and winter conditions on the section of Interstate 93 in question.

STATEMENT OF INJURIES TO TERRY GUSTAF

After seeing the Goshen vehicle crash into the Gustaf vehicle, Dale Gustaf raced back to find the Goshen vehicle resting on the rear left corner of the Gustaf vehicle. Terry Gustaf was unconscious in the front passenger seat. Emergency responders took Terry to the Parkland Medical Center, and it was Dale Gustaf's recollection that Terry remained unconscious until sometime after arrival at the emergency room.

At the Parkland Medical Center, in addition to receiving emergency treatment, Terry was seen by Dr. Jeffrey Rand. It was Dr. Rand's assessment that Terry Gustaf had suffered a significant concussion, grade 3 to grade 4, depending upon the rating system, but certainly the worst grade in either system. Terry was suffering from double-vision and lethargy as well as decreased sensation to light touch on the left side of the face. An MRI done on February 16 was interpreted by Dr. Rand as indicating a contusion of the corpus callosum on the right of the midline. Terry also complained of neck and back pain. X-rays were negative and further treatment was postponed because of the head injury.

Terry was discharged from the Parkland Medical Center on the 18th of February and later admitted to Northeast Rehabilitation for one day of rehabilitation treatment. Nearly a year later, on February 5, Terry was seen by a neurologist named Dr. Ronald Sprague. On physical exam Dr. Sprague detected slight abnormalities in Terry's right eyelid with the right pupil set slightly larger than the left and some limitation of the movement of the eyes. It was Dr. Sprague's assessment that Terry was recovering from traumatic brain injury and diplopia or double-vision.

Terry Gustaf began receiving chiropractic care for the neck and back injuries at Straight Chiropractic and those treatments continued from March 18 through August 26 on the year of the accident. Terry was seen for continuous speech and language therapy at the Southern New Hampshire Medical Center for more than a year. Terry was also seen by Joseph Romer, M.D. at the Massachusetts Eye and Ear Infirmary for a neuro opthomological evaluation. The first assessment by Dr. Romer two months post-accident found that Terry had traumatic brain injury; at his follow-up assessment a year later, Dr. Romer stated that it was his impression Terry had traumatic brain injury with residual right hypotropia with diplopia. This is the same assessment that Dr. Romer gave after a further follow up two years post-accident, that Terry still had traumatic brain injury with residual double-vision on the extremes of vision.

At the time of the accident Terry Gustaf was a junior at Banter High School. Terry was out of school for nearly five weeks. During that time Terry received speech and language therapy assistance from New Hampshire Medical Center. It was recommended that Terry receive a 504 accommodation plan and that plan was approved by the high school to provide Terry untimed and extended times for tests, a reduction of work load per course limitation, limitation on oral presentations, limiting team work to one partner, limiting homework to two hour blocks with teachers monitoring and encouraging walks, water, breaks, snacks to minimize fatigue.

Terry Gustaf received a comprehensive neurological assessment by Margaret Dana, PhD, and in her report eighteen months post-accident she concluded that although Terry had a history of having a learning disorder prior to the motor vehicle accident on February 15, it was her assessment that the continued problem with rapidly alternating attention was likely secondary to the traumatic brain injury from the motor vehicle accident. Dr. Dana did recommend continuing academic accommodations for Terry at UNH.

It is Terry's assessment that it takes a longer period of time to complete mental tasks since the accident and that it is harder to concentrate. Terry manages these problems as best as possible. As a result of the accident, with the exception of track and field, Terry did not return to any pre-accident sports at high school, which included lacrosse and basketball, because of the fear of having another concussion causing a more severe brain injury. Terry does continue to experience headaches when working on mental tasks for a long period of time. Terry feels it takes longer to do academic tasks because things have to be repeated more often. Terry continues to have double-vision when looking out of the corner of the eye and sometimes sees double when sitting at a desk and looking up at a screen. Generally, Terry Gustaf has been able to overcome or compensate for any difficulties and has worked hard to achieve a 3.5 grade point average at UNH.

Total medical expenses for Terry Gustaf are $49,809.42.

DEMAND

Terry Gustaf suffered a brain injury and other serious injuries that caused substantial pain and suffering and impacted on Terry's future quality of life. Demand is made against Noonan and Goshen in the total amount of $650,000.00.

> Respectfully submitted,
> Terry Gustaf
> By Terry Gustaf's attorneys,

Date:_____

(Attorney for Gustaf) NHBA #3333
9855 Apple Street
Manchester, NH 03104
(603) 668-0000

CERTIFICATE OF SERVICE

I hereby certify that on this date I emailed a copy of the above Arbitration Submission for Plaintiff Terry Gustaf to all counsel of record and to the arbitrator(s).

Counsel for Terry Gustaf

ARBITRATION SUBMISSION OF DEFENDANT NOONAN IN GUSTAF CASE

STATE OF NEW HAMPSHIRE

Hillsborough, ss.   Superior Court
Northern District

Terry Gustaf
v.
Charlie Goshen and Fran Noonan
Docket #: 216-2011-CV-000

DEFENDANT, FRAN NOONAN'S ARBITRATION SUBMISSION

NOW COMES the Defendant, Fran Noonan and respectfully submits the following:

STATEMENT OF THE FACTS:

This suit arises from an accident which occurred two years ago February 15, in Windham, New Hampshire. Defendant, Fran Noonan, fell asleep while driving north on Interstate 93 at approximately 11:37 p.m. and was involved in a one vehicle accident in which the Noonan vehicle came to rest in the left hand lane.

Upon seeing Noonan's disabled vehicle, co-defendant Dale Gustaf, who had been travelling in the same direction as Noonan, pulled over into the right hand breakdown lane of I-93 N to see if Noonan needed assistance. Gustaf activated emergency flashers, stepped out of the Gustaf vehicle and was attempting to contact emergency personnel while the passenger, Plaintiff Terry Gustaf, remained in the vehicle. After several vehicles had driven by the Noonan vehicle, Goshen approached, swerved abruptly to the right to avoid the vehicle, lost control and proceeded to roll approximately 2-3 times, landing on the roof and rear compartment of Gustaf's vehicle. Goshen was able to exit the vehicle without assistance and was ambulating at the scene.

DAMAGES:

Injuries and Treatment:

Terry Gustaf claims to have the following injuries as a result of the motor vehicle accident: upper back, neck and head injuries with loss of consciousness, vision problems and short term memory loss as well as cognitive dysfunction.

Gustaf was brought by ambulance to Parkland Medical Center early morning on February 16, and was treated for a concussion and diplopia (double vision.) Gustaf was discharged on February 18 with orders of no lifting, no running and no driving. Gustaf was referred to outpatient neuro-rehabilitation.

Gustaf was seen at Northeast Rehab Health Network on February 19, where prognosis was reported as excellent. Gustaf was told to wear an eye patch on alternating eyes to assist with the diplopia.

At Gustaf's March 5 neurology appoint with Dr. Sprague, less than a month after the accident, he noted the patient was improving and that the diplopia occurred with up and down gaze, but not lateral gaze. Gustaf was eager to go to school and participate in activities. No difficulty with balance or coordination was noted. Dr. Sprague stated that other than the diplopia, which was improving, Gustaf was virtually asymptomatic. Gustaf was released to resume activity, return to school for half days. Gustaf was restricted from playing lacrosse and contact sports but was otherwise free to participate in athletics.

In the meantime, Gustaf attended 6 therapy sessions. The March 18 therapy notes indicate the patient was making rapid gains and was not having double vision, even at night. Gustaf continued with a busy social life going to the mall without difficulty and planning for track, running cross-country. By March 26, about six weeks after the accident, Gustaf reported no difficulty while presenting a speech at school. Gustaf had almost complete resolution of symptoms and only noticed diplopia with extreme upward or downward gaze. No further physical therapy was recommended and Gustaf was discharged.

In March, about 5 weeks post-accident, Gustaf had an evaluation for speech language rehabilitation. At this testing Gustaf indicated concern about a slower reading rate, which was not a new problem. When young, Gustaf needed speech therapy and reading help as early as kindergarten. It was recommended the patient have a 504 School Accommodation Plan in place to modify the work load, accommodate learning needs with testing and projects as well as be given additional time to accomplish tasks and take home tests. This plan was put in place at school in May following the accident. An SAT prep course was also recommended to assist in learning test-taking skills and strategies (no course was taken). Gustaf was referred to a neuro-optometrist for reassessment of visual tracking vs. reading rate differences. Speech and language therapy was also recommended, though Gustaf did not follow through on this treatment and recommendation until August.

At an April 9 neuro-ophthalmological consult less than 2 months post-accident, Gustaf reported that the diplopia had resolved 2 weeks prior and had not returned. Gustaf's parents reported that functioning was almost back to baseline. The exam was normal with the exception of a small left hypertropia in upgaze to the right but given that the patient was asymptomatic it was felt there was no need to address this small misalignment.

In August following the accident, Gustaf returned for speech and language therapy after not having been seen since the March evaluation. Gustaf attributes the gap in treatment to a decision to take the summer off and also due to family illnesses. At this point in time, Gustaf's mother wanted Terry re-assessed partially due to the fact that Terry did not want an IEP plan in place at school. Gustaf was retested and the scores had improved since spring testing. In the spring Gustaf had tested "baseline normal" but now had an 11 point gain and was scoring "average normal." Though Gustaf continued to test within normal limits and managed to do well at school, speech and language therapy continued and focused on SAT preparation and college essay writing.

Throughout the school year Gustaf managed to hold on to a busy school schedule and social life while maintaining a 3.13 GPA in school. It is important to note that at the pre-accident baseline Gustaf was an A-B student. Now, upon return to school, not only did Gustaf have a heavy course load, but also participated in the following activities and events during the school year:

- math and robotics team;
- community service at a local elementary school;
- part-time at the Info Center;
- track and field;
- a very active social life, going out with friends on Friday nights;
- a rock concert in November;
- SATs in October and November;
- ACTs in December;
- part-time work in the high school library;
- 30 weekly speech and language therapy sessions to assist with organization and executive functioning;
- applied to colleges

By October, it was reported that Gustaf's reading skills were closer to pre-morbid levels and by January the following year Gustaf's mother felt Terry was 90% back on track. Throughout the speech and language therapy sessions Gustaf's overloaded school and social calendar were continually addressed as the late nights and long hours were causing fatigue. Gustaf was continually urged by medical providers and parents to make better use of time for school work.

Upon discharge from speech and language therapy, Gustaf was urged to develop goals for a 504 plan at college and to register with the Study Support Center at college, neither of which was followed through on.

A neuro-ophthalmological exam 15 months post-accident showed Gustaf to be doing well with no diplopia or change in vision. Neither Terry nor the parents noted any cognitive impairment. Terry's exam was normal except for the right hypotropia in upgaze with a slight limitation of elevation of the right eye in abduction. The exam was stable and no further neuroradiographic workup was recommended. Given that Terry was asymptomatic, there was no need to address the continued small misalignment.

At a psychology/neuropsychology evaluation 15 months post-accident, it was again documented that the diplopia resulting from the motor vehicle accident had resolved. During this evaluation Terry's prior developmental history was reviewed. It was noted that early in Gustaf's developmental stages there had been some issues with language delay and Terry had received early intervention. Terry had Title 1 Programming for reading and language arts in kindergarten through 3rd grade. In addition, Terry was monitored because of concerns about varying levels of attention. At this evaluation, Gustaf reported to Dr. David that Gustaf currently had a significant problem with spelling and was always a slow reader. Despite this, Terry had always maintained A and B grades with a lot of hard work. Also noted was a family history of ADHD and learning issues.

Dr. David concluded that Gustaf's developmental history suggested learning difficulties early on in elementary school which continued to manifest. He suspected that what Terry was experiencing was residual from a learning disorder. The continued difficulty with rapid word retrieval was consistent with a history of reading difficulties from earlier in childhood. While math and problem solving skills were in the high average to above average range, reading and writing skills had always been a problem area for Terry. Because of this, Dr David said it was unknown whether the results of the neuro-psych testing stemmed from a learning disorder, or from the motor vehicle accident. He suggested Terry have appropriate college level accommodations including a reduced course load while in college.

Gustaf graduated high school on time with a 3.3 GPA, grades ranging from A+ to B- and had served 42 community service hours. Terry began classes at UNH the next fall and had a 3.83 GPA during the first semester. Terry did not use the resources available at college, such as the Study Support Center recommended by the therapist and Dr. Davis, though Terry did reportedly file paperwork allowing additional time for tests. As of the fall semester of sophomore year, Gustaf was maintaining a 3.66 GPA.

Medical Specials:

The plaintiff is claiming medical specials of approximately $51,126.75. There is no claim for lost wages.

Conclusion:

Terry Gustaf claims to be suffering from lingering problems of diplopia (double vision) but medicals since 5 weeks post-accident have indicated that the double vision has resolved. Gustaf has a history of a reading disability and has always had to work hard at school. Since the accident, Terry has continued to do well in school and is an A-B college student with a 3.6 GPA. Terry has opted not to use the Study Support Center resources which are readily available. Gustaf has made an excellent recovery and is no longer treating.

                                  Respectfully submitted,
                                  Fran Noonan
                                  By Fran Noonan' Attorneys,

Dated: _____

                                  By: /s/_____
                                  Attorney
                                  NH Bar No. 9999
                                  1838 Apple Street
                                  Manchester, NH 03104
                                  (603) 634-0000

CERTIFICATE OF SERVICE

I hereby certify that a copy of the within Arbitration Submission has this day been sent to all counsel of record and the arbitrator(s).

/s/
_____
Attorney for Noonan, Esq.

Manchester, NH 03101
(603) 612-0012

CERTIFICATE OF SERVICE

I hereby certify that on this day, a copy of the within was forwarded electronically to all counsel of record and to the arbitrators.

_____/s/_____
Attorney for Goshen

ARBITRATION SUBMISSION OF PLAINTIFF CHARLIE GOSHEN

STATE OF NEW HAMPSHIRE

HILLSBOROUGH, ss.   SUPERIOR COURT
                                                               216-2010-CV-00000

CHARLIE GOSHEN
v.
DALE GUSTAF AND FRAN NOONAN

PLAINTIFF, CHARLIE GOSHEN'S ARBITRATION SUBMISSION

NOW COMES the Plaintiff, Charlie Goshen, and submits the following:

FACTS AND LIABILITY

Charlie Goshen was 43 years old at the time of the accident. Charlie is single and resides in Allenstown, New Hampshire.

Charlie earned a BA from St. Anslem's College in Manchester. Since graduation, Charlie has worked at Bowling Lanes in Allenstown. At the time of the accident, Charlie was the League and Marketing Supervisor, which involved mostly desk work, outside sales, and mechanical work. Charlie was earning $1,344.00 per week.

MEDICAL HISTORY

Charlie Goshen was in very good health at the time of the accident. There was no history of smoking, alcohol or recreational drug use. Charlie had no surgical history.

Prior to the accident, Charlie enjoyed golf, and performed the usual household duties and yard work. There were no orthopedic restrictions. In short, Charlie was in overall good health.

FACTS OF THE CRASH

The crash occurred two years ago on February 15, while Charlie was traveling north on Route 93 in Windham, NH. Charlie had just finished work at 11:00 p.m. and was headed home. Defendant Fran Noonan ("Noonan") moments earlier had been traveling north on Route 93 and fell asleep, crashed off two guard rails and ended up in the left travel lane at 11:37 p.m. Noonan's vehicle had no lights on and it was completely dark at the crash scene. Charlie, traveling within the speed limit of 65 mph, approached by turning to the right on a curve and going over a hill so that the view of Noonan was impaired. In a last-second attempt to avoid crashing into Noonan's vehicle, Charlie swerved to the right and lost control of the motor vehicle which rolled over and collided with the automobile operated by Defendant Dale Gustaf ("Gustaf") which was parked in the right breakdown lane.

The evidence will show that Noonan had taken an unorthodox and unauthorized psychotropic cocktail of Tesretrol (800 mg), Klonopin (.5 mg), and Zoloft (100 mg) prior to the accident.

The New Hampshire investigating officer, Trooper Chris Rose, placed fault squarely upon Noonan. His report stated in part:

> *"Vehicle 1 fell asleep while driving in the left hand lane and left the roadway, striking the guard rail along the left side of the roadway. Vehicle 1 then moved across both marked lanes of travel and struck the guard rail along the right side of the roadway. Vehicle 1 came to rest in the left lane of Interstate 93 northbound, blocking the entire lane of travel . . . As a result of this crash, a subsequent crash occurred wherein a vehicle attempted to avoid Vehicle 1, which was blocking the left lane of travel, lost control and rolled over onto a second vehicle which was parked in the breakdown lane . . . Based on the investigation of the crash scene, the driver of Vehicle 1 was found to be at fault for causing the crash, and the subsequent crash . . . The driver of Vehicle 1, who had admitted to falling asleep and leaving the roadway, was found to be in violation of RSA 265:22."*

Trooper Rose estimated Goshen approached Noonan's vehicle in the left hand lane at 11:39 p.m. Noonan's vehicle had no lights on and it was dark. Goshen also approached by turning to the right on a curve and going over a hill so view was impaired. In fact, Windham Police Officer Brian Smyth, when responding to the accident and already aware of the location of the Noonan vehicle, reported that he barely missed Noonan's vehicle because it was impossible to see it due to the curve, hill and darkness.

In addition to the obvious negligence of Noonan, Dale Gustaf bears responsibility. As Charlie explained during deposition, the location of the Gustaf vehicle made it necessary to attempt a sharp swerve around the Noonan vehicle. As motor vehicle accident reconstructionist Robert G. Laton will testify, the combination of the location of the Noonan vehicle and the Gustaf vehicle made it nearly impossible for Charlie Goshen to avoid this crash while going the authorized speed limit of 65 m.p.h., and the fault thereof rests solely on Defendants Noonan and Gustaf.

DAMAGES

As a result of the collision, Officer Rose reported (with regard to Goshen):

> *"the driver of Vehicle 2 sustained a head injury. The driver was unable to remember anything about the crash, had a bloody nose, and was complaining of pain to the ribs, left ankle, and neck."*

At the hospital, Charlie underwent a plethora of x-rays and scans. Charlie spent approximately six hours at the hospital because of injuries, diagnostic studies and treatment. Charlie was in significant pain and was prescribed Vicodin and Zofran. Charlie was diagnosed with head injury, multiple rib fractures (left 4th and 5th). Injuries also consisted of a large lump on the head, 4 smashed/fractured teeth, and a severely sprained ankle that required crutches for 2 weeks. In addition, Charlie's neck was very stiff and hurt for many months after the accident.

Throughout the months of June, July, August and September following the accident, Charlie underwent a total of eleven (11) post and core, root canal and crown procedures for broken and fractured teeth. During that four month period, Charlie could not eat solid food and suffered significant pain and discomfort.

Three months after the accident, Charlie's primary care physician, Dr. Khalil Khan, reported in part: "The patient was taken to the ER at Parkland, was diagnosed with 2 fractured ribs and multiple bruises from head to toe. Patient was on pain meds and it took 7-8 weeks before the pain subsided. Patient was regaining normal activities slowly. Patient continues to have pain with bending over anteriorly and when carrying objects with arms extended, . . . persistent rib pain vs neuropathic pain vs de-conditioned, will start high dose NSAIDS for 2 weeks and then stop, if still persist may consider referral to ortho for further eval and management."

Charlie returned to see Dr. Khan as instructed. There was no improvement. The physician reported: "The patient was placed on high dose NSAIDS for 2 weeks and stopped. Patient continues to have pain in the sternum with bending forward and with attempts to lift anything with arms extended straight in front . . . rib pain . . . persistent pain . . . will refer to ortho and follow recommendations."

Gradually Charlie's condition improved, but there has not been a complete recovery. Eighteen months post-accident, Charlie visited an orthopedic specialist who reported: "Today patient reports mild dull aching pain predominately over the left sternal border, which is noted when patient bends over. Patient also has pain when lifting something heavy with arms outstretched in front. Patient has had some difficulty sleeping and, therefore, has been sleeping in a recliner. At worst the pain is 3/10 on the pain scale . . . Assessment: rib sprain/strain, possible costochondritis on the left side . . . consideration may be given to trigger point injection to the tender areas."

Costochronditis is an inflammation of the cartilage that connects a rib to the breast bone (sternum). It causes short pain in the costesternal joint and/or dull and gnawing pain, usually on the left side. The only treatment is to ease the pain while waiting for costochronditis to improve on its own.

SPECIAL DAMAGES

As a result of the injuries sustained by Charlie Goshen, a total of $26,505.55 were incurred. The detailed breakdown has been provided to all counsel.

LOST WAGES

At the time of the accident, Charlie Goshen was salaried at the rate of $1,344.00 per week. According to Charlie's employer, Bowling Lanes, Charlie was absent from work from February 16, to March 1, and worked half days from March 2 to March 16. **Total lost wages are $4,002.00.**

CLAIM FOR DAMAGES

As to the question of damages, in addition to the special damages stated above, we have taken into consideration Charlie Goshen's traumatic emergency room and hospitalization experience lasting over 6 hours on February 16, plus extreme pain, not only with the head to toe bruises, soft tissue injuries, but fractured ribs, and extensive dental repair work. We have also considered the residual pain that Charlie still has although admittedly on a more occasional basis than before.

DEMAND: $300,000

Dated: _____

> Respectfully submitted,
> CHARLIE GOSHEN
> By Charlie Goshen's attorneys
>
> /s/ _____
> (Attorney for Goshen) NHBA #2222
> 9800 Peach Street
> Manchester, NH 03104
> (603) 666-0000

CERTIFICATE OF SERVICE

I, (Attorney for Charlie Goshen), hereby certify that on this date I emailed a copy of the above to all counsel of record and to the arbitrator(s).

> _____/s/_____
> Counsel for Charlie Goshen

ARBITRATION SUBMISSION OF DEFENDANT FRAN NOONAN IN GOSHEN CASE

STATE OF NEW HAMPSHIRE

Hillsborough, ss.   Superior Court
Northern District

Charlie Goshen
v.
Fran Noonan and Dale Gustaf
Docket No: 216-2011-CV-0000

DEFENDANT, FRAN NOONAN'S ARBITRATION SUBMISSION

NOW COMES the Defendant, Fran Noonan, and respectfully submits the following:

STATEMENT OF THE FACTS:

This suit arises from an accident which occurred two years ago February 15, in Windham, New Hampshire. Defendant, Fran Noonan, fell asleep while driving north on Interstate 93 at approximately 11:37 p.m. and was involved in a one vehicle accident in which the Noonan vehicle came to rest in the left hand lane.

Upon seeing Noonan's disabled vehicle, co-defendant Dale Gustaf, who had been travelling in the same direction as Noonan, pulled over into the right hand breakdown lane of I-93 N to see if Noonan needed assistance. Gustaf activated emergency ¹ashers, stepped out of the Gustaf vehicle and was attempting to contact emergency ʟ ʳsonnel while the passenger, Plaintiff Terry Gustaf, remained in the vehicle. After se ₂ral vehicles had driven by the Noonan vehicle, Goshen approached, swerved abr ɒtly to the right to avoid the vehicle, lost control and proceeded to roll appr ximately 2 – 3 times, landing on the roof and rear compartment of Gustaf's vehicl Goshen was able to exit the vehicle without assistance and was ambulating at the sce e.

DAMAGı S:

Injuries and Treatment:

At the scene of the accident, Goshen initially refused treatment but was convinced by Derry Fire and EMS to be checked out at the emergency room. Goshen was transported to Parkland Medical Center and was diagnosed with 2 fractured ribs and a head injury. Goshen was released the same day.

More than a year later, Goshen met with primary care provider Dr. Shamin for persistent rib pain. Goshen was treated with NSAIDs. Dr. Shamin referred Goshen to an ortho for further evaluation.

It was not until eighteen months post-accident that Goshen consulted with Dr. Batlivala for mild pain on the left side of the sternum when bending over or lifting with outstretched arms. X-rays did not reveal any issues and no treatment other than basic stretching and strengthening were recommended. No other doctor's visits have taken place since this appointment.

In the few years prior to the accident, Goshen had been seeing a dentist regularly, correcting teeth that needed posts and crowns or other repairs. Just two months prior to this accident, Goshen's dentist made a treatment plan of the teeth that needed repair or treatment which included 15 out of Goshen's 21 teeth. Included on this chart were upper front teeth 2-1, 1-1, 1-2 (also known as 7, 8, 9) all needing root canals, post/core and crowns. When Dr. Ferramo called Goshen's house coincidently a few days after the accident to report on the cost estimate for a tooth needing repair, Goshen informed him that Goshen had injured teeth in an accident and would need these teeth looked at prior to the crown repair Dr. Ferramo was calling about.

Only days after the call, Dr. Ferramo wrote up an insurance estimate that included work on the four upper front teeth, 1-2, 1-1, 2-1 and 2-2 (also known as teeth 7, 8, 9 and 10.) His treatment plan for these teeth was identical to the pre-accident treatment plan, with the exception of tooth #10. Tooth #10 had previous root canal, post/core and crown treatment and was not on the earlier list.

Goshen made no complaints to any of the EMS attendants at the scene of the accident regarding an injury to teeth, nor is there any injury of that type recorded in the emergency room records. Goshen's teeth 7, 8 and 9 were scheduled for root canal, post/core and crown treatment prior to the accident taking place. Further, there is no indication that Goshen's tooth #10 was injured in the accident requiring it to have a replacement crown. Therefore, the defendant Noonan disputes the dental bills Plaintiff Goshen has claimed in this incident.

Past Medical History:

Goshen's history is significant for extensive ongoing dental treatment.

Medical Specials:

The plaintiff is claiming medical specials of approximately $26,505.55. This total includes $7,050 in dental treatment.

Goshen's lost wage claim totals $4,002.00.

Conclusion:

There is no question that Goshen did in fact sustain 2 fractured ribs on the night of the accident. However, that a total of 2 doctors' visits in the years since the accident took place proves that Goshen has been well enough to continue day to day activities without any lingering problems. The last of the 2 visits occurred just 2 months prior to filing suit in this matter. What does draw a red flag is the fact that Goshen is claiming the $7,050 incurred in dental fees to be related to this incident, with no medical records following the accident to prove Goshen had sustained any dental injuries. Further, this dental work was already scheduled to take place prior to the accident even occurring.

Many vehicles came upon the Noonan crash and were able to slow down and drive between the Noonan and Gustaf vehicles safely. Goshen's speed and/or inattentiveness contributed to the inability to keep the vehicle in control, which ultimately caused the injury. Goshen created an emergency situation by failing to slow down and by failing to be on the lookout for an accident when it was easy to observe several cars parked in the breakdown lane including Gustaf's which had its emergency flashers activated. Goshen was the only driver whose car flipped over on the night in question.

Respectfully submitted,
Fran Noonan
By Fran Noonan's Attorneys,

Dated: _____

By: _____/s/_____
Attorney
NH Bar No. 9999
1838 Plum Street
Manchester, NH 03104
(603) 634-0003

CERTIFICATE OF SERVICE

I hereby certify that a copy of the above has this day been sent electronically to all counsel of record and the arbitrator(s).

_____/s/_____
Attorney for Noonan, Esq.

ARBITRATION SUBMISSION OF DEFENDANT DALE GUSTAF IN GOSHEN CASE

THE STATE OF NEW HAMPSHIRE

HILLSBOROUGH, SS   SUPERIOR COURT
Northern District

Charlie G. Goshen

v.

Fran Noonan

and

Dale Gustaf

216-2010-CV-00000

ARBITRATION SUBMISSION OF DEFENDANT
DALE GUSTAF

NOW COMES defendant Dale Gustaf and submits the following:

Facts: Two years ago, on February 15, at approximately 11:30 PM defendant Gustaf was driving a vehicle northbound on Interstate 93 in Londonderry, NH, with Terry Gustaf riding in the front passenger seat. Defendant observed a car traveling in front (later determined to have been driven by defendant Fran Noonan) bouncing from one guard rail to the other, eventually coming to rest perpendicular to traffic flow in the left of the two northbound travel lanes. The defendant slowed down and passed the stopped Noonan vehicle and parked in the right breakdown lane about 100 yards beyond the Noonan car, leaving the motor running, headlights on, and activating the flashers to warn approaching traffic of the danger. Terry Gustaf stayed in the car. Defendant then called 911on a cell phone to report the accident and walked down the breakdown lane toward the Noonan car to see if Noonan needed assistance. Meanwhile, somewhere between two and seven northbound vehicles came upon and through the scene without losing control, and one or two of them of them pulled over and parked beyond Gustaf's car in order to be of assistance. One of them was operated by witness Karen Cantor, who (as she related to the investigating trooper) pulled into the breakdown lane herself and stopped to render aid, just as Dale Gustaf had. As Cantor and defendant Gustaf walked toward the Noonan car to determine if Noonan needed help, both Cantor and Gustaf (who was still on the cell phone with the 911 operator) saw the vehicle operated by defendant Goshen approach the scene from the south, lose control as it passed by them and flip onto the roof of the Gustaf car parked in the breakdown lane, causing physical injury to passenger Terry Gustaf. Charlie Goshen also sustained physical injury in the impact with the Gustaf car.

Liability: Dale Gustaf has been sued by Charlie Goshen on the theory that Gustaf's actions on the night in question did not meet the standard of ordinary care and were the proximate cause of injuries sustained by Goshen. Terry Gustaf has not brought suit against Dale Gustaf.

The injuries in this case were the proximate result of the loss of vehicular control by Fran Noonan and/or Charlie Goshen, for which Dale Gustaf bears no legal liability. The actions of motorists encountering the Noonan accident scene, even as it appeared after Gustaf had parked in the breakdown lane and was walking with others back to the Noonan car, prove that the scene could have been, and was, encountered safely and without loss of vehicular control by oncoming traffic. Several cars came upon, and through, the Noonan accident scene without incident, and even stopped to offer aid, as did Gustaf. These other people have not been joined as defendants. Only Goshen lost control, and Goshen has no recollection of the accident.

Dale Gustaf's actions on the night in question were reasonable and responsible under all the circumstances and did nothing to cause Goshen's loss of control. The only thing Dale Gustaf could have done differently that might conceivably have prevented the injuries to Gustaf's child, Terry Gustaf, was to have ignored the plight of distressed fellow motorist Noonan and to have kept on driving. The law does not require a motorist to turn an indifferent eye toward the predicament of others on the highway. While there may be no clearly defined statutory or common law duty of a motorist to stop and render aid to a fellow motorist in need of it (but see, e.g., *Soule v. Stuyvesent Insurance Co*, 116 N.H. 595 (1976)) nevertheless Gustaf's actions in so doing cannot be said to reflect a lack of ordinary care. Gustaf acted with prudence and circumspection in light of all the circumstances and none of Gustaf's actions were proximately causal of any injury.

Respectfully submitted,
DALE GUSTAF
By Dale Gustaf's attorneys,

Dated: _____

By: _____
(Attorney for Dale Gustaf)
74 Proctor Street
Newmarket, N.H. 03857
(603) 293-0000
NH Bar #6666

State of New Hampshire
Rockingham, s.s.

I hereby certify that I have this day electronically forwarded a copy of the foregoing to all opposing counsel of record and the arbitrator(s).

_____
(Attorney for Gustaf)

EXERCISE 13.1
PRACTICING THE ARBITRATION PROCESS
MULTI-PARTY ARBITRATION

"THE MULTIPLE CAR ACCIDENT CASE"

REFLECTION

1. In what ways did your preparation for arbitration differ from your preparation for mediation?

2. In what ways did the arbitration submissions differ from the mediation submissions? Why?

3. Do you think your arbitration strategy would differ if the arbitrator had/had not been the mediator? In what ways?

4. If you had your choice with this case, would you first try to mediate it or go straight to arbitration? What are your reasons?

5. Would your decision to Question 4, above, be the same in all cases? What factors would you consider?

6. In what ways did this arbitration differ from a trial?

7. What things would you have to do for a trial of this case that you would not need to do for an arbitration?

Chapter 14

VARIOUS KINDS OF ARBITRATION

As we discussed in Chapter 13, there are numerous different areas in which arbitration is employed. In this chapter, we discuss some of the more common.

A. UNINSURED/UNDERINSURED MOTORIST (UM/UIM) CASES

Most drivers have automobile insurance that insures them in the event that they are responsible for injury to another person or to another person's property. Many states require motor vehicle owners to carry minimum amounts of insurance. For example, a state statute may require that all automobile insurance policies provide personal injury liability coverage of not less than $25,000 per injured person, up to a total amount of $50,000. But what happens when someone does not have insurance, or if they have insurance of only $25,000 per person and they seriously injure another person? While they remain liable for the full amount of damages, many defendants are "judgment proof." That is, they do not have any assets to satisfy a judgment even if the plaintiff obtains one.

Uninsured/underinsured (UM/UIM) motorist coverage is designed to protect drivers and passengers who are injured through the fault of someone else (usually another driver) who does not have insurance or who does not have sufficient insurance to cover the full extent of injuries. The insurance is part of an automobile insurance policy that contains other coverages. For example, Driver A and Passenger A are in an automobile proceeding down Main Street. Driver B is driving up Side Street, toward the intersection with Main Street. Driver B fails to see that the light has turned red and she collides with the car driven by Driver A. Driver A and Passenger A are both seriously injured. Driver A has over $35,000 in medical bills, permanent injuries and lost wages of over $20,000. Passenger A has $25,000 in medical bills, a broken leg, and lost wages of over $13,000.

Driver B is a young driver who has the minimum policy required in the state, which is $25,000 per person and $50,000 per accident. Without even considering pain and suffering and other intangible damages, the claim for medical bills and lost wages for both Driver A and Passenger A exceed Driver B's $25,000 per person coverage. Fortunately for Driver A and Passenger A, Driver A carried UM/UIM insurance in the amount of $500,000 per person and $1,000,000 per accident. Driver A and Passenger A would first obtain the insurance of $25,000 each from Driver B's insurance company.[1]

---

[1] Most UM/UIM policies require the injured party to obtain written permission from the UM/UIM carrier before settling with Driver B's insurance company. Language varies, and lawyers must always

At this point, they could make a UIM claim to Driver A's insurance company. The claim is processed in accordance with the language of the insurance contract.[2] Driver A and Passenger A would make separate claims, seeking up to $500,000 per person, reduced by a credit of $25,000 per claim for the amount already paid on behalf of Driver B.

Most insurance contracts call for UM/UIM cases that cannot be voluntarily settled to be resolved through arbitration. Most lawyers first make a demand on the insurance company under the terms of the policy. They then attempt to negotiate with the insurance adjuster. If negotiation is not successful, the parties might agree to mediate the matter. Or, the parties might proceed directly to arbitration.

UM/UIM arbitration is *pre-dispute, boilerplate* arbitration. The contract was written by the insurance company and was approved by the state insurance department before it could be used. There is no contract negotiation. The contract often requires that the arbitration must be filed with the American Arbitration Association (AAA) and sets forth the rules of the arbitration. *In the absence of a negotiated agreement to the contrary*, the parties proceed under the process set forth in the contract — including the rules set forth by any referenced administrative body. But lawyers making claims sometimes negotiate with the insurance company and agreement is reached to select a private arbitrator or a private panel of arbitrators. Often, the parties agree that they each select one arbitrator, and that the third arbitrator is chosen by agreement of the two selected arbitrators. Modification of the contract language is often cheaper and less cumbersome for both sides. In almost all types of arbitration, *remember that the parties can always negotiate the rules after the dispute arises.* The pre-dispute contract language is the *default* language in the absence of later modification.

UM/UIM awards are usually very short. For example, "The plaintiff is awarded the gross amount of $_____ in full satisfaction of all claims" or "The defendant prevails." Usually, there are no findings of fact or rulings, except for the amount of the award, if any.

B. OTHER KINDS OF INSURANCE DISPUTES

UM/UIM insurance is a common example of insurance arbitration, but there are other kinds. Sometimes, there is an event where more than one insurance policy may apply. For example, assume a commercial chicken farm in Brazil sells breeder chickens to commercial chicken farms around the world. A commercial poultry farm in Ohio buys chickens from the breeder over a period of 5 years. It is discovered that the breeder chickens have a genetic disorder that requires their destruction and the destruction of all offspring. The Ohio farm is forced to destroy hundreds of thousands of chickens, with damages in the millions of dollars. The Ohio farm brings an action against the Brazilian breeder. The Brazilian breeder has liability insurance, but has changed insurance carriers on a yearly basis — always shopping for the best price.

---

carefully read the contract language and comply with it. This is not intended to be a thorough discussion of UM/UIM law, but is only meant to explain how the UM/UIM arbitration cases arise.

[2] Remember from Chapter 13 that Congress gave states the right to regulate insurance contracts. *See* McCarran Ferguson Act 15 U.S.C. § 1011 available at: http://www.law.cornell.edu/uscode/text/15/1011.

can be pursued. In the alternative, the contract may call for immediate arbitration. The AAA is usually identified as the administrator. When that occurs, the AAA Construction Industry Arbitration Rules and Mediation Procedures (Including Procedures for Large, Complex Construction Disputes) are used.[9] The rules provide separate procedures for regular track, fast track, and large complex construction disputes.

As with other commercial disputes, most awards in construction arbitration are succinct, stating the minimum amount necessary to inform the parties of the decision, without stating the reasons leading to the decision. Sometimes, parties agree that they want more detailed findings.

E. EMPLOYMENT ARBITRATION

1. When There is a Collective Bargaining Agreement

When employees are represented by a union, a collective bargaining agreement (CBA) is negotiated between the employer and the union which sets forth terms and conditions of employment and establishes dispute resolution procedures. Almost all of these agreements include binding arbitration.[10] Unlike most arbitration, this type is usually fairly formal in nature. There are usually written, published awards stating reasons for the decisions.

CBA arbitration clauses for resolving employment disputes for matters involving the terms and conditions of employment are now favored by the Supreme Court and are clearly enforceable. But what about matters that are not part of the collective bargaining agreement, such as statutory claims of discrimination? Can an employer contract with the union to require that all employment-related claims, including statutory claims, be arbitrated and not litigated? Can the union bargain away a statutory cause of action on behalf of individual members? To the extent that the Supreme Court has addressed this to date, the answer by a 5-4 vote is "yes." In *14 Penn Plaza v. Pyett*, 129 S. Ct. 1456 (2009), the Supreme Court was asked to resolve whether an age discrimination claim under the Age Discrimination in Employment Act of 1967 (ADEA), 29 U.S.C. §§ 621 *et seq.*, was subject to mandatory and binding arbitration based upon a CBA that stated the following:

> § 30 NO DISCRIMINATION. There shall be no discrimination against any present or future employee by reason of race, creed, color, age, disability, national origin, sex, union membership, or any other characteristic protected by law, including, but not limited to, claims made pursuant to Title VII of the Civil Rights Act, the Americans with Disabilities Act, the Age Discrimination in Employment Act, the New York State Human Rights Law, the New York City Human Rights Code, . . . or any other similar laws, rules, or regulations.

---

[9] These AAA rules are available online at: http://www.adr.org/aaa/faces/rules/searchrules/rulesdetail?doc=ADRSTG_007210&_afrLoop=84119783037751&_afrWindowMode=0&_afrWindowId=3z2o6ozy6_3 4#%40%3F_afrWindowId%3D3z2o6ozy6_34%26_afrLoop%3D84119783037751%26doc%3DADRSTG_007 210%26_afrWindowMode%3D0%26_adf.ctrl-state%3D3z2o6ozy6_86.

[10] *See* MENKEL-MEADOW ET AL., *supra* note 7, at 397.

All such claims shall be subject to the grievance and arbitration procedures (Articles V and VI) as the sole and exclusive remedy for violations. Arbitrators shall apply appropriate law in rendering decisions based upon claims of discrimination."

The Court found that, under the National Labor Relations Act (NLRA), 29 U.S.C. § 159(a), the employees had "designated the Union as their "exclusive representativ[e] . . . for the purposes of collective bargaining in respect to rates of pay, wages, hours of employment, or other conditions of employment." *14 Penn Plaza, supra* at 1463. The Court noted that the union is required to bargain on behalf of the employees in good faith. The Court stated, "In this instance, the Union and the RAB, negotiating on behalf of 14 Penn Plaza, collectively bargained in good faith and agreed that employment-related discrimination claims, including claims brought under the ADEA, would be resolved in arbitration. This freely negotiated term between the Union and the RAB easily qualifies as a 'conditio[n] of employment' that is subject to mandatory bargaining under § 159(a)." *Id.* at 1464.

The Court went on to determine that there was nothing in the ADEA that prohibited arbitration as the exclusive process for resolving an alleged violation of the statute. "We hold that a collective-bargaining agreement that clearly and unmistakably requires union members to arbitrate ADEA claims is enforceable as a matter of federal law." *Id.* at 1474. Although the Court was only looking at the ADEA, it appears that this language would apply to the broad category of discrimination claims set forth in the CBA.

Since *14 Penn Plaza*, some lower courts have attempted to limit and distinguish the holding, by stating that it applies only when the CBA arbitration provision expressly covers both contractual and statutory discrimination claims. *See Mathews v. Denver Newspaper Agency LLP*, 649 F.3rd 1199 (10 Cir. 2011). And courts have found that various CBA arbitration provisions are not "clear and unmistakable." *See Jackson v. O.K. Grocery Co., Inc.*, 2011 U.S. Dist. LEXIS 59272 (W.D. Pa. June 2, 2011). It is likely that caselaw will continue to develop in this area and cases will be decided based upon the particular facts, the express language of the CBA, the nature of the statutory claims, and whether the statute prohibits arbitration as an exclusive forum. Given the 5-4 nature of the *14 Penn Plaza* holding and the lower court activity since the decision, it seems likely that the law in this area will continue to develop.

2.   When There is no Collective Bargaining Agreement (CBA)

Most employees in the United States do not belong to unions and so are not covered by CBAs. This includes employees who are management and employees who are labor. Management employees often have written employment contracts that may or may not have been negotiated with the employer. Many non-management employees have no written employment contracts and are employees at will. Non-management employees who have written employment contracts usually have non-negotiated "take it or leave it" contracts written by their employer. These contracts may have arbitration clauses in them for the resolution of employment disputes. Even though the employees are not involved in the negotiation of these contracts and do not have unions negotiating the contracts on their behalf as with CBAs, discussed above, the arbitration clauses are generally enforceable. In *Circuit City Stores, Inc. v. Adams*, 532 U.S. 105 (2001), the Supreme Court found that employment contracts are subject to the jurisdiction of the FAA (with narrow exceptions for "seamen," "railroad employees" and "transportation workers" excluded by § 1).

But what about matters that are not strictly part of the terms and conditions of employment, such as statutory claims of discrimination? Can employers contract with employees to require that all employment-related claims, including statutory claims, be arbitrated and not litigated? Based upon the holding in *Circuit City Stores, Inc.*, the answer seems to be a qualified "yes."

In *Circuit City Stores, Inc.*, an applicant for employment named Adams signed an application which said:

> I agree that I will settle any and all previously unasserted claims, disputes or controversies arising out of or relating to my application or candidacy for employment, employment and/or cessation of employment with Circuit City, *exclusively* by final and binding *arbitration* before a neutral Arbitrator. By way of example only, such claims include claims under federal, state, and local statutory or common law, such as the Age Discrimination in Employment Act, Title VII of the Civil Rights Act of 1964, as amended, including the amendments of the Civil Rights Act of 1991, the Americans with Disabilities Act, the law of contract and [the] law of tort.

Two years later, Adams sued Circuit City in California state court for various California statutory claims of discrimination and general tort theories under state law. Circuit City filed suit in federal court seeking to enjoin the state court action and to compel arbitration under the employment contract. As noted above, this issue wound up at the Supreme Court, where the employment contract calling for arbitration was found to be subject to the FAA and the case was remanded back to the Ninth Circuit. But on remand, the Ninth Circuit found that the arbitration agreement was procedurally and substantively unconscionable under California law, that the unconscionable provisions could not be severed, and that the entire arbitration agreement was unenforceable. *Circuit City Stores, Inc. v. Adams*, 279 F.3d 889 (9th Cir. 2002). Certiorari was denied by the Supreme Court. *Circuit City Stores, Inc. v. Adams*, 535 U.S. 1112 (2002).

Where does this leave the mandatory enforcement of statutory claims in employment contracts as distinguished from CBAs? *Circuit City* was decided eight years before *14 Penn Plaza*. Given that the Court has now put CBAs and employment contracts on essentially the same footing, it seems likely that the same rules apply to the enforcement of arbitration clauses regardless of whether the clause is in a CBA or an employment agreement. It is expected that this area of law will continue to evolve and practitioners should be aware of the issues as they continue to develop.[11]

---

[11] For further discussion and an analysis of the status of non-CBA arbitration agreements requiring arbitration of federal civil rights statutes, see Comment Note: Enforceability Under Federal Arbitration Act of Arbitration Clause Not Within Collective Bargaining Agreement With Respect to Claims Under Federal Civil Rights Statutes, 39 A.L.R. Fed. 2d 253 (originally published in 2009).

F. SPORTS ARBITRATION

Sports has become a huge business. The parties are usually involved in an ongoing relationship and need resolution as quickly as possible. Mediation is always available as a first resort, but sometimes the parties cannot resolve their disputes voluntarily. Arbitration is a common method of resolution in many sports, including baseball, football, hockey and basketball. As between players and owners, there is usually a CBA calling for arbitration.

Sometimes, sports arbitration employs an interesting method of dispute resolution. Rather than asking the arbitrator to make a decision out of whole cloth, the parties are each required to make a proposal to the arbitrator. The arbitrator must accept the more reasonable proposal. This is called "final offer arbitration," also commonly known as "baseball arbitration." In salary disputes, teams and players each propose a salary, knowing that one will be accepted and one will be rejected. The theory is that this will force both parties to be reasonable, because they know that the arbitrator must choose one of the proposals and cannot compromise. This type of arbitration is sometimes used in other areas (e.g., public sector bargaining disputes over the terms to be included in future contracts) and can always be agreed to by the parties.

EXERCISES

EXERCISE 14.1
PLANNING FOR ARBITRATION

"ALPHA AND OMEGA COMMERCIAL SUPPLY CONTRACT"

GENERAL DESCRIPTION OF EXERCISE: Negotiation of inclusion of ADR clause in supply contract.

SKILLS INVOLVED: Negotiation.

PARTICIPANTS NEEDED: Two.

ESTIMATED TIME REQUIRED:

45 minutes research and preparation of ADR clause; 30 minutes for negotiatic 15 minutes for discussion: 90 minutes

LEVEL OF DIFFICULTY (1-5):

ROLES IN EXERCISE: You are acting as attorney for one of the partie

THE EXERCISE

You will be divided into pairs. Your professor will assign one perso to represent Alpha, Inc. and one person to represent Omega, Inc. Start by readi ; the General Information below. After that, read the Confidential Information pe aining to you assigned role and follow the instructions that are provided.

GENERAL INFORMATION
AVAILABLE TO ALL STUDENTS

Alpha, Inc. is a wholesale provider of fresh produce to national grocers. Omega, Inc. is a national grocer. Alpha and Omega want to enter into a supply contract.

EXERCISE 14.1
PLANNING FOR ARBITRATION

"ALPHA AND OMEGA COMMERCIAL SUPPLY CONTRACT"

REFLECTION

1. What elements did you want to make sure to include in your contract language? Why?

2. If you had total control over your preferences in this exercise, what would you have done? Why? How do you plan to resolve those tensions when you represent a client?

EXERCISE 14.2
PRACTICING THE ARBITRATION PROCESS

"HAMMER AND NAIL DISPUTE"

GENERAL DESCRIPTION OF EXERCISE: Arbitration of construction dispute.

SKILLS INVOLVED: Arbitration.

PARTICIPANTS NEEDED: You will be assigned one of five roles.

ESTIMATED TIME REQUIRED:

60 minutes for arbitration and 45 minutes for discussion: 105 minutes

LEVEL OF DIFFICULTY (1-5):

ROLES IN EXERCISE: You are acting as a Contractor, Attorney for Contractor, Owner, Attorney for Owner, or Arbitrator.

THE EXERCISE

You will be divided into groups of five – Contractor, Attorney for Contractor, Owner, Attorney for Owner and Arbitrator. Your professor will tell you whether you have a single arbitrator, a panel of three, or how it will be determined. Start by reading the General Information below. After that, read the Confidential Information pertaining to your assigned role and follow the instructions that are provided. For the purposes of this arbitration, the parties will stipulate that all of the *facts* stated in the General Information would be the subject of an affidavit by a person with personal knowledge of the particular facts stated. In other words, the arbitrator(s) may consider, but need not accept, any factual representations contained in the General Information. The rules that apply to the arbitration hearing shall be the Construction Industry Arbitration Rules of the American Arbitration Association. This case has been assigned to the Fast Track under the Construction Industry Arbitration Rules of the American Arbitration Association.

GENERAL INFORMATION
AVAILABLE TO ALL STUDENTS

Owner purchased a house in Hampton, Va. The house needed repair. Owner selected Contractor. Owner and Contractor both signed a contract prepared by Contractor that complied with both state and federal law. Among others, the following provisions were included:

CONSTRUCTION CONTRACT

I. Project Description

A. For a price identified below, Contractor agrees to complete the remodeling work (identified as the Project in this agreement) for Owner.

B. Description of the work, materials and equipment to be installed:

All materials and equipment needed to remove, replace and tape sheetrock on first floor, including all baseboard trim and addition of electrical outlets to meet code in locations as designated by Owner; all materials and equipment needed for prepping, priming and painting entire exterior and interior, including paint in colors to be specified by owner. It is agreed that this bid is intended to provide a completed project.

II. Contract Price

Owner agrees to pay Contractor $92,500 for completing the Work described as the Project.

IV. Scheduled Completion of Project

Work under this agreement will be complete and property will be ready for occupancy no later than May 1. It is agreed that time is of the essence.

XII. Payment Plan

Owner will pay to Contractor the Contract Price in 2 installments, an initial payment and a final payment upon completion of the Work.

XIV. Interest

A. Payments due and not paid under the Contract Documents shall bear interest from the date payment is due at a monthly rate of 1.5 percent.

B. When payment is withheld pending settlement of a bona fide dispute on the quantity, quality, or timeliness of the Work, interest shall accrue only on the amount ultimately paid.

XVI. Arbitration

Any controversy or Claim arising out of or relating to this contract or contract warranty or the breach thereof which cannot be resolved between the Contractor and Owner shall be settled by arbitration by the American Arbitration Association under its Construction Industry Arbitration Rules, and judgment on the award rendered by the arbitrator(s) may be entered in any court having jurisdiction thereof.

After the Contract was signed, Contractor promptly started the work. Owner made a timely first payment of $42,250. When Contractor removed all of the sheetrock, Contractor discovered that the wiring on the first floor had been eaten in places by mice. Based upon the damage, Contractor felt the existing wiring was a fire hazard and should be removed and replaced. Contractor offered to do this for the additional sum of $16,000 over and above the contract price. Owner refused to pay. Contractor stated that the work would not continue without payment of the additional amount in full. Owner continued to refuse, taking the position that the work was included in the bid for a "completed project." Contractor left the job. After 10 days with no progress, Owner made the additional payment. Contractor returned to the job site 4 days later – a total of 14 days after leaving. Contractor completed the project on May 17 and asked for final payment under the contract. Owner refused, based upon the damages claimed from late completion. Contractor filed a demand with the AAA which complied with Construction Industry Arbitration Rule R-4. The pertinent demand language is below:

CONTRACTOR'S DEMAND FOR ARBITRATION

Nature of the Claim:

Contractor fully performed the Contract and is entitled to final payment of $42,250, plus interest at the rate of 1.5% per month since May 17, as called for in the contract.

Owner filed a timely answer and counter-claim, pursuant to Construction Industry Arbitration Rule F-2, which included the following statement, pursuant to R-4(c):

OWNER'S ANSWER AND COUNTERCLAIM

Contractor knew that time was of the essence, as stated in the Contract. Contractor also knew that Contractor had assumed the risk of unknown problems with the electrical work. The Contract specifically referred to electrical work and stated that "this bid is intended to provide a completed project." When Contractor discovered that some of the wiring was frayed and would need to be replaced, Contractor wrongfully refused to do further work unless immediately paid by Owner an additional sum of $16,000. When Owner rightfully refused to pay, Contractor wrongfully left the job and refused to return until full payment was made by Owner. Even after receiving full payment, Contractor failed to show up for an additional 4 days, while knowing that time was of the essence. Despite Contractor's contractual duty to complete the Project by May 1, Contractor did not complete the Project until May 17. As a direct and proximate result of Contractor's breach, Owner was required to pay moving and storage fees for household contents that were scheduled to be brought to the Project premises, live in a motel for 11 nights, rent a function room in a hotel to host a wedding reception for Owner's daughter that was scheduled for the Project premises, and experience tremendous stress and aggravation at a time when Owner had scheduled a sabbatical. Owner claims direct damages as identified below and mental and emotional damages.

Owner's Damages

A.	Cost of hotel lodging from May 1-17. 11 nights @ $200 per night —	$ 2,200
B.	Cost of eating out (no kitchen) for 11 days and nights @ $50 per day —	$ 550
C.	Cost of moving from House 1 to storage —	$ 8,200
D.	Cost of storage (one month minimum rental) —	$ 925
E.	Cost of hotel function hall for wedding, all inclusive —	$ 27,500
F.	Loss of deposit to original caterers —	$ 3,000
	Total Damages (not including emotional distress)	**$ 42,375**

EXERCISE 14.2
PRACTICING THE ARBITRATION PROCESS

"HAMMER AND NAIL DISPUTE"

REFLECTION

1. In what ways did your preparation for an arbitration differ from what your preparation would have been for a mediation? For a trial?

2. In what ways did the arbitration submissions differ from you would expect for mediation submissions? Why?

3. If you had your choice with this case, would you first try to mediate it or go straight to arbitration? What are your reasons? Does it make any difference which side you are on? Why or why not?

4. Would your decision to Question 3, above, be the same in all cases? What factors would you consider?

5. In what ways did this arbitration differ from a trial?

6. What things would you have to do for a trial of this case that you would not need to do for an arbitration?

7. How, if at all, did the lack of a discovery process affect the case? Can you think of situations where lack of discovery might be more significant?

Chapter 15

PUTTING IT ALL TOGETHER

In Chapter 1, we told you that "ADR" was a misnomer, because it was no longer considered "alternative." But now that you have studied the various methods for resolving disputes, we encourage you to think of "***ADRM***" — "Alternative Dispute Resolution *Methods*." You have now been exposed to a variety of ways to resolve disputes — direct negotiation, mediation, collaboration and arbitration. Within each of those categories, you have seen that there are various approaches, nuances and strategies. These are now all tools in your tool box, and you can practice using the right tool for a specific job. A craftsperson knows whether to use a hammer, a saw, a sander or a screwdriver. If more than one tool is required, a craftsperson knows the order to use them in and why.

In this same way, creative lawyers know how to approach dispute resolution. They understand that one size does not fit all. Each situation is unique. Facts vary, personalities vary, and stakes vary. The best lawyers are creative and intentional. If they are drafting contracts, they do not just stick in the clause they used last time. They work to understand the parties, the nature of the relationship and the goals to be accomplished. They consider timing and cost. In the event of a dispute, should the parties first attempt to work it out between CEOs? Is there a role for collaborative law? Should mediation be built in as the next step? If so, should it be through an administrator like AAA or through private selection? If mediation does not resolve the matter, should arbitration be the next step? If so, what kind? By now, you know that there are many variables to consider, and experienced lawyers try to balance a desire for flexibility with a need for predictability.

When disputes do arise, the best lawyers remain open and creative. They help their clients to move forward. They do not engage in behavior that generates unnecessary hostility and expense. They remember the story of the Gingham Dog and the Calico Cat who destroyed each other. Good lawyers evaluate the various disputes and look for ways to resolve them. They are proactive, not reactive. They gather the facts and carefully examine any contracts and other dispute resolution laws or rules that apply. Even if there are pre-dispute resolution mechanisms in place, they are open to looking at the situation as it now exists, and thinking deliberately about whether there is a better approach given the actual situation. They understand that pre-dispute mechanisms are valuable but cannot anticipate every event. Sometimes, if they remain open, the parties can fashion a better post-dispute resolution process. If not, good lawyers know how to follow the rules and proceed under them.

As you go forward, we encourage you to practice what you have learned in this course. It will make you better client representatives. Be intentional. Think three moves ahead. Stand in the other person's shoes. Negotiate every day. Be curious. Read your lease and your cell phone contract. Read all of the fine print in your software agreement. How many dispute resolution processes have you "agreed" to? In what ways do they differ? Who wrote them? Why are they written that way? What was the lawyer who drafted them hoping to accomplish?

Set your computer to track newspaper articles on mediation and arbitration. Look for occasional books dealing with the various aspects of dispute resolution, and attend continuing legal education programs covering this critical area. Follow the cases. Ask your professor if she knows of any mediations or arbitrations that you might be allowed to observe. The more you see, the more you will understand and the more creative you will be when you are representing clients.

The next 25 years are going to bring a lot of changes to the practice of dispute resolution. We believe that the economic pressures of litigation will continue to mount. Creative lawyers will continue to look for methods of resolving disputes in ways that add value to their clients. We assume that you have read articles about the retrenchment of the legal profession, but you are entering the practice of law at an exciting time for people who are problem solvers. We hope that you find it exciting and fulfilling.